COGNITIVE

THERAPY

SECOND EDITION ⁱⁱ

FHSW

Praise for the Book

Diana Sanders and Frank Wills have produced a splendid introduction to the theory and process of cognitive therapy. They reference the traditional approach along with some of the latest ideas, and they do so without losing accessibility and clarity. They blend matters of theory, conceptualisation, relationship issues, and difficulties in therapy in a way that makes this work unique. Their own sensitivity, knowledge and skill in the process of treatment delivery have undoubtedly contributed to the quality of this book. This volume should be the first stop for mental health practitioners from all disciplines looking for an introduction to the basic art and ideas of cognitive therapy.

Adrian Wells, Professor in Clinical Psychology,
University of Manchester

COGNITIVE THERAPY

AN INTRODUCTION

SECOND EDITION

DIANA SANDERS AND FRANK WILLS

SAGE Publications

London ● Thousand Oaks ● New Delhi

First edition published 1997
Reprinted 2000, 2002, 2003, 2004
This second edition first published 2005
Reprinted 2006

 SAGE Publications Ltd
1 Oliver's Yard
55 City Road
London EC1Y 1SP

SAGE Publications Inc.
2455 Teller Road
Thousand Oaks, California 91320

SAGE Publications India Pvt Ltd
B-42, Panchsheel Enclave
Post Box 4109
New Delhi 110 017

British Library Cataloguing in Publication data

A catalogue record for this book is available
from the British Library

ISBN-10 1-4129-0788-8   ISBN-13 978-1-4129-0788-0
ISBN-10 1-4129-0789-6 (pbk)   ISBN-13 978-1-4129-0789-7 (pbk)

Library of Congress Control Number: 2005926187

Typeset by C&M Digitals (P) Ltd., Chennai, India
Printed on paper from sustainable resources
Printed and bound in Great Britain by TJ International Ltd, Padstow, Cornwall

Contents

Preface to the Second Edition

We were delighted to be asked to write a second edition of *Cognitive Therapy*. The first edition arose out of our training experience in Oxford in 1994 when we both did the Oxford Diploma in Cognitive Therapy. We realized that cognitive therapy is an exciting and effective approach, which really seemed to make a difference both to ourselves and to our clients. Coming as we both do from counselling traditions, we felt strongly that these methods could, and should, be valuably integrated into counselling practice, enabling more counsellors to train in cognitive therapy, and add such methods and approaches to their range of practices. We also wanted to write a book that was slightly different from other texts available, one that was more honest about what cognitive therapy is all about in practice, describing some of the realities of trying to apply what seem to be straightforward and clear methods to the mess and complexity of humans and their lives. Whilst many cognitive therapy books have been manualized and clear, in reality the people we see, and ourselves as therapists, are less simple and do not fit into pretty boxes – we cannot be tidied away with the application of rationality and positive thinking.

In the years since the first edition was published, we as authors have gone through our own processes of change. Frank has changed from being a trainer who also did therapy to a therapist who also does training. He has experienced at first hand the huge tidal wave of demand that seems to be developing for cognitive therapy. He has also experienced the fascinating and sometimes baffling problems that clients can bring. It is really very inconsiderate of them to have so many issues not described in the literature! Writing a new edition has shown how much cognitive therapy has changed and also how much more is available to aid us in our work with these more elusive problems.

I (Diana) am literally a new woman. When writing the first edition, I worked in the Department of Psychology in Oxford, as part of a primary care service and in a community mental health team, as a therapist and trainer in cognitive therapy. At the beginning of 2001, everything changed when my health deteriorated due to a heart condition. I left my job, believing that my career had come to an end. However, thanks to a successful heart and lung transplant in 2002, everything changed once again and I am back to work. I am now looking at this book, and cognitive therapy, with not only a different heart and set of lungs, but also a fresh set of eyes, and realize that cognitive therapy had changed a great deal whilst I was away. I came back to a different approach, a different tone, where therapists talked more about their issues, the therapeutic relationship had come centre stage, and experiential methods and mindfulness were the flavour of the day. The therapy seemed, to my view, richer and more human, a place where human suffering, and what Leahy (2001) describes as the 'awe-ful' things that happen, were not to be challenged and re-framed, but to be accepted with a more compassionate mind. It took me a while to check out that my new way of seeing the therapy was not simply a function of being born again, or a side effect of the medications I take to stay alive, but a genuine change in the model and approach. Cognitive therapy has retained much of what makes it work, but somehow has blossomed and spread its wings.

In this second edition, we aim to introduce the reader not only to the traditional model but to these new developments, in metacognition, mindfulness, therapist beliefs, experiential methods, behavioural experiments and imagery. A surprise from the first edition was its readership. We aimed mainly to appeal to counsellors; in fact, the book has been used in clinical and counselling psychology training courses, nurse training, educational settings and social work, to name a few. We therefore, in the second edition, write for a wider audience of professionals who use psychological therapy in any way and to any degree. We believe that this approach can be used to inform cognitive practice whatever the therapist's core profession. The term 'therapist' used throughout the book describes the practitioner, whether you are a nurse, doctor, registrar or consultant, psychologist, counsellor, psychotherapist, social worker, occupational therapist or coach. Similarly, we have interchanged he and she, at random, and used the term client as being the people we are seeing in therapy, without losing sight of the fact that they are, like us, people, and that the issues that arise for them are those that can arise for us as therapists.

ACKNOWLEDGEMENTS

We would both like to re-acknowledge the inspiration we received from our original Oxford course supervisors: Melanie Fennell, Ann Hackman and Adrian Wells. We are pleased to have been able to stay in touch with them and to be able to receive their on-going support: delivered in their individual and unique ways. We also thank Alison Poyner and Louise Wise at Sage Publications for all their help.

I (Diana) would like to acknowledge my husband Mo Chandler, who has, once again, supported my writing with love and humour, expertise in disk- and sanity-recovery, tea and a reminder that there is life beyond the little screen. James Bennett-Levy gave helpful comments on the manuscript as well as providing a fresh approach to cognitive therapy through his research and work on behavioural experiments – not to mention many good laughs. Thanks, also, to Oxford Cognitive Therapy Centre and the Department of Psychological Medicine, particularly Christina Surawy and Jill Roberts, for their on-going inspiration.

Frank would like to acknowledge the huge help and support from his wife, Annie, and his children Joe and Laura (for her occasionally entertaining interactions with his clients). The book has been strengthened by comments on the manuscript from Brian Hunter, Utsa Das and Kathy Baines. He has benefited from the support and singing of the School of Social Studies, led by Amelia Lyons, at the University of Wales Newport. Whilst greatly appreciating his professional and social contact with James Bennett-Levy, Frank would have to remind James that if Tranmere Rovers ever have to play Aldershot, all bets are most definitely off!

Introduction
Cognitive Therapy: An Image Transformed?

Cognitive therapy is a fast-growing and fashionable form of psychological therapy. It is widely used not only in the US, where the therapy originally developed, but also across the world. It has developed very strongly in the UK, appealing particularly to British pragmatic and empirical traditions. The British Association for Behavioural and Cognitive Psychotherapies (BABCP) has made internationally significant initiatives in spreading good practice. There is great demand for cognitive therapy, with research on its applications increasing to an ever-widening range of emotional and other problems. Cognitive therapy has been thought of as being conducted mainly within the domain of the mental health professions – by psychologists, psychiatrists and nurses – but is now being increasingly used by many other helping professions, such as psychotherapists, counsellors, social workers, probation workers, to name but a few.

Cognitive therapy, as developed by Aaron T. Beck, is a model of psychological therapy that proposes that how we feel, how we think and how we behave are all inter-related, and changes to thoughts and behaviour will influence feelings. The therapy is collaborative, structured, educational and empirical, and uses a variety of methods, some specific to cognitive therapy, others integrated from behavioural therapy, and yet others borrowed and adapted from the wider world of psychotherapies and counselling. Therapy proceeds by modifying thinking processes in an experimental way to see whether this may have a positive effect on the client's symptoms and/or underlying problems.

Cognitive therapy is one of the wider cognitive-behavioural approaches to therapy including CBT, REBT, behaviour therapy and constructivist therapy. We are often asked 'what is the difference between cognitive therapy and CBT?' It is not an easy question to answer since, in our view, there are few really significant differences: all good cognitive therapists these days will be using a range of behavioural strategies to enable people to make cognitive, emotional and behavioural changes; similarly, behavioural approaches will be targeting, directly or indirectly, cognition. Sometimes we call ourselves Cognitive Therapists, at other times Cognitive Behavioural Therapists. The difference may well be historical, CBT representing a coming together of the cognitive and behavioural traditions. In this book we focus mainly on the invaluable contribution made initially by Beck and then elaborated upon by new waves of therapists and researchers to develop cognitive therapy as it is today. We acknowledge that other therapeutic traditions have also made very valuable contributions to cognitive behavioural therapies and aspects of these models will be reflected in the book and described in terms of the wider cognitive behavioural therapies.

All practitioners, particularly those working in the public sector, are now encouraged to practise the most appropriate and most effective form of therapy for our clients, alongside the development of evidence-based mental healthcare. Evidence-based practice requires practitioners to search out the most effective treatment plan for their individual clients, not just one that falls under their own present treatment modality. The evidence for cognitive therapy is strong. In the UK, a Guidelines Development Committee of the British Psychological Society authored a Department of Health (2001) document entitled *Treatment choice in psychological therapies and counselling: Evidence-based practice guidelines.* This document states that there are now over 325 clinical trials of cognitive or cognitive behaviour therapy for a range of populations and difficulties (Butler, 2001). Cognitive therapy is well established as first-line therapy for depression and works well in combination with medication. Cognitive therapy also helps people avoid relapsing with future episodes of depression, and its effects and benefits carry on even after therapy has ended (Strunk and DeRubeis, 2001). Cognitive therapy is well-established therapy for a range of problems (Barlow, 2001; Nathan and Gorman, 2002). Cognitive therapy is based on empirically grounded research that feeds into practice (Salkovskis, 2002) and in general does have long-lasting effects:

> CBT interventions have been shown to have an enduring effect that extends beyond the end of treatment; they reduce risk for relapse in chronic disorders and risk for recurrence in episodic disorders. Whether CBT is truly curative remains to be seen, but there is more good evidence for CBT having an enduring effect than for any other intervention in the field today. (Hollon, 2003: 71).

None of these points are made in the spirit that other types of therapy are not effective. It may be, however, that other therapies can learn from the strong tradition of quantitative research developed in the field of cognitive therapy. In this book, however, we also argue that cognitive therapy itself can learn much from the tradition of qualitative research favoured by other traditions, especially in furthering its own debate about how its general methods can be best adapted to individual clients. Such exchange symbolizes the kind of assimilative integration that we favour.

Despite its popularity and endorsements, the cognitive approach does not rest easily with some. At the time of the first edition of this book[1] we had asked trainees to describe their images of the different therapies and their respective therapists. The image then attributed to cognitive therapy and cognitive therapists was remarkably consistent, revolving around the adjectives rational, cold, intellectual, analyzing, clever and unemotional.

How did this rather unappealing and Vulcan image come about? One factor seemed to be that psychotherapy and counselling had been until quite recently dominated by psychodynamic and person-centred models. The behavioural model was unattractive to trainees from other traditions because of its disdain of psychodynamic principles and because of its supposed 'mechanical' model of human nature, tending to make it, to paraphrase Oscar Wilde, 'the model that dare not speak its name'. Another factor was the relative newness of the cognitive model. Albert Ellis did not fully develop rational-emotive behaviour therapy until the mid-1960s and Aaron T. Beck's work did not really gain wide currency until the late 1970s.

Although the passage of time since the first edition has seen more acceptance of cognitive therapy, some of the old prejudices re-emerge at times when treatment guidelines promoting cognitive approaches appear (Salkovskis, 2002; Sanders and Wills, 2003). The flames of these 'conflicts' have sometimes been fanned by the claims, not so much of cognitive therapists themselves but from certain parts of the medical world, that carry prejudice against the supposed vagaries of other forms of counselling and therapy. The cognitive and cognitive-behavioural therapies do claim to be effective, at least within prescribed areas. Some perceive these claims as threatening to established beliefs and methods of those practising other forms of therapy. Beck's work on depression, for example, carried a well-developed research profile to back up its claims of effectiveness. Even when people were prepared to accept the effectiveness of cognitive therapy in the treatment of depression, there was scepticism with regard to the approach's value when applied to a wider range of problems. The notion of 'evidence-based health care' is also open to questioning (Grant et al., 2004; Marzillier, 2004; Rowland and Goss, 2000).

After its initial arrival, a critique of the cognitive approach quickly developed around the following points:

- Cognitive therapy was only useful in relatively specific areas such as depression.
- Cognitive approaches downplayed or ignored emotions.
- Cognitive approaches paid insufficient attention to 'real life' events and could be over-confrontational with and even detrimental to vulnerable clients.
- Cognitive approaches did not take into account early experience and developmental issues.
- Cognitive approaches downplayed or ignored the importance of the therapeutic relationship and over-focused on rational change processes.
- The research base relied heavily on randomized controlled trials based on standard therapy with people with relatively circumscribed problems, and was not necessarily so applicable in the 'real world'.

All these criticisms had some merit then and do so even today. The cognitive field, however, is a rapidly developing one and we think many of these points have already been successfully addressed and all of them are being worked on in significant ways. The challenge for us as educators and trainers has often been to keep minds of trainees open long enough to hear some of the more sophisticated nuances of the approach whilst, at the same time, teaching basic concepts from the early seminal works.

In this revised edition of *Cognitive therapy* we aim to introduce cognitive therapy, past and present, bearing in mind the criticisms as well as the huge amount of new and innovative work developing cognitive therapy as it is today. We particularly focus on the recent developments in seven main areas:

- Expanding the range of applications of cognitive therapy.
- The ways in which cognitive therapy now conceptualizes and works with emotions.
- Ways in which cognitive processes (for example, attention to negative and self-conscious thoughts and images), as well as cognitive content play a central role in maintaining people's difficulties, particularly in problems such as worry, obsessive compulsive disorder and relapsing depression.
- The integration of concepts of acceptance and mindfulness within cognitive therapy.
- How cognitive therapy has conceptualized environmental influences on psychological difficulties.
- How cognitive therapy has been adapted for work with personality issues and longer-term work.
- How the model's thinking about the therapeutic relationship has developed.

The book is divided into three parts. In Part I, we begin our description of cognitive therapy with an up-to-date account of the theory and practice of cognitive therapy as it has developed from Beck's original model, particularly stressing the adaptations in light of earlier criticisms. We go on to look in detail at two of the most important features of cognitive therapy: conceptualization, developing a cognitive model for each individual client that will guide therapy; and the therapeutic relationship in cognitive therapy. In Part II, we get down to the nuts and bolts of the work. Starting with the initial contacts, we describe the processes of assessment and engagement and building an individual conceptualization. We then devote three chapters to the variety of methods used in cognitive therapy – some unique, others borrowed from different psychotherapeutic traditions – and how to use these methods with individual clients. We look at issues such as using protocols in therapy and when and how to weave these into individual work. Chapters follow on the subjects of working with difficulties in therapy, and the issues surrounding endings. In Part III of the book we look at the wider field of cognitive therapy. In our chapter on cognitive therapy's many and varied applications, we describe how therapy interventions develop from an understanding of the individual models for each problem area, illustrated with the two most common problems of anxiety and depression. We look at some of the psychological processes across different problem areas and ways of working with these.

In the final chapter, we offer some ideas about where next for practitioners coming from diverse fields – whether to dip in a toe and dabble, or whether to go the whole hog, dive in and become a fully paid up member of the large family of cognitive therapists. We look at training issues, and some of the difficulties faced by trainees struggling to make sense of the structure and methods of the therapy, balancing the art and science of cognitive therapy resources. The book aims to be an introduction rather than an encyclopaedia and in the Appendix, as well as at the end of each chapter, we give details of where to go for more information, including books, websites and audiovisual.

Throughout *Cognitive therapy*, we aim to provide an honest account of what it is like, in practice, to be cognitive therapists, rather than always giving 'the party line'. At times we speculate, at times we disagree with some of the traditions in cognitive therapy. We are happy to debate. At the same time, we hope to share with our readers our enthusiasm and support for cognitive therapy, with all its new exciting developments and debates. More ambitiously, we hope that we have been able to inspire the reader to regard, at least as a testable hypothesis, our belief that cognitive therapy is a comprehensive approach drawing from an exciting cornucopia of imaginative and effective techniques, integrated into a rich overall conceptual model. This model can help therapists to work with most of the clients who will come their way. We have also taken good note of Paul Gilbert's entreaty, still as relevant as it was at the time of our first edition, that cognitive therapists should 'take more time out of their technique-oriented approaches and consider what it is to be a human being' (in Dryden and Trower, 1988: 66).

NOTE

1 Wills, F. & Sanders, D. (1997). *Cognitive therapy: Transforming the image.* London: Sage Publications.

Part one

Cognitive Therapy - the Theory, Model and Structure

1 The Original Model and its Recent Developments

Cognitive therapy, as developed by A. T. Beck, is built on the assumption that thinking processes both influence and are influenced by emotional difficulties such as anxiety and depression. Therapy therefore aims to modify thinking processes in an experimental way to see whether this may have a positive effect on the client's emotions, behaviour or underlying problems. While clients may well come to therapy asking for help with their negative thoughts, more often they come because they are feeling bad. Despite its focus on thinking, cognitive therapy is actually all about reaching and working with emotion. Cognitions and cognitive processes are emphasized because they can often provide the most direct and useful paths to emotions. Furthermore, understanding specific thoughts and styles and processes of thinking can go a long way to explain negative feelings to clients themselves, who may well have been experiencing these negative emotions as particularly incomprehensible and frightening. The way in which cognition influences emotion and behaviour is at the heart of cognitive therapy and the basis of both the early models, developed in the 1970s, and current theory and practice.

Since the first model evolved, both the theory and practice of cognitive therapy have been advancing, with fast-moving developments. In this chapter, we look first at the original model and original therapy process and then at the subsequent developments which have led cognitive therapy to be what it is today. Such developments include an integration of the interpersonal and the therapeutic relationship within both the theory and practice of cognitive therapy. In addition, they include contributions from both behavioural and cognitive theorists that have added new dimensions through increased understanding of the role of cognitive and emotional processes in psychological disturbance (Papageorgiou and Wells, 2003; Segal et al., 2002; Wells, 2000). Even after 30 years, the theory and practice of the approach are still developing, with what has been called the 'third wave' entering the arena (Hayes et al., 2004). We end the chapter with a look at some of these new contributions, the 'third wave', bringing an experiential focus, mindfulness and acceptance to the practice of cognitive therapy.

THE ORIGINAL MODEL OF COGNITIVE THERAPY

With his two major publications of the 1970s, *Cognitive Therapy and the Emotional Disorders* (1976) and *Cognitive Therapy of Depression* (Beck et al.,

1979), Beck and his colleagues established what many now regard as the original model of cognitive therapy. The model contained a theory of how people develop emotional problems; a model of how they could alleviate and eliminate disturbance; and a model of how further problems might be prevented. The links between emotion and cognition were initially most clearly demonstrated in the treatment of depression; opportunely because depression is often regarded as one of the most frequently presented psychological problems (Fennell, 1989). The model was also supported by what was, for the psychotherapy field, an impressive range of research validation for both its processes and its outcomes.

THE THOUGHT–EMOTION CYCLE

One of the aims in cognitive therapy is to look at the meaning that the client gives to situations, emotions or biology, often expressed in the client's 'negative automatic thoughts'. The valuable concept of cognitive specificity demonstrates how particular types of thoughts appraise the impact of events on the 'personal domain' (all the things we value and hold dear) and thereby lead to particular emotions, as shown in Figure 1.1. It is then possible to discern the influence that such thoughts and feelings have over our behaviour. The appraisal of 'danger' to our domain, for example, raises anxiety and primes us for evasive, defensive or other reactions. The appraisal of 'loss' is likely to invoke sadness and mourning behaviour. An appraisal discerning 'unfairness' is likely to arouse anger and may lead to an aggressive response.

Figure 1.1   Key themes: cognitive specificity

Appraisal	Emotion
Loss to domain	Sadness, Depression
Threat to domain	Fear, Anxiety
Violation of domain	Anger
Expansion to domain	Delight

In themselves, the responses to our appraisals are not necessarily problematic and are often functional: for example, we all know that driving carries certain risks and thinking about those risks may, hopefully, make us better drivers. Our specific appraisals of events may begin to be more problematic, however, as the appraisals themselves become more exaggerated. If we start to become preoccupied with the risks of driving, and begin to see ourselves as likely to have an accident, then our emotion of slight, functional anxiety becomes one of unease or even panic. Furthermore, if this feeling increases, the chances of our driving ability being adversely affected also increase. Similarly, we may feel a certain comforting sadness about a loss in our life, but if we begin to see the loss as a major erosion of our being, we could then feel corrosive depression rather than relatively soulful melancholy. If the depression cycle goes on, we tend to become lifeless, lacking energy and enthusiasm, and are thereby less likely to engage in the things that give our life meaning; as a result we become even more depressed. In another example, appraising meeting people as 'worrying' raises anxiety and primes us for evasive, defensive or other reactions. Rather than the anxiety being functional, if we start to become preoccupied with the risks of meeting people, and begin to see ourselves making *faux pas*, then our emotion of slight, functional anxiety becomes one of unease or even panic. Furthermore, if this feeling increases, the chances of our making *faux pas* may increase, which further increases our anxiety and so maintains the problem.

The essence of the model is that there is a reciprocal relationship between emotional difficulties and seeing events in a way that is exaggerated beyond the available evidence. These exaggerated ways of seeing things tend to exert further negative influences on our feelings and behaviour, and may begin to constitute a vicious cycle.

Critics sometimes wrongly regard Cognitive Therapy as being based on a generalized formula that claims people are disturbed by their thoughts. In fact, a good cognitive therapist would try to understand the client in a highly individualized way. Rather than reducing a client's mediating cognitions to a formulaic set of 'irrational beliefs', the cognitive approach aims to understand why the client is appraising events in particular ways and why she feels the way that she does. An external event will have a very different impact on different people because each individual has, first, a different personal domain on which the event impinges. Second, each person has an idiosyncratic way of appraising events because cognitions, perceptions, beliefs and schemas will have been shaped by the individual's unique personal experiences and life history. The aim of cognitive therapy is to understand both the person's personal domain and their idiosyncratic way of appraising events.

While, on a simplistic level, a person's thoughts and emotions about an event may appear 'irrational', the response may be entirely rational, given his way of seeing the world. In the later section on the second wave of cognitive therapy, we will also see that it may be that the content of the thinking itself is not so problematic. It turns out that, perhaps in a good, democratic fashion, 'irrational' content is by no means confined to people with psychological problems. For example, the thoughts that are problematic for clients who suffer with obsessive-compulsive disorder (OCD) are shared by 90 per cent of the population (Salkovskis et al., 1995). OCD sufferers, however, pay attention to these thoughts in a different way. Non-sufferers can let these thoughts go – OCD sufferers cannot. Similarly, the kind of worrying, intrusive thoughts that are a problem for 'worriers' may also go through the minds of just about everyone at times. The worriers, however, will focus more time and attention onto the worries and will be less able to let them go.

COGNITIVE DISTORTIONS: NEGATIVE THOUGHTS

Cognitive themes are expressed in specific thoughts. Rather than thinking in literal themes, such as 'There is a loss to my personal domain', such themes are expressed in situationally specific cognitions which, when added together, amount to a theme. These themes become elaborated and maintained by the day-to-day 'dripping tap' effect of the client's 'negative automatic thoughts' (NATs). Often the client is barely aware of these thoughts until highlighted. Beck (1976) first discovered the negative commentary constituted by negative thoughts when a client became anxious while talking about past sexual experiences. The client went on, however, to reveal that it was not the fact of describing these experiences that was causing the emotional pain but rather the thought that Beck would think the client 'boring'. In depression, thinking has a characteristically negative tone centred on loss – not just of loved objects but of a sense of self-esteem and, crucially, for depression, a sense of loss of hopefulness about the world and the future. The triangle of negative views of self, of the world and the future comprise Beck et al.'s (1979) 'cognitive triad', in which the dynamics of depression operate.

In his 1976 book, Beck describes a range of cognitive distortions, shown in Figure 1.2. For example, the thought, 'I'm stupid', a very common negative automatic thought in emotional disturbance, betrays 'all-or-nothing' thinking because it usually refers to the actually narrower reality that the person may occasionally do some things which, with the benefit of hindsight, may be construed as 'stupid'. The depressed client, however, will often go on to conclude that this makes him a 'stupid person'. In this type of reasoning, there are only two possible conditions: doing everything right and being 'not stupid' or doing some things wrongly and being 'stupid'. Thus the negatively biased person begins to use self-blame, thereby depressing mood even further in the vicious cycle described below.

Identifying and labeling negative thoughts and seeing how emotions and thoughts interact in a vicious cycle are the first steps towards enabling the client to understand her emotions. When a client detects specific thoughts, it can be useful to ask her what effect these repetitive thoughts will have on her mood. Many clients will conclude that such thinking is bound to get them down. Thus the simplest form of the cognitive model (Figure 1.3) links the thoughts and emotions that are most relevant to the client's situation.

FROM THOUGHTS TO SCHEMAS

Negative automatic thoughts (NATs) are those cognitions that are closest to the surface of consciousness and may refer to a limited range of situations. Beck recognized, however, that there were also deeper cognitions that incline the person to interpret wider ranges of events in relatively fixed patterns. Working with ideas that parallel those of personal construct theorists (Kelly, 1955), he began to conceptualize the idea of cognitive structures. Beck initially used, and then

Figure 1.2 Common Thinking Biases

BLACK AND WHITE THINKING	Seeing things in black and white, all or nothing categories, missing the 'grey' areas: '*I've completely failed*' '*Everyone else gets it right*'
MIND READING	Concluding that other people are thinking a certain way: '*I feel really embarrassed and stupid*' '*People must think I'm really stupid*' '*Everyone thinks I'm boring*'
GAZING INTO A CRYSTAL BALL	Looking into the future and making predictions: '*This therapy won't work*' '*There's no point in trying it, it won't work*'
OVER-GENERALIZATION	Seeing a negative event as an indication of everything being negative: '*I didn't get the job so I'll never get another job again*'
MENTAL FILTER	Picking out a single negative feature and dwelling on it without reference to any good things which might have happened: '*I had an awful day, my computer crashed and I couldn't do anything for the first hour*'
DISQUALIFYING MINIMIZING THE POSITIVE	Recognizing something good in yourself or your life and rejecting it as invalid or unimportant: '*I'm a good mother to my kids but that doesn't matter, anyone can do that*' Or shrinking it inappropriately: '*I'm being promoted at work, but I'm still not at the top so it doesn't count*'
MAGNIFICATION or DRAMA QUEEN	Exaggerating the importance of events: '*I've got a pain in my chest, it must mean I'm having a heart attack and am going to die*' '*I can't find my keys, I must be losing my mind*'
EMOTIONAL REASONING	Assuming that what you feel is true: '*I feel like a bad person, I must be a bad person*' '*I feel like I'm dying so I must be*'
UNREALISTIC EXPECTATIONS	Using exaggerated performance criteria for yourself and others. Using 'shoulds' and 'oughts' in your expectations of yourself and your demands of others: '*I should always be interesting when talking to other people*' '*I must keep going even though I'm tired*'
NAME CALLING AND LABELLING	Attaching a highly emotional negative label to yourself or to others: '*Idiot*' '*Silly cow*'
SELF BLAME	Seeing yourself as the cause of a bad event for which you were not responsible: '*She's looking cross, it must be my fault*'
CATASTROPHIZING	Predicting the very worst: '*Nothing is ever going to work out for me again*' '*This lump in my breast must be cancer, the treatment won't work and I'll die a horrible death*'

Figure 1.3   Vicious cycle: simple form

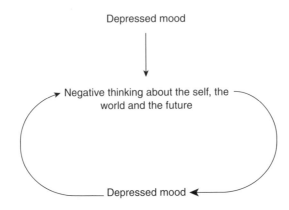

abandoned, Kelly's term 'constructs', preferring the descriptions of earlier psychologists, such as Bartlett (1932), thus going on to use the term 'schemas' to describe the deeper cognitive structures.

Schemas are not, of course, all problematic. For example, following the work of John Bowlby (1969), it appears that children who have experienced satisfactory bonding to primary care-givers will develop a basic set of rules or schemas that contain the inner working model that 'people can generally be trusted'. If a person who has this kind of 'trust' schema meets untrustworthy behaviour in another, she is likely to think, 'Something went wrong there, I may have to be more cautious in future', which is an adaptive response. When a person with a 'mistrust' schema encounters untrustworthy behaviour, however, he is likely to conclude, 'I was right. You can't trust anyone. I won't do so again', which is an overgeneralized and, therefore, less adaptive response.

Negative schemas are seen as having an underlying relationship to NATs. The assumptions or rules contained within schemas are triggered by events and lead to NATs. Sometimes the assumptions persist after the NATs and the other symptoms of depression have abated and may then be targeted as a method of preventing later relapse into depression. As cognitive therapy has developed, schemas have been given a more significant and autonomous role in therapy. It is important to remember when working with schemas that they are not 'objects' but are 'schematic processes'. It has been difficult for cognitive therapy researchers to show the autonomous existence of these processes but the concept remains a useful one. (For a good discussion of this point see Wells (2000): Chapter 1).

So far we have established that there is a strong link between thought and feeling. We do not argue, as Beck did not, that this is a *causal* link, but is best understood as a two-way process. It is also likely that clients will experience the link in this reciprocal way. Thoughts and feelings are often experienced as a unitary phenomenon and it is likely that our labeling of 'thought' and 'feeling' is more a useful heuristic device for therapy than a truly knowable reality.

THE ROLE OF BEHAVIOUR IN DISTURBANCE

A similar line of reasoning to that applied to the relationship between thought and emotion is best applied to fitting behaviour into the picture. Again, the behaviour may seem to come as an instantaneous reaction – 'I couldn't help blurting it out'. Often, it will be helpful to the client to become aware of the thoughts and feelings that accompany the behaviour, enabling him to make a response that is less automatic and therefore less problematic. The behavioural response often seems to play the role of final link in the chain, locking the whole sequence of thought–feeling–behaviour into persistent, repetitive and unhelpful patterns.

Below are some examples of linking thoughts, behaviour and disturbance.

KEITH

Keith is aged 40. He is a computer project manager in the Civil Service and has experienced recurrent depression since his teenage years. His current depression has lasted for two years, since the threat that his work section might be privatized. He is somewhat isolated at work, works hard, stays late and takes work home. He also considered that his performance was deteriorating, thus making him even more vulnerable to redundancy. Keith's pattern is shown in Figure 1.4.

Figure 1.4   Keith's vicious cycle

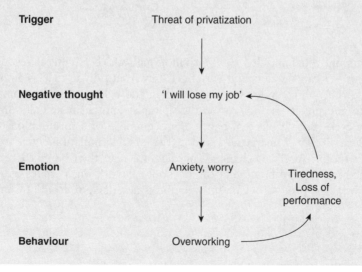

BEN

Ben had lost his mother when he was 12-years-old. He came to believe that 'Nothing lasts. People leave you'. When he meets a potential girlfriend, he feels very anxious because he can't help but imagine her leaving him. He then tends to become 'over the top' in the relationship, thus making it more likely that the relationship will not last. Ben's cycle is shown in Figure 1.5.

Figure 1.5 Ben's vicious cycle

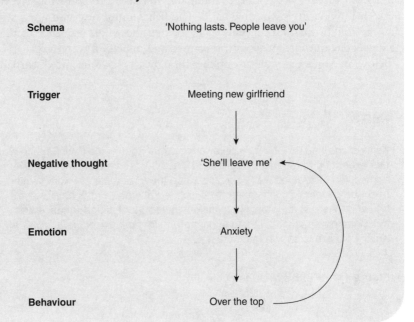

Clients are often puzzled by their emotional and behavioural reactions to situations – 'I can't understand why I get drawn into doing that' is a common response. The whole cycle of thought, feeling and behaviour can become more concrete and understandable when the therapist and client actually draw the 'vicious cycle' onto a piece of paper, the beginnings of a formulation or conceptualization. The concreteness and clarity of a formulation often seems to enhance the prospects of change. The diagram may then be given to clients as something to take home and think about or work on, perhaps as part of homework. The process of case formulation is described in detail in Chapter 2.

THE ORIGINAL MODEL OF THE THERAPY PROCESS

Cognitive therapy aims to be an accessible and practical mode of therapy, one that can be related to common sense (Wills, 1997). One of its attractions is its immediacy, achieved by the fit with the client's experience. Formulation often appears relatively simple and straightforward to students of the approach. Although such terminology may belie the complexities and sophistication of the cognitive model and cognitive therapy, its congruence with our client's experience enables the therapy to make sense and, therefore, to fit the facts.

The basic therapeutic processes of cognitive therapy specified in the early models and continued in recent developments involved three elements: a collaborative therapeutic relationship; a scientific, empirical method; and a parsimonious form of therapy.

In Chapter 3 of *Cognitive Therapy of Depression*, Beck and colleagues describe a view of the therapeutic relationship which draws heavily on the work of Carl Rogers, stressing the 'core conditions' of 'warmth, accurate empathy and genuineness' (1979: 45). They add, however, that these conditions are not in themselves sufficient to produce optimum therapeutic effect. Trust, rapport and collaboration are also needed. It is the concept of collaborative empiricism that marks the real point of departure from Rogers:

> In contrast to 'supportive' or 'relationship' therapy, the therapeutic relationship is not used simply as the instrument to alleviate suffering but as a vehicle to facilitate a common effort in carrying out specific goals. In this sense, the therapist and the [client] form a 'team'. (1979: 54)

The emphasis is on a working relationship: one that perhaps carries with it a little of the Protestant work ethic, offering a contrast to other therapies which stress the importance of 'being' rather than 'doing' in the relationship with the client. The nature of the cognitive work to be carried out is that of identifying unhelpful cognitive processes and challenging or modifying them.

A second aspect of the therapy process is that cognitive therapy is a scientific and empirical form of therapy. The client's problem is, first, collaboratively assessed and then therapy proceeds from the findings of this assessment. As will be discussed in greater detail in Chapter 4, assessment involves full understanding of the presenting symptoms and underlying factors, allowing a clear direction for the therapy. The 'base line' of current functioning is established so that the outcome of therapy can be measured, using tools such as the BDI (Beck Depression Inventory) and the BAI (Beck Anxiety Inventory). By the time the usual allocation of around 12–20 sessions (for depression, 5–12 for anxiety) is coming to an end, the scores should be considerably reduced. Therapeutic interventions undertaken in this way can therefore be regarded as a series of scientific 'single case experiments' to be judged by their results (Kirk, 1989). The degree of symptom relief would be one of several factors to consider when determining whether the therapy may best end as planned. Further, cognitive therapy seeks to elicit feedback from the client, both during and at the end of each therapy session, so that client and therapist can evaluate progress in therapy from several interlocking points of view. A final aspect of the scientific approach is the relative standardization of therapy. The degree to which the therapist appropriately stays with prescribed interventions and yet also applies them individually and artfully can be assessed using measures such as the Cognitive Therapy Scale and its revisions (James et al., 2000; Wills, 1998; Young and Beck, 1980). These measures of therapist skill reflect the ingredients of cognitive therapy that are known to represent effective practice. They help to ensure that cognitive therapy is conducted in a way that is consistent across different settings of therapy.

The third aspect of the therapy process is the parsimony of cognitive therapy (parsimony meaning achieving the greatest benefit from the least effort). Parsimony involves commencing work at a symptom level and advancing to work on the level of underlying belief only when it becomes necessary either from the way therapy unfolds or from the need to militate against later relapses. For example, in depression, behavioural withdrawal is a profound feature. The resulting draining away of pleasure from the client's life is a powerful factor that reinforces the maintenance of low mood and depression. Therefore, cognitive therapy with people who are depressed often starts at the behavioural level, moving to working on cognitions and underlying assumptions only when behavioural approaches have produced some improvement in mood (Fennell, 1989). The client would often be encouraged to schedule activities and then try to insert more 'achievement' and 'enjoyment' into the day (see Chapter 5). The overall aim of these behavioural tasks and experiments is to loosen the grip of depressogenic thinking. Thus, a pleasurable activity can be used to test and, hopefully, disconfirm the client's negative automatic thought 'I never enjoy things any more'. As the mood lifts, it should then be possible to address negative thoughts more directly.

The parsimonious approach is also evident in the recommendation that therapists usually start to work at the most accessible level of cognition – that of the automatic thought – and only later work at the deeper levels of assumption and schemas. The great array of both behavioural and cognitive techniques gives flexibility to 'mix and match' therapeutic interventions. Good cognitive therapy should, however, always be carefully fitted to the individual client. Although the usual recommendation for a depressed client may be to move from working with behaviour to working with negative automatic thoughts and then with assumptions, the actual therapy process will need to be modified according to the needs of the client and the events that unfold in the therapy.

Clients who did not respond to the parsimonious models may have been described at one time as presenting 'technical problems' for cognitive therapy. Among the responses to such clients would be adjustments to therapeutic procedures and perhaps different treatment mixes, including drug and group therapy. Cognitive therapists have, however, now come to the view that some clients might benefit from a form of cognitive therapy that focuses more on interpersonal and schema-based problems. These developments in the original model of psychological problems and the processes of cognitive therapy are described next.

THE NEWER MODEL OF PSYCHOLOGICAL PROBLEMS

Since the development of the original cognitive model of psychological problems, a number of new ways of thinking about psychological processes have been integrated into the cognitive model. One main area of development concerns the integration of an interpersonal perspective into the model (Gilbert, 2000c). Other developments have seen a more explicit integration of cognitive processes into cognitive therapy (Harvey et al., 2004). Such work includes that of identifying the meaning that clients attribute to symptoms and working with their meta-cognitive (thinking about thinking) framework (Wells and Matthews, 1994; Wells, 2000).

INTERPERSONAL PROCESSES AND THE COGNITIVE MODEL

Safran and Segal (1990) added strength and depth to traditional cognitive therapy by building in a clearer understanding of the client's relationship issues outside therapy and emphasizing the interpersonal aspects of the therapeutic relationship itself. They follow on the earlier work of Guidano and Liotti (1983) and integrate such interpersonal issues into the context of a perspective that owes much to John Bowlby, especially to his concept of attachment. These approaches recognize the strong, and almost universal, imperative for humans to relate to each other. Relatedness has crucial survival value not only to the infant during the long period of dependency but to all of us, as our lives are usually dependent on large degrees of social cooperation. Attachment behaviour is seen as a 'wired-in' propensity of human behaviour, evident right from the first moments of a newborn baby's experience. Infants quickly develop the ability to send and receive attachment-based communication with the caregiver. Misattunements in sending or receiving attachment information, if persistent, can have a highly negative effect on development.

As a result of our imperative to relate, many of the key core beliefs and assumptions that we hold about life and the world are likely to be interpersonal. Attachment schemas are internalized and may become very persistent, independently of subsequent experience. They can therefore become locked into, in Safran and Segal's terms, a cognitive-interpersonal style. The process is illustrated with Jane.

JANE

Jane remembered her childhood as one in which she felt that she did not get the parental recognition that her siblings got. She summed this up in the core belief, 'I do not measure up'. Consequently she developed a strong desire to please others during her childhood. Forty years later, she could not understand why her work colleagues 'didn't respect her'. Her tactic was to try very hard to please them and to win their respect. Unfortunately, as often happens with this tactic, it made her colleagues irritated and actually less respectful of her.

As Harry Stack Sullivan (1953) points out, the client's attempted solution is often part of the problem, that is, the client, understandably, tries to counter the unhelpful belief, yet in a way that only leads to its perpetuation. Part of the therapist's assessment of the client is to see how pervasive and enduring these patterns are and to identify when they are replayed within the therapeutic relationship itself. Safran and Segal suggest that therapists need to be aware of 'interpersonal markers', not only because such awareness is likely to facilitate the therapeutic process but also because such markers can prove to be 'windows into the client's whole cognitive-interpersonal style' (1990: 82). We turn again to Jane.

> The first time that I (FW) met Jane, she asked me a lot about my qualifications as a therapist. I initially made what I guess is the standard interpretation of her actions – that they might conceal an anxiety about trust. In a later discussion, however, she told me that her inquiries were linked to her cognitive-interpersonal belief that: 'People will only be interested in me if I am even more interested in them first'. As part of training in sales techniques undertaken as an adult, she had been taught that customers were more likely to buy from her if she showed interest in them first. A look back at the previous extract on her childhood will, however, show how well this belief fitted into her existing cognitive-interpersonal schema, 'I am only able to gain love and respect by pleasing people'.

Safran and Segal (1990) link the need for an interpersonal focus with the work of Greenberg and Safran (1987) on the need for 'felt meaning' and deep emotion to be activated in therapy. This work criticized earlier models of cognitive therapy as being overly rationalistic and utilitarian in their approach, viewing painful emotions as needing to be brought under control. There has, however, been a growing realization in most forms of cognitive therapy that, as Beck has long said, emotion is the key to successful therapy.

The need to work with emotionally significant material can be linked to the development of interpersonal schemas. These schemas are likely to be encoded in highly emotional ways, so unless the therapeutic process activates at least some of these emotions, processing their meaning is unlikely to have much therapeutic impact. As indicated earlier, the relevant interpersonal beliefs may have been established in the client's earliest days and therefore much of the influential encoding will have been done in non-verbal ways. This means that such encoded meanings may not be touched by directly verbal interventions. This again highlights the role of the therapeutic relationship, especially as a context within which 'interpersonal markers' may be reviewed as possible samples of the client's interpersonal style. The recognition of the importance of interpersonal schemas and their role in the therapeutic relationship is now more fully integrated into cognitive therapy. This has started to change cognitive therapy from being a therapy in which the therapist could appear as the stereotyped cool, detached, logic-chopping technician, to a therapy in which 'emotion and thinking and behaving' are the central concerns. The therapist has to have a crucial awareness of how the client's issues may be played out in the 'here and now' in the therapeutic relationship itself, as well as in the client's life outside therapy. Such awareness demands a high degree of self-knowledge – awareness emphasized more readily in other therapies but now also recognized as a necessary part of cognitive therapy (Bennett-Levy, 2001).

In many ways, however, these new developments leave the original structure of cognitive therapy much as it was. The difference lies in the quality of what goes on inside the structure. Although the interpersonal model of cognitive therapy is still very much developing, the clearest accounts of it are emerging as 'schema-focused therapy' (Beck et al., 1990; Layden et al., 1993; Young, 1994; Young et al., 2003) described further in Chapter 7.

WORKING WITH COGNITIVE PROCESSES

A new addition to cognitive therapy is the focus on cognitive *processes* as well as cognitive content, and how these affect the development, maintenance and treatment of psychological problems. To some extent, this focus is evident in the original model with the highlighting of processes such as cognitive avoidance in anxiety, and how rumination, or continually thinking and worrying, maintains depression. An interest in the role of physiology in anxiety and work on meta-cognition ('thinking about thinking'), mindfulness and attention all served to bring cognitive processes centre stage. These new developments also chime in with some parallel thinking on the need to distinguish between the processes of acceptance, commitment and change, discussed in the final section of this chapter.

Cognition and Physiology

Physiological factors have always played an important role in the cognitive model, particularly in the understanding of anxiety (Beck and Emery, 1985). Models of anxiety have looked in greater detail at the way people interpret bodily cues (interoception), which has been shown to play a key role in panic attacks (Clark, 1986). People prone to panic attacks tend to make catastrophic interpretations of normal bodily symptoms. They are often prevented from learning that these symptoms are normal and benign by using 'safety behaviours' (Salkovskis, 1991; Salkovskis et al., 1996). The following examples illustrate how thinking about physical symptoms may be integrated into the cognitive model.

KEVIN

Kevin is a student nurse, prone to panic attacks. When he feels his pulse suddenly racing, he feels as if he is going to collapse and believes that collapsing in this way would lead colleagues to conclude that he is unable to do his job. Such catastrophic thoughts lead to a growing sense of panic, with increasing physical symptoms to match. He then uses a safety-seeking behaviour – he sits down. After a worrisome half hour, the symptoms begin to subside. Because he has not collapsed, he deduces that sitting down has saved him. He is not able to learn that he probably never would have collapsed, and even if he had, this would have been unlikely to lead to the catastrophe he fears. His panic-inducing belief therefore remains intact and able to strike again another day.

The role of physiology is also important in conceptualizing depression, as the following example illustrates.

JIM

Jim reported that every morning he awoke feeling physically uncomfortable, stiff and 'down'. He habitually thought, 'Oh no, not another day feeling like shit'. When he was able to step back and monitor this feeling more closely, he realized that he often felt some bladder or bowel discomfort because he wanted to go to the toilet. When he simply went to the toilet and set about getting ready for the day, he noticed that he felt much less uncomfortable and 'down'. He was then more able to resist making negative predictions about the rest of the day. He also discussed his physical sensations on waking with his wife. Although she did not get such symptoms, she reported feeling very tired in the early evening. As Jim felt better in the evening, he was able to redefine himself as 'different from' rather than 'inferior to' his wife. These two pieces of learning were a significant part of his successful attempts to get out of the vicious cycle of depression.

Meta-Cognition

Traditionally, cognitive therapy has tended to work with the language (declarative) content of negative thoughts and beliefs. When new therapists first try cognitive methods, they often report the difficulty that the client may report being intellectually convinced that they are not 'stupid', yet may continue to 'feel as if' they are stupid. This may be because traditional cognitive methods that challenge the content of thought are only challenging the output of the relevant cognitive processes whereas they would be more effective if they addressed the processes themselves, that is, explored how people arrive at what they 'know'.

The concepts of meta-cognition include an analysis of how individuals' thinking about their thinking plays a key role in the development of psychological problems. For example, the client who is anxious about everything has numerous negative, anxious thoughts. What is of interest is not simply the content and meaning of specific thoughts, but the meaning of thinking in this particular way. Wells and Matthews (1994) distinguish between direct (type 1) worries and these meta-cognitive (type 2) worries. Wells (2000), Clark and Wells (1995) and Wells and Butler (1996) show the importance of meta-cognition in the problems of both general anxiety and social phobia. They show how beliefs such as 'Worrying keeps me protected from nasty surprises' reinforce the problem and incubate further difficulty.

The case of Sasha, a 43-year-old insurance clerk, illustrates this process:

SASHA

Sasha worried about everything. She woke up worrying about the day, and went to bed worrying about what had happened in the day and what might happen the next day. She worried about her husband, her daughter, and her health and world affairs. Therapy initially focused on the content of these worries, her cognitive distortions, and learning to spot and challenge her thinking. She reported that the process of evaluating her thoughts made sense in her head, but she continued to feel awful, worrying as much as before. The therapy then moved to a meta-cognitive level, looking at the meaning of her worrying thoughts. She believed that not worrying would mean the things that she worried about would be more likely to happen. Worrying somehow alerted her to the possibility of danger, so she could act more quickly, and indeed prevent terrible things happening in the first place. If she did not worry, she might forget to do things. Therefore, stepping outside her thought content to look at the meaning of the process was necessary before Sasha could begin to change her worry patterns.

Salkovskis offers a similar analysis for people with obsessive-compulsive difficulties, where the client may believe that the fact she is having 'bad thoughts' in itself proves something 'bad' about her. Bad thoughts may also be taken as an indication that something bad might happen, indicating a sense of the client's excessive degree of personal responsibility for harm to self or others (Salkovskis et al., 1995). To try to deal with their thoughts, these clients often combine ritualistic behaviours, such as compulsive washing or checking, with 'neutralizing', such as trying to stop the thoughts or replace them with 'good' thoughts. As a result they are prevented from learning that the thoughts are normal and harmless. Therefore, as well as working on the specific content of the thoughts, analysis of the meaning of the thought processes is a more effective and fruitful intervention.

CHRISTOPHER

Christopher felt plagued with anxiety after walking past someone in the street and imagining him or her slipping on the wet pavement and hurting themselves. He felt extremely guilty, believing that the fact he had those thoughts was as good as him wanting the accident to happen, and may even increase the likelihood of an accident for which he would be responsible. If someone were to slip and hurt himself, he would not only be responsible for injury to that person, but doubly responsible because he had the chance to prevent catastrophe but did nothing about it. Christopher attempted to assuage his guilt by praying several times an hour.

Mindfulness and Attentional Processes

We have already shown how cognitive processes have increasingly pushed themselves forward for consideration as factors in both the understanding and treatment of psychological problems. It should perhaps not be forgotten that paying attention to the content of unhelpful cognitions might in itself lead to changes in the way that clients pay attention to such cognitions. Clients often refer to a process of moving on from such thinking styles by 'becoming heartily sick of them'. This kind of statement seems to refer to the experience of looking at the content of such thoughts and finding them ridiculous and/or revolting. While this does seem to represent a new view of content, it also reveals a determination to disengage with thinking about them at all.

This manoeuvre, however, seems a difficult one to achieve in certain kinds of more perseverative and ruminative thinking, particularly prominent in some of the anxiety disorders but also in some experiences of depression.

SALLY

Sally suffered from a disabling combination of panic attacks and health anxiety. An intervention based on changing the way she paid attention to her 'symptoms' at the start of the day was one of a number of successful interventions that helped to greatly reduce the overall effects of these problems. Rather like Jim, presented earlier in this chapter, Sally often awoke and immediately experienced aches, pains and discomforts. She then began to scan her body for other 'symptoms' and this scanning often escalated quite quickly to the conclusion that she had a major illness such as cancer. Attempts to counter this type of thinking via a thought record proved unsuccessful, partly because proof that she didn't have cancer was not easily or quickly obtainable. At this point, the therapist reflected on the way he himself handled this type of early morning feeling and suggested that Sally could try an experiment, during which she would endeavour merely to 'notice' such symptoms on waking and to postpone any serious evaluation of them until 11 am. Sally accepted the rationale for this manoeuvre – that if the aches and pains were only a passing phenomena, they might well have gone by that time. This proved a revelation to her in that not only had such aches overwhelmingly gone by that time but also on the rare occasions when they had persisted, they seemed less serious and intrusive.

This kind of relatively informal approach to attentional processes has been greatly supplemented in more recent years by the development of more systematic treatment approaches to problems of attention. In this book, we will particularly focus on MBCT (mindfulness based cognitive therapy; Segal et al., 2002) and ATT (attentional training; Papageorgiou and Wells, 1998, 2000), both discussed later in more detail. Mindfulness, drawing on the traditions of meditation and yoga, has developed ways of helping people view life experiences in a less driven and more mindful way. Attentional training has developed systematic ways of helping clients to shift their focus of attention while they are experiencing modes of negative experience.

THE NEWER MODEL OF THE THERAPY PROCESS

The scope of cognitive therapy is ever widening both in terms of its application to an increasing number of difficulties and in terms of a wider use of therapeutic interventions within its overall structure. In this new scenario, the concept of formulation or conceptualization, described in detail in Chapter 2, becomes even more useful. If we think of the formulation as a map of the client issues that are likely to be relevant to therapy, then we can see that it offers us many different points from which we may start and many different possible directions in which we may proceed. We could, for example, choose to proceed in the way of orthodox cognitive work and begin to work at the symptom level – the 'bottom-up' approach. The emphasis on working with emotions in cognitive therapy allows us to work in a primary way on the feeling level, perhaps taking techniques from experiential therapies such as Gestalt (Beck, 1995; Edwards, 1989). There is also a growing interest in working with emotions and imagery within a cognitive framework (Hackmann, 1997, 1998; Layden et al., 1993). Wells and Hackmann (1993), for example, show that clients' negative images in health anxiety, such as images of coffins, death or permanent disability, play a strong role in maintaining anxious symptoms, and that these negative images can be greatly attenuated as part of both symptom relief and general therapeutic change. Interestingly, working with imagery was advocated at an early stage by Beck (1970a), yet this seems to have been, until recently, a neglected clarion call. Beck's initial interest was in using imagery as a way of understanding the meaning that the client attributes to images or dreams. Emery, in a later work on anxiety (Beck and Emery, 1985), pointed out, however, that merely repeating the image several times often resulted in the development of more functional imagery. Influenced by Gestalt therapy, more recent cognitive approaches have shown a greater capacity to experiment with transforming imagery (Hackman, 1997, 1998; Layden et al., 1993).

As new ways of working in cognitive therapy evolve, rather than necessarily starting at the level of automatic thoughts, there is always the option of 'top-down' work, starting with work on the deeper level of cognitions – assumptions, core beliefs and schema. These cognitions can be deeper and less conscious than the more surface level of negative automatic thoughts, so that this style of therapy may bear some resemblance at times to psychodynamic therapy. The more explorative style of the 'constructivist' approach advocated by Mahoney (2003), Guidano (1991) and Liotti (1991), emphasize taking a developmental history and spending time working at that level. Assessment in cognitive therapy now includes more historical and developmental analysis, allowing for greater understanding of the origins of the client's core beliefs. This trend also allows many of our clients to tell their stories from the beginning, giving a top-down historical perspective of their difficulties.

In the newer models of the therapy process events in the therapeutic relationship may be used as markers, for both client and therapist, of unhelpful patterns of relating that are frequent outside therapy. Safran (1998), Safran and Muran (2003) and Safran and Segal (1990) have borrowed many ideas from both experiential and psychodynamic therapy to build a cognitive-interpersonal style for working with the therapeutic relationship. For example, if a client has had a poor attachment experience, then they are likely to develop the core belief, among others, that 'People are not trustworthy'. It is possible that they will carry that belief with them into therapy and that 'incidents' will happen in which lack of trust in the therapist will occur.

These incidents offer golden opportunities to highlight the client's immediate 'hot' thoughts and schemas about trust. The interpersonal tangles resulting from such schemas can be worked through in the relative safety of the therapy setting, for example by what Young et al. (2003) call 'limited re-parenting' which will be discussed further in Chapter 9.

JANE

Jane was able to see the origin of her 'people pleasing' and how it was driven by a lack of self-validation and self-esteem. She also detected the unhelpful assumption that 'I must work harder and harder and harder to please people if I am to ever get respect and recognition'.[1] Her people-pleasing style was sometimes active in therapy when she showed 'pleasing' behaviour towards the therapist. The therapist's supervisor advised him to look at how Jane could be a little more playful both with her colleagues and with the therapist. With statements like, 'I bet I really get up your nose sometimes', Jane could express empathy for others and, at the same time, get some useful feedback from them. Jane's pattern was so ingrained that it took some time for her to be able to stay with the experiment of being 'playful', firstly, with the therapist and, then, with her colleagues at work. Yet eventually she did begin to get experiential and emotional disconfirmation of her belief. One day she refused to clear up the office. She sought feedback from a colleague by asking, 'I bet that surprised you, didn't it?' The colleague laughed and said that people would respect her more if she surprised them more often.

THE 'THIRD WAVE' IN COGNITIVE THERAPY: THE NATURE OF CHANGE AND THE STANCE OF THE THERAPIST

Steven Hayes has referred to different 'waves' in the development of the cognitive behavioural therapies (Hayes et al., 2004). The first wave was classical behaviour therapy, rooted in behavioural principles, using empirical methods and aiming at changing behaviours. Later came the second wave, based on the cognitive models we have described, and integrating the behavioural model in the form of behavioural methods and experiments, aiming at changing thinking, meanings and beliefs. The third wave then began to question some of the basic assumptions and models of the previous waves: Is change always a good thing? Is doing always better than being? The newer cognitive therapies are developing approaches based on acceptance, moving between acceptance and change rather than automatically aiming for change and using experiential strategies, with broad, flexible and effective repertoires. There is more emphasis on the relevance of issues for clinicians as well as clients, and this wave is open to older traditions of meditation, mindfulness, spirituality, personal values and relationships (Teasdale, 2004). What does this mean in practice?

Hayes et al. (2004) have pointed out that although many people believe that they can 'get better' by changing negative patterns in thought and behaviour, these patterns are remarkably persistent and seem at times to defy rational analysis and treatment. Cognitive therapy has sometimes seemed guilty of being overly rational in its treatment objectives, assuming that the client will want to take on board a therapy and model of change which makes so much sense to the therapist. The client may, however, still be secretly dedicated to pursuing his old pattern strategy and may even be hoping that the therapist will design a strategy that will confirm or at least be compatible with it (Leahy, 2001). Sometimes the old pattern may be based on a lack of acceptance of the real problem, perhaps concealed in the blaming of another person or in a grandiose plan to transcend the difficulty. The grandiosity may be blind to the fact that change is actually hard work and takes a great deal of commitment. If cognitive therapy is undertaken before the client has fully accepted the fact that he does have a problem or before he has really committed himself to the hard work of change, it is likely to founder. Thus Hayes and colleagues (2004) have termed their approach to cognitive behavioural therapy 'Acceptance and Commitment Therapy' (ACT). This approach demands a subtle shift in the role of the therapist, including ensuring that both acceptance and commitment are tackled first before engaging in the more problem-centred and active aspects of cognitive therapy.

DAVE

Dave came into therapy following the development of depression after a separation with a long-term partner. She had convinced him that his way of thinking was the reason why their relationship was not working. There were indeed unhelpful and biased aspects to his thinking and he was therefore trying to use cognitive therapy to remake his thinking in order to make it and him acceptable to her again. He was secretly resentful of needing to do this and this resentment was only held in check by a strong fear of being left alone. In the event, however, no matter how humble and sensitive and how much of a 'new man' he made himself, he could not succeed in making her want him back. Cognitive therapy was channelled into a new version of the way he had always tried to 'win her back' before. Working on his thinking and feeling were potentially helpful to him and yet the goal for such work had been subverted by his old pattern. The therapist, though not quite seeing this at the time, felt that this 'putting on of an identity' was not a productive strategy but could not find a way of effectively conveying this to Dave. It was only when Dave discovered that his partner had been having an affair with another man for years, even before their separation, that the fury released him from this nonsensical strategy and he moved quite quickly thereafter towards psychological health and a new partner. A Scotsman, he eventually emigrated from the UK to the USA to marry and sent the therapist a wedding photograph of himself (in a kilt) and his very attractive new partner. Although that is what I call a therapeutic result, on reflection, addressing acceptance and commitment might have got us there more quickly.

Hayes et al. (2004) suggest that therapists who are over-reliant on rational change processes need to get smarter in understanding and responding to the kind of irrational factors that influence change. Therapists need to find ways for clients to really accept their problems and to commit to experimentation with new styles of being. These authors maintain that the tracks leading to change are mined with behavioural patterns and language traps and suggest many helpful ways of defusing such impediments throughout therapy.

A further aspect of the 'third wave' is the integration of mindfulness into cognitive therapy, as discussed earlier, not only in the form of explicit mindfulness practice such as that taught in Mindfulness Based Cognitive Therapy (Segal et al., 2002), but in a more mindful way of conducting therapy. The pull between acceptance, mindfulness and change is well developed in the model of Dialectical Behaviour Therapy for people with severe, long-term difficulties. Dialectical Behaviour Therapy aims to teach people to examine, accept and change patterns of thought and behaviour using meditation and acceptance strategies in order to stay with bad feelings, and make informed choices about change (Linehan, 1993a, 1993b).

The full implications of these more strategic ways of thinking about cognitive therapy are very new and are still being worked out. They suggest to us, however, a new angle on an old chestnut. How do we keep the clarity of the cognitive and behavioural models and yet at the same time make them flexible enough to be adapted to the differing needs of individual clients? The ideas of 'acceptance' and 'commitment' and 'mindfulness' can perhaps help us to elaborate on questions that have long been suggested as part of an initial assessment interview (Oxford Diploma in Cognitive Therapy, 1994):

- What is/are your exact goal/s at this time?
- What other solutions have you tried with this problem?
- How hopeful are you that therapy can help you at this time?

CONCLUSION

Now 40 years old, cognitive therapy is no longer the 'new kid on the block' but is an established psychotherapy and counselling model. It continues to show a great and youthful vibrancy and a capacity to develop very quickly. Cognitive therapy has also shown a capacity to listen to criticisms, and to change where appropriate. Although constructivist, schema-focused and attention-related models of cognitive therapy seem to have many differences from the original model, they also carry much of the older paradigm with them. For example, it is indeed debatable whether a true reading of Beck's earlier works does sustain the later accusations of being over-rational (Weishaar, 1993). It is probably more accurate to see the different ways of working as being on a continuum. Rather than replacing the old, newer approaches represent extensions of the original model that allow cognitive therapy to tackle a broader range of problems. The newer models have been put forward as being particularly appropriate for those difficulties with which the older model was not so successful – especially when clients have more intransigent anxiety problems, disrupted and traumatic histories and more fundamental personality issues rather than supposedly straightforward emotional disorders. It would be easy in this book to get carried away by the excitement of the new, and dive headlong into the third wave. These new developments are still in their very early stages and we look forward to their greater elaboration and secure location within the cognitive therapies. In the next chapters, we look at the core and well established features of cognitive therapy, conceptualization and the therapeutic relationship.

Further Reading

Classic texts with history and origins of cognitive therapy:

Beck, A. T. (1976/1989). *Cognitive therapy and the emotional disorders*. New York: Penguin.

Beck, A. T. & Emery, G. with Greenberg, R. L. (1985). *Anxiety disorders and phobias. A cognitive perspective*. New York: Basic Books.

Beck, A. T., Rush, A. J., Shaw, B. F. & Emery, G. (1979). *Cognitive therapy of depression*. New York: Guilford Press.

NOTE

1 The repetition of the word 'harder' indicates the driven nature of this thought.

2 Conceptualization: The Heart of Cognitive Therapy

Therapeutic models have tended to polarize between those that emphasize therapy as an experiential encounter, and those that stress therapy as a process wherein techniques are applied to a problem. As we have described in Chapter 1, initial models of cognitive therapy tended to locate themselves within the latter tradition. However, as the cognitive approach has evolved, the concept of case conceptualization or formulation (the two words carry the same meaning and are used interchangeably) has enabled us to integrate different aspects of therapy: experiential and technical information about the client's difficulties and the process of therapy. While case conceptualization was implicit in the older models of cognitive therapy – Beck et al. (1979, 1985) stress the importance of having an overall conceptualization for each client – the conceptualization or formulation model has become much clearer as cognitive therapy has evolved (Bruch and Bond, 1998; Tarrier and Calam, 2002). Jacqueline Persons (1989) was the first to explicitly describe how to link presenting problems to underlying psychological mechanisms, an approach which has subsequently developed, both in its application to specific problems, and in its integration of concepts concerning the role of emotion (Greenberg, 2002; Greenberg et al., 1997; Greenberg and Paivio, 1997) and the therapeutic relationship (Layden et al., 1993; Safran and Muran, 2003; Safran and Segal, 1990). In cognitive therapy, the conceptualization becomes the central driving force of the therapy process – a guide for understanding new material, the choice of strategies and the therapeutic relationship itself.

In this chapter, we look at what is meant by conceptualization or formulation in cognitive therapy, and the value of conceptualization. Formulation goes on at many levels and we start by looking at the 'basic level' or maintenance conceptualization, focusing on the client's immediate problems in terms of an interaction between thoughts, feelings, behaviour and biology as well as the individual's environment. We then go on to look at beliefs and assumptions that may be 'running the show' and how these underlying mechanisms fit into an overall, longitudinal formulation. We look at some of the 'off the shelf' conceptualizations that are increasingly developing in cognitive therapy, and discuss some of the hazards of using conceptualization. We also address the role of diagnosis, the pros and cons of using a diagnostic system and how diagnosis and formulation, together, can be helpful in understanding the individuals we see in therapy.

WHAT IS A COGNITIVE CONCEPTUALIZATION?

A cognitive conceptualization or formulation is a means of making sense of the origins, development and maintenance of a person's difficulties. It represents an overview which is essentially a hypothesis, open to testing and verification, arrived at collaboratively with the client, which then leads to a plan for intervention and therapy (Tarrier and Calam, 2002). The idea of formulating or conceptualizing a person's difficulties as part of therapy is not unique to cognitive approaches, but has been developed within other therapeutic models (Eells, 1997; McWilliams, 1999; Westmeyer, 2003). In cognitive analytic therapy, for example, case formulation is overtly used to build a shared understanding of the client's presenting issues, develop the therapeutic relationship and guide interventions (Ryle and Kerr, 2003).

There are many models of conceptualization or formulation in the cognitive therapy literature (see for example, Beck et al., 2003; Blackburn and Davidson, 1995; Bruch and Bond, 1998; Butler, 1998; Chadwick et al., 2003; Hawton et al., 1989; Persons, 1989, 1993; Persons and Tompkins, 1997; Tarrier and Calam, 2002; Young et al., 2003). As we have seen in Chapter 1, the cognitive model, in brief, proposes that thoughts and feelings are interrelated. At its simplest, a cognitive conceptualization focuses on vicious cycles linking thoughts and emotions (pp. 4–9). The conceptualization also includes behaviour and biology, and how these impact on and are affected by thoughts and emotions. As well as looking at the issues the client brings to therapy, a conceptualization also enables an understanding of problems in terms of underlying psychological mechanisms, namely assumptions and beliefs the client holds about him/herself, others and the world (Beck et al., 2003; Young et al., 2003). Formulation provides a bridge between what we know about psychological difficulties in general – such as how particular thoughts and behaviours might maintain anxiety problems, or how patterns of negative thinking and rumination make depressed people feel even worse – and an understanding of the client as an individual.

Conceptualization is an active and continuing process of developing a working hypothesis to provide a map or overview of the individual's problems and their origins. The map, made collaboratively with the client, is open to continuous modification, but acts as a useful guideline to any issue that crops up either in the client's life outside the therapy, or in the therapy relationship itself, and can act as the 'therapist's compass' (Persons, 1989). A good conceptualization helps the client answer questions such as 'Why me?', 'Why now?' and 'Why doesn't the problem just go away?', as well as 'How can I get better?'.

WHAT IS THE VALUE OF CONCEPTUALIZATION IN COGNITIVE THERAPY?

Formulation is one of the cornerstones of cognitive therapy for a number of reasons. It provides a bridge between cognitive theory and the practice of therapy, and helps make sense of individual's issues and difficulties. Conceptualization in itself is therapeutic, being a means of understanding, predicting and normalizing what people experience. Conceptualization provides a structure to therapy and guides the choice of interventions and treatments. It aids collaboration and is a means of dealing with problems in the process of therapy. Conceptualization is also useful in dealing with therapists' own issues (Beck et al., 2003; Persons, 1989; Persons and Davidson, 2002; Persons and Tompkins, 1997). In these and other ways, formulation 'drives' the therapy.

CONCEPTUALIZATION: MAKING CRYSTAL OUT OF MUD

Conceptualization is a means of linking the theory and practice of cognitive therapy. Theories of cognitive therapy are relatively clear and simple. In practice, we are dealing with the complexities of people. People we see in therapy describe their problems as seemingly intractable, incomprehensible, unending and unpredictable. If the client's problems are well conceptualized, they become more understandable and predictable both to themselves and to the therapist. The process of clarification and differentiation between problems, defining apparently unrelated problems as part of one issue, or conceptualizing a mass of issues into a smaller number of problems, helps the client make sense of the problems and believe that change is possible. Clients are likely to feel understood and, by gaining a greater understanding of why they are the way they are, it is likely that the therapist will feel greater empathy towards them, thereby improving the therapeutic relationship. Conceptualization can be a powerful therapeutic method in itself: a good conceptualization is likely to increase the client's understanding of and control over her problems, and enable her to predict future problems, thereby giving her the scope to avoid setbacks or relapse. An accurate conceptualization aids understanding of the picture for the individual rather than making generalizations based on a broad diagnosis. For example, two people seeking help for panic attacks may both be terrified of fainting. One may fear fainting because it would indicate that there was something seriously wrong with her, an as yet undiagnosed illness that would have terrible repercussions for her life. For this person, the key themes concern the meaning of physical symptoms and a personal sense of vulnerability. The other person fears fainting because he would make a fool of himself and lose others' respect. For him, the underlying mechanisms relate to being seen to be strong, to cope and not to show vulnerability to others. Thus, something reported by many people experiencing panic has very different meanings depending on the individual, understood in terms of differing psychological mechanisms.

CONCEPTUALIZATION FOCUSES AND GUIDES THERAPY

It is not unusual for people to bring to therapy a range of seemingly unrelated problems and, for any of these problems, a range of therapeutic strategies is available. While one strategy might be to throw solutions at the various problems in the hope that one or more might prove effective, the client may become discouraged and some interventions may be counterproductive. Short et al. (2004) report that many practitioners use cognitive methods without a formulation. For example a person-centred therapist might say they 'give thought records' to people without this method being used as part of an integrated formulation or therapy plan, and methods such as relaxation, distraction and controlled breathing may be used routinely for people with anxiety without an individual formulation. For an individual whose anxiety can be conceptualized by a belief that relaxing and letting go is dangerous, learning progressive muscular relaxation to activate and challenge the belief may be useful. However, for another client who believes that 'If I'm anxious, I may die' relaxation may be counterproductive, in that always relaxing when feeling anxious acts as a safety behaviour and prevents the client finding out that anxiety, while unpleasant, is not terminal. The conceptualization can therefore guide the choice of the many approaches to treating anxiety and worry (Sanders and Wills, 2003; Wells, 1997).

A more effective method is to base the choice of approach on an understanding of both the overt problems and the underlying mechanisms. The conceptualization is therefore a means of structuring and focusing therapy and enabling decisions to be made about the choice of intervention strategies and even which questions to ask during the process of guided discovery detailed in Chapter 5.

CONCEPTUALIZATION AIDS COLLABORATION AND HELPS DEAL WITH PROBLEMS IN THERAPY

Working with a formulation actively involves the client in therapy and improves collaboration. By learning how to conceptualize problems, the client becomes his own therapist. An understanding of underlying mechanisms alerts him to particular attitudes and beliefs that might be 'running the show', as well as teaching strategies for solving problems.

The conceptualization enables the therapist to understand and predict difficulties and 'off the ball' incidents in therapy, such as persistent lateness or non-attendance, or the client not doing homework. Such issues or difficulties can be conceptualized in terms of the client's overall picture, as understandable problems for both client and therapist, collaboratively, to work on. The conceptualization helps clients and therapists to consider how particular moves and interventions will influence the overall pattern of therapy.

BRENDA

Brenda had a long-standing tendency to ruminate and worry about things she had to do, starting to plan in her mind, mull over and think about any potential problems before they came up to surprise her. She believed, to some extent, that this rumination and thinking in advance enabled her to plan and predict difficulties, and be prepared whatever happened. At the start of each therapy session, Brenda would appear on guard, problems and issues spouting out of her in a way which seemed at times almost hostile. She appeared as though she arrived with 'all guns blazing', picking up on issues from the last session, putting words and ideas into the therapist's mouth, and finding it difficult to plan an agenda. In turn, the therapist felt 'on guard', having to get every word just right, not say the wrong thing, and the sessions started to get out of control, as planning an agenda became more difficult. The therapist started to dread the sessions. She asked Brenda what happened in the few hours before each session. Brenda would think through and plan in her mind everything she might say; everything the therapist might ask her and how she would answer the questions. This related to her need to be prepared, to have the right answers, to make the very best use of the therapy time, and not to be 'caught out' by the therapist as she had felt others had caught her out, and teased her, earlier on in her life. By identifying her beliefs, and how these led her to ruminate and worry before the sessions rather than think through, constructively, what she wanted to work on, the therapist felt more understanding of Brenda and why she was so 'prickly' to begin with. They collaboratively discussed and tested new ways of starting sessions, such as Brenda only allowing herself 20 minutes of problem solving to identify her session goals before each session.

The formulation helps the therapist understand and work with difficulties in the therapeutic relationship, by assuming that the client's behaviour with the therapist is similar to behaviour with others, and that both are driven by the central underlying problem (Flecknoe and Sanders, 2004; Persons, 1989). For example, if the client seems to constantly need reassurance from the therapist, this may be something that goes on in the rest of the person's life. The therapy can be used to explore such beliefs and the client's need for reassurance from others, and then test out means of her being more confident in her own decisions and opinions. Interpersonal beliefs regarding dependence can be allowed for and used in therapy, by discussing how dependence might be successfully overcome by working through a well-planned and resolving end to therapy.

CONCEPTUALIZATION FOR THERAPISTS

Conceptualization can also be usefully applied to therapists: by conceptualizing our reactions to our clients, we can work with difficulties we have with particular clients or clinical problems (Persons, 1989). For example, perfectionist therapists may find themselves overly concerned with getting the technical or manualized aspects of therapy 'right' or using the 'right' method even if it does not fully fit with the formulation or stage of therapy. Trying to do perfect, textbook cognitive therapy may mean we lose the sense of the individual client, and never risk the occasional forays into the murk and mess from which we may well learn something new or have startling revelations. If the therapist shares the same, not altogether functional, beliefs as the client, then it can be difficult for either to see or predict difficulties or blocks in therapy, and the therapist may unwittingly 'collude' with, rather than challenge, the client's assumptions. When therapists find strong emotion difficult, believing 'I must be in control at all times' or 'emotion is dangerous', they are more likely to guide the client towards managing strong feelings rather than allowing expression and exploring their meaning. Having a conceptualization of our own views of clients' issues may be a way of avoiding such collusion.

The method of conceptualization enables the therapist to work with a variety of people with a variety of problems, some of which may be new to the therapist. Although the problems may seem different, applying a general method of conceptualization is possible over a wide range of work in therapy. Many of the processes that cause psychological difficulties, such as difficulties with over-general memory, attention, thinking, rumination or safety behaviours, are common across many problems (Harvey et al., 2004). By using formulation, and understanding how to identify and work with these processes, we are able to work with people with a range of difficulties and issues. For example, I (DS) instinctively shy away from clients with OCD (obsessive compulsive disorder), believing that I 'do not understand' or 'am no good at' working with these problems. If I conceptualize myself, and some of my own near-obsessional beliefs, then I can understand part of my reluctance. But I am always happy to work with clients who worry and ruminate, those with health anxiety, and have a good understanding of spotting and working with safety behaviours. When I realized that these processes are very similar across different diagnostic groups, I also realized that, to my relief, I do not need to be so nervous of clients bearing the label of OCD.

CONCEPTUALIZATION IN PRACTICE

Developing a cognitive conceptualization or formulation is an ongoing process throughout the course of therapy. It often starts even before client and therapist meet. The therapist may have information about the client from referral letters, discussion with colleagues, a body of knowledge about the problem based on training and experience, and information from contact with the client, such as telephone calls or difficulties in making an appointment. Likewise, clients will have an understanding of their problem based on their experience and knowledge, reading, surfing the net, previous experience of psychological therapies and discussions with others. Both therapists' and clients' assumptions about the problems can be a rich source of material for the conceptualization, or may equally be a rich source of misinformation that needs revising.

CONCEPTUALIZATION: A SHARED PROCESS

At all stages, a conceptualization is a working hypothesis, which may or may not be useful to both client and therapist. We have seen how formulation aims to help the therapist think about how things fit together, what might change and what the difficulties of change might be. Formulation also needs to have exactly the same functions for the client. Hence, cognitive therapy leans towards trying to share as much of the conceptualization with the client as possible. In many instances, clients can be given a full diagram (as shown later in the chapter) at an early stage of therapy to play with and reformulate as therapy proceeds and their own ideas develop. There are sometimes reasons not to look at the full conceptualization until later in therapy – perhaps some clients might not be able to follow it or, at the other extreme, some clients might treat it as an excuse to 'intellectualize' their issues. In Kuyken's words:

> To use an analogy, a navigator who shares the whole road map with the driver may hinder rather than help the driver to keep on track because the driver is given information not directly relevant to the current task and the amount of information may be overwhelming. Collaboratively and gradually developing shared understandings and responding to feedback is an important method in CBT for ensuring understanding is developed constructively. (in press)

Another reason to hold back some of the model might occur when the therapist has hypotheses about the client's underlying schema or experience, on which it may be counterproductive to focus too early in therapy, possibly because the issues raised would be too painful for the client to deal with all at once. In our experience, most clients are able to make good use of a conceptualization in some form and we would encourage therapists to err on the side of sharing. With these cautions in mind, a general principle is that sharing and discussing the conceptualization in an overt and open way with the client is an integral and important part of the therapy process. It is also a means of working collaboratively with the client, and introducing them, at an early stage, to the process of collaborative empiricism.

CONCEPTUALIZATION: A WRITTEN EXERCISE

Cognitive therapists are never without pen and paper, and, ideally, a white board. Cognitive therapy has most things 'out on the table' or illustrated in a written form. The conceptualization, often linked to key points of the therapy, is illustrated, in black and white, during the session, for both client and therapist to think about during and between sessions. There are many ways of drawing up a conceptualization, such as drawing vicious cycles, with pictures, metaphors or ready-made conceptualizations with boxes to fill with negative automatic thoughts and underlying beliefs. General conceptual models for different problems can be adapted to the individual client (see for example Bruch and Bond, 1998; Clark and Fairburn, 1997; Sanders and Wills, 2003; Tarrier, in press; Wells, 1997; see also Fennell, 1999 for a formulation of low self-esteem that can be adapted to the individual). Literally drawing out the formulation as a diagram begins to trace out patterns and chains of different reactions in a readily understandable way and offers a means of finding a point where intervention and change can start.

BASIC CONCEPTUALIZATION: LINKING THOUGHTS, FEELINGS, BEHAVIOUR AND PHYSIOLOGY

The essence of the model is that emotional difficulties begin when the way we see events gets exaggerated beyond the available evidence; these exaggerated ways of seeing things tend to have negative influences on our feelings and behaviour, in a *vicious cycle*. Basic conceptualization, therefore, aims to identify and focus on the *meaning* people give to situations, emotions or biology, expressed as patterns of thinking and beliefs. At the beginning of therapy, we ask the client for a specific, recent example of the problem brought to therapy. Rather than asking 'How do you generally feel ...?', We ask 'Can you describe in detail a recent example of ...?' This way, the conceptualization can be specific, concrete and relevant to the client's concerns.

THE THOUGHT–EMOTION CYCLE

In the first stages of conceptualization, the therapist and client work together to draw out the links between thoughts and feelings specific to the individual, looking in particular at how each relates to the other. This forms the rudimentary conceptualization in cognitive therapy, as the following brief dialogue with a depressed client illustrates:

Therapist: So, yesterday, you were finding it difficult to write your essay. What was going through your mind?
Client: I kept thinking 'I'm such a failure: a useless failure'.
Therapist: And when you say to yourself 'I'm a useless failure', how does that make you feel?
Client: Terrible, really depressed.
Therapist: And when you feel really depressed, what goes through your mind?
Client: ... I'm such a useless failure.

This kind of dialogue leads to the simplest level conceptualization, linking specific thoughts with feelings, leading to a drawing such as that shown in Figure 2.1.

EXPANDING THE CYCLE: THE ROLE OF BEHAVIOUR

The next section of the vicious cycle, often identified and drawn up at the same time as the simple level conceptualization described earlier, is to begin to add behaviour and physiology to the equation. For example, a common behaviour pattern in depression is that people will become withdrawn,

Figure 2.1 Linking thoughts and feelings

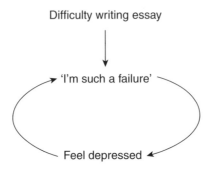

Figure 2.2 Linking thoughts, feelings and behaviour

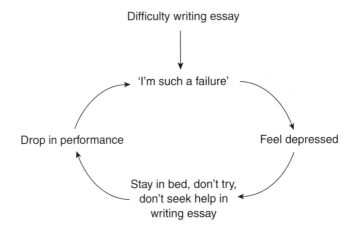

not going out or staying in bed for long periods. At these times, they often feel a lot worse – the ease of rest does not help. The inactivity gives them more opportunity to think, which often seems to turn into moping and morbid rumination, including negative thoughts about the self for staying in bed. For the client of Figure 2.1, the cycle can be expanded as illustrated in Figure 2.2.

A further example is given in Figure 2.3.

JOHN

John is a 52-year-old farm labourer. He has had considerable family problems, with two of his four sons getting in trouble with the law. His marriage has been very strained, with his wife spending long periods with her sister in a nearby village. John became withdrawn and very depressed, unlike his old, generally quite cheerful, self. His GP asked the practice counsellor to try to help but warned that John might not be very psychologically minded. The counsellor found John easy to get on with and they began to make some progress to help him understand his depression by drawing and discussing the diagram shown in Figure 2.3.

Figure 2.3 Linking thoughts, feelings and behaviour

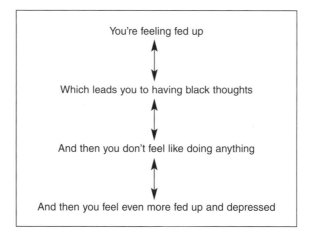

The way we behave and what we do in response to our thoughts and beliefs can, inadvertently, maintain our problems. The notion of 'safety behaviours' was originally introduced by Paul Salkovskis (1991) to explain why people who experience panic attacks continue to believe that something bad will happen to them despite repeated episodes where their feared catastrophe does not happen. For these people, something they do during a panic attack, such as sitting down, breathing deeply, escaping from the situation or seeking help, reinforces the beliefs that the feared catastrophe would still have happened if not for their behaviour, and that they are still at risk of the consequences of panic. The notion of safety bahaviours has been developed and expanded to cover many different problems (see Bennett-Levy et al., 2004; Harvey et al., 2004; Wells, 1997). The following example illustrates the role of behaviour in social anxiety.

MIKE

Mike, a 24-year-old student with social phobia, is describing a recent incident where he was required to make a presentation to a group of his classmates. He had been anxious and preoccupied about this for several weeks beforehand, but had worked out strategies to get him through. Notice that the therapist has asked Mike to describe what is going on in the incident as though it is happening now.

Therapist: You're describing being asked to begin your presentation. How are you feeling?

Mike: Actually, I'm feeling as if I'm not really here, like my mind has gone off somewhere else, and that scares me. So, I try and really concentrate on what I've got to say, and keep an eye on how I'm feeling.

Therapist: How are you doing that, keeping an eye on how you're feeling?

Mike: I'm scanning what's going on. I'm beginning to notice a sort of churned up feeling inside, like my guts are just getting busy, and I'm feeling quite shaky. I realize I've got to get a grip... otherwise....

Therapist: Otherwise...?

Mike: Otherwise I will lose it completely. Just spurt the words out all over the place and not make any sense at all. Like we've been talking about – like a complete prat.

Therapist: And that's an awful fear for you. How do you prevent this happening? What do you mean by 'getting a grip'?

Mike: I do everything in my power to relax. I bust a gut to relax. I say to myself over and over, 'Get a grip, Mike, get a grip', and try and let my muscles go. I start taking deep breaths and concentrate on watching the air go in and out.

Therapist: Does that help? How are you feeling now you're trying so hard to relax?

Mike: I know it is the only way I'll get through. I must relax, otherwise...

Therapist: Otherwise...?

Mike: Well, it's back to the same old thing, the same old Mike being a complete prat.

In this example, Mike is trying to relax and breathe deeply in order to get through his presentation, and has very strong beliefs that if he did not do this, catastrophe would happen – in his case he gets a strong image of himself shaking, stuttering, saying words in random order, and being 'a complete prat'. The behaviours of trying to keep himself safe are not helpful for several reasons: they keep Mike focused on himself and how he is feeling. This means he takes his many physical reactions as evidence of losing control, and averts his attention from his audience which means he cannot see the evidence to counteract his beliefs that people see him as a prat; trying to relax and breathe deeply may

Figure 2.4   Formulation of Safety Behaviours

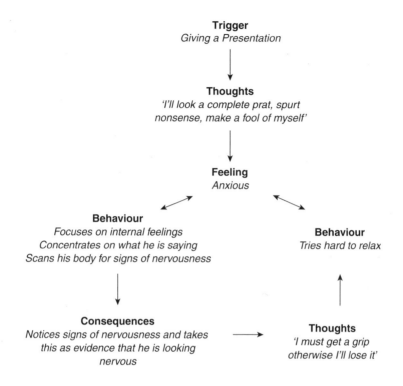

themselves increase symptoms of anxiety (an experiment readers can try for themselves – I find trying hard to relax can feel stressful); and continually trying to control his anxiety means that Mike is unable to disconfirm his worst fears, that people will notice he is nervous, that the anxiety means he will spurt out nonsense and so on. The formulation for Mike is shown in Figure 2.4

Avoidance is a very common, and important, safety behaviour that maintains anxiety, depression and other difficulties. Individuals may avoid going into situations just in case something bad happens, such as not going out of the house in case they collapse. Not doing what is feared may, in the short term, alleviate some of the anxiety. In the long term, however, avoidance prevents the individual from learning how to deal effectively with situations. Neither will the person learn that what is feared is very unlikely to happen. Avoidance erodes the individual's confidence. A depressed person may avoid going out or trying to do something they previously enjoyed, believing, for example, that 'there is no point', or 'if I try and do something I won't feel any better, and that will just confirm there is something wrong with me'. By not attempting to involve themselves in enjoyable activities, people do not get the chance to test out and disconfirm such beliefs.

The fact that distraction can sometimes be a helpful way of dealing with negative thoughts leads to the question: when is a behaviour a safety behaviour and when is it a useful way of getting through life? Many of us might feel nervous before, say, an interview, giving a workshop or lecture, meeting our partner's parents for the first time, giving evidence in court and so on. It is quite reasonable and helpful for us to calm ourselves down by some deep breathing, relaxing, or making sure we take time not to be stressed before the event by getting a good night's sleep. These strategies can all be either helpful coping methods or safety behaviours, depending on the individual's beliefs. The key questions are what the person believes would happen if they did not do these things, and whether they believe that such behaviours are the only ways of coping. If we know that whatever happens we will get through, and that, once we start talking, we'll get engaged in the social event and then will no longer be so self-focused, it is likely that the anxiety will then recede and we will be able to get on with the task in hand. This coping behaviour is now more a way of helping ourselves feel better than a way of averting catastrophe. So, as the example of Mike illustrates, it is important to check not only what someone does when anxious, but what they believe would happen if they did not do it.

Similarly, when very low, taking time out and not attempting to deal with or fight the situation may be in some situations adaptive or helpful. Taking an evolutionary perspective, depression and withdrawal may be an appropriate response when the situation means that no change is possible, and the person or social group is better off withdrawing and conserving their energy than wasting energy on fruitless attempts to change, or where submissive behaviour is valuable as a form of social defense (Gilbert, 2000a, 2001). For example, in evolutionary terms, during a long, cold winter, people who stayed in, withdrew and did not attempt to do too much were more likely to survive than those who tried to actively tackle the environment with limited resources. This does not mean that total withdrawal during depression is always a good thing, but it may help people to understand why we instinctively withdraw, and be more compassionate towards this behaviour, and then begin to do more and become more active on a gradual basis.

The fourth stage in developing a conceptualization is to bring in the client's physical symptoms or somatic state. In anxiety, physical symptoms often predominate: the initial problem may be interpreted as 'There's something wrong with my body: I'm ill'. The aim of conceptualization is to help the client to look at how the physical feelings interact and trigger off the other components of the cycle, well illustrated by the cognitive models of panic and health anxiety (Clark and Fairburn, 1997). The following example illustrates how physical symptoms play a role in panic attacks.

MAVIS

Mavis had been referred to the community psychiatric nurse (CPN) for help with anxiety and panic attacks. Mavis had not initially thought about the possibility that she was anxious, and did not know what a panic attack was. She had been feeling awful, with 'out of the blue' episodes of shaking, difficulty in breathing, a tight chest and tingling in her arms. She was extremely concerned that this was the beginnings of heart disease, and had been checked up by the cardiologist, who had diagnosed anxiety and sent Mavis off to 'sort herself out'.

The nurse asked Mavis to describe a recent example of feeling awful, in this case in the supermarket. The conceptualization proceeded as follows:

CPN: What was the first thing you noticed?
Mavis: I started to feel awful, really odd, completely out of the blue. I couldn't breathe, I started to get these pains in my chest and the tingling … I felt quite shaky.
CPN: So, you were feeling really awful … when you felt like this, what was going through your mind?
Mavis: Well, I know it's stupid since I know there's nothing wrong with me, the cardiologist said so … but I really thought I was having a heart attack and this was it!
CPN: It sounds like you were feeling pretty bad, but you sound a bit embarrassed about what you made of it … I guess it makes sense if you were feeling that bad.
Mavis: Um …
CPN: So, you felt awful, chest pains, couldn't breathe, and you said to yourself, 'I'm having a heart attack, this is it'. When you said that to yourself, how did that make you feel?
Mavis: Terrified.
CPN: And when you felt terrified, what was going on in your body?
Mavis: I guess it didn't help. I felt much worse.

The nurse writes down the sequence as illustrated in Figure 2.5.

CONCEPTUALIZING THE PROCESS OF COGNITION

While early approaches to cognitive therapy aimed to identify and change the content of thoughts, newer models also focus on the process of cognition, meta-cognition, thinking about thinking, and the meanings people attach to cognitive phenomena in their own right (Wells, 2000).

People have characteristic thinking styles and processes, for example a black and white style, a ruminatory style, or difficulty in moving between different styles or modes of thinking, such as getting 'stuck in a groove' of negative thoughts, or

Figure 2.5   Linking thoughts, feelings, behaviour and biology

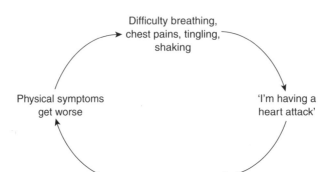

trying to suppress thoughts (Harvey et al., 2004). Rumination is described as 'behaviour and thoughts that focus one's attention on one's depressive symptoms and on the implications of these symptoms' (Nolen-Hoeksema, 1991: 569). People can believe that rumination is a good strategy for solving problems or preventing bad things happening whereas, in reality, too much focus on bad feelings can perpetuate depression and low mood, and impair the ability to solve problems (Papageorgiou and Wells, 2003). A ruminative style, mulling things over and over, asking 'Why do I feel this way? Why me?' and trying to come to some kind of conclusion about questions without solutions is not helpful. Such rumination, however, may often be confused with the analysis, understanding and insight that is such an important component of emotional processing and change (Watkins, 2004). Rumination also plays a major role in the processes of worrying and generalized anxiety.

Thought suppression, when the person tries not to think certain thoughts, or actively 'neutralizes' them by engaging in behaviours such as counting, hand washing or other rituals, is characteristic of obsessive-compulsive disorder. Metacognition refers to specific negative and 'positive' beliefs about thoughts, such as 'Worrying will kill me' or 'I need to worry, it's the only way to be prepared if bad things happen'. Sometimes it is clear in the early stages of therapy that thinking styles and metacognition are key areas of concern, as is often the case for people who worry or ruminate excessively; for other clients, conceptualizing the process of thinking comes later in therapy.

CONCEPTUALIZING ENVIRONMENTAL, SOCIAL AND CULTURAL FACTORS

All therapies aim to emphasize the unique qualities of the individual, and to understand the issues the client brings into therapy in terms of an overall, holistic, picture. Psychotherapy in general has been criticized for not paying sufficient attention to the wider social, environmental and cultural context in which the individual operates, and cognitive therapy is no exception (see Hays, 1995). Therefore the conceptualization must always take into account the client's cultural background and environment (Tarrier and Calam, 2002). The context includes a person's gender, sexual orientation, ethnicity, family upbringing, social support or lack of, socio-economic circumstances, accommodation and employment status. We would also include in the environmental formulation positive factors in the person's life, such as good, confiding relationships, the ability to solve problems in the past and their financial status, which will facilitate rather than hinder change.

Environmental factors, too, are of vital importance in determining how we react in the world and the meaning given to situations. Socially isolated women with young children are at particular risk of depression; mental health correlates strongly with economic factors. The conceptualization must consider these, and remind both therapist and client alike that we do not operate in isolation, and therefore any change has to take into account the wider context.

OTHER MODELS OF CONCEPTUALIZATION

Cognitive conceptualization may be as varied as our clients, and require creativity on the part of the therapist. Not all problems fit into vicious cycles or straight lines; for some clients, behaviour, biology or even thoughts may play little role in the conceptualization. The challenge for the therapist is to be sufficiently flexible and creative to develop a workable conceptualization with the client that takes into account what she is saying and believing, regardless of whether it fits into the cognitive model in the therapist's head.

A generic model, shown in Figure 2.6, is a means of integrating thoughts, emotions, behaviour and biology as well as the effect of the environment (Padesky and Mooney, 1990). The model illustrates the impact of the different components on each other and means that, wherever the client starts to describe his

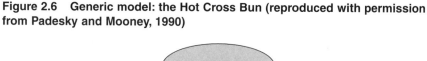

Figure 2.6   Generic model: the Hot Cross Bun (reproduced with permission from Padesky and Mooney, 1990)

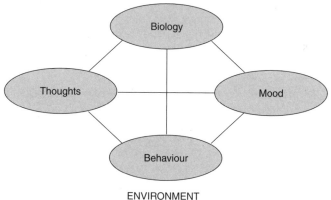

©1986 Center for Cognitive Therapy, Newport Beach, CA.

problems, the therapist can look at the other components and include these in the conceptualization. The generic model was valuable in engaging Philip in cognitive therapy.

PHILIP

Philip, a 50-year-old man who had been depressed for two years, had only reluctantly agreed to see a psychologist. Antidepressant medication had not proved all that helpful, and Philip was still very low. Initially, he was adamant that his problems were due to chemical imbalances in his brain, and therefore psychological factors were not relevant. The psychologist developed a model of Philip's problems as follows:

Philip:	I really don't see much point in talking about it. Depression is an illness – it's the chemicals in my brain that need fixing. I don't know what else to do about it.
Therapist:	Yes, there's no doubt that depression is a chemical imbalance. But, there may be other things you can do to help, despite what's causing the depression. Would you be happy to talk a bit more about it to see if there are any other ways of tackling the depression?
Philip:	Well, OK …
Therapist:	Tell me a bit about how you've been feeling.
Philip:	Really low. I've no energy and I just can't get on and do anything. I just want to sleep all the time.
Therapist:	So, the depression is making you feel very tired so it's hard to get on with anything. How does the tiredness make you feel in yourself?
Philip:	Very fed up really. Like there's not much point in anything.
Therapist:	It sounds like you've been feeling very fed up, and that makes you say 'There's no point'. When you say that to yourself, how does that make you feel?
Philip:	More fed up, I guess.
Therapist:	And when you feel fed up, what do you want to do?
Philip:	I just want to sleep.
Therapist [Summarizing]:	I've been drawing up a model as you've been talking. What you've told me is that the depression is making you feel very low: the chemicals really affect your energy levels. When you feel physically low, you want to sleep all the time, which makes you feel low and tired, and feeling low makes you think there's no point, which makes you feel fed up [*draws up diagram – Figure 2.7*].

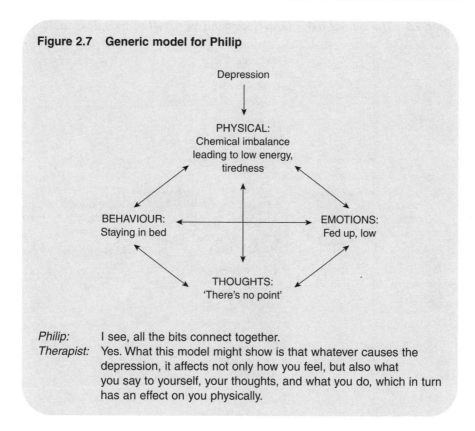

Figure 2.7 Generic model for Philip

Depression

↓

PHYSICAL:
Chemical imbalance
leading to low energy,
tiredness

BEHAVIOUR:
Staying in bed

EMOTIONS:
Fed up, low

THOUGHTS:
'There's no point'

Philip: I see, all the bits connect together.
Therapist: Yes. What this model might show is that whatever causes the
              depression, it affects not only how you feel, but also what
              you say to yourself, your thoughts, and what you do, which in turn
              has an effect on you physically.

As a result of using the diagram, Philip agreed to try to tackle the depression in different ways, such as working out how to behave differently when depressed, and looking at his patterns of thinking. Such models can be valuable when working with people who see their problems as primarily physical, but where psychological factors play a role in maintaining them. This might include people with chronic medial illnesses (White, 2000), somatization and health anxiety, or unclear medical problems such as chronic fatigue syndrome (Burgess and Chalder, 2005). A formulation focusing on components that maintain the problems avoids getting into a debate about what causes the problems in the first place. For example, chronic pain may have been triggered initially by physical injury, but is maintained by a combination of emotional factors (depression about the pain), environmental factors (stress, financial difficulties from being unable to work), behavioural factors (avoiding activities due to pain) and cognitive factors (catastrophizing about the pain, constant worry about the future; see Winterowd et al., 2004).

Another clinically valuable conceptualization is the 'vicious daisy', where the central problem is maintained by a number of 'petals' made up of different factors. For example, a client's thoughts, feelings and behaviour may be both the result and cause of low self-esteem, as illustrated in Figure 2.8. The model shows how, as a result of low self-esteem, a person picks unhealthy relationships, abuses themselves in

Figure 2.8 The vicious daisy (Ann Hackmann, personal communication, 1996)

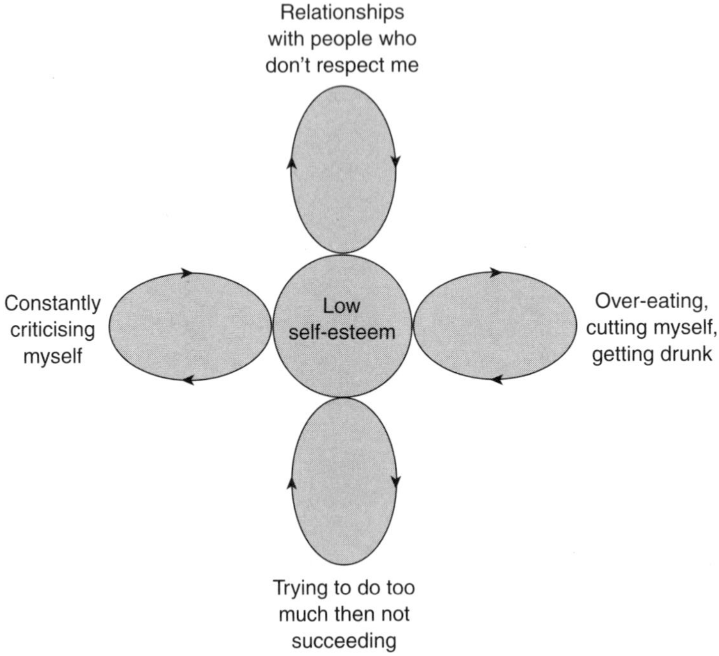

Relationships
with people who
don't respect me

Constantly
criticising
myself

Low
self-esteem

Over-eating,
cutting myself,
getting drunk

Trying to do too
much then not
succeeding

various ways, attempts impossible tasks and castigates themself for not succeeding, and continually gives themself very negative messages, all of which reinforce the person's lack of self-esteem. Petal diagrams are used by Salkovskis to conceptualize obsessional problems and health anxiety (Salkovskis and Bass, 1997).

CONCEPTUALIZING ASSUMPTIONS AND CORE BELIEFS: A LONGITUDINAL PERSPECTIVE

So far we have discussed formulating the links between thinking and emotions, and the role of behaviour, biology and the environmental context. The next stage is to begin to conceptualize the problems in terms of underlying psychological mechanisms, namely unhelpful assumptions and beliefs which are related to, and which 'drive', the negative automatic thoughts and emotions. Assumptions and beliefs can be understood in terms of the client's early, or later, experiences, and cultural, biological and environmental factors, as relevant. The client's fleeting thoughts are often only the immediate manifestations of deeper cognitive levels. If these thoughts are seen as a cross-section of a tree, then the core beliefs relating to early experience are the original growth of the tree and the assumptions and automatic thoughts are subsequent rings of growth. Thoughts, assumptions and beliefs can be seen as three different levels of meaning, as illustrated in Figure 2.9.

Figure 2.9   Level of Thoughts and Beliefs

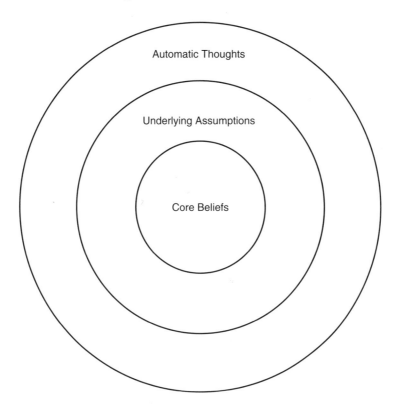

Source: Padesky, 1995–2000. Centre for Cognitive Therapy. Reproduced with permission

WHAT ARE BELIEFS AND ASSUMPTIONS?

We all have beliefs and assumptions about the essential nature of our selves, others and the world. Such beliefs and assumptions may be thought of as the key elements of our frame of reference, or set of rules determining our 'way of being' in the world, how we judge ourselves, situations or others, and how we interact with other people (Beck, 1976; Beck et al., 2003; Young et al., 2003). Our rules are formed mainly from our early experience, and often become revised as we develop and encounter different experiences. Rules of this sort are 'silent assumptions' and generally operate without us being aware of them. We pay selective attention to the world around us, screening, sorting and integrating information according to our rules. Core beliefs, which are discrete parts of more general mental structures called schemas, are often expressed in absolute terms such as 'I am a bad person', 'I'm a failure', 'I'm vulnerable' or 'I'm worthless'. As well as beliefs about the self, we have beliefs about others, such as 'Other people can never be trusted', and beliefs about the world such as 'The world is a dangerous place'. Assumptions, in contrast, are often conditional, 'if/then' statements, developed to some extent in order to enable the individual to live with the particular beliefs. For example, a woman who feels herself to be a bad person, may develop a rule: 'If I am nice all the time, and put others' needs first, then they won't see what a bad person I am', or for someone who believes 'I am a failure', an assumption may develop such as 'I must be perfect and in control of everything. To make a mistake means I'm a complete failure'. Beck (1996) identifies three types of conditional rules: negative conditional rules ('If I get close to others, they will reject me'); compensating conditional rules ('If I avoid others, I can avoid rejection'); and imperative rules ('I must be perfect').

Assumptions and beliefs that may underlie emotional problems have been labelled 'dysfunctional' or 'maladaptive'. In practice, our set of rules may well have been functional and adaptive at some stage in life. For example, it may have been useful for the child to believe 'I am responsible for bad things happening' and 'If I am extremely careful and do everything just right, then bad things may not happen', in order to survive childhood abuse. It is safer for children to conclude that they are wrong than it is to conclude that their parents, on whom they are very dependent, are wrong. Problems may arise, however, when our rules are not adjusted and revised in the light of later experience, or when we take on board rules that are the result of someone else's distorted or unhelpful way of seeing things: in the earlier example, the individual's rules may lead to obsessional problems and self-blame or disgust. As these beliefs and rules may have had some rationale at the time, describing them as 'dysfunctional' may be rather harsh. Terms such as 'unhelpful' or 'out-of-date' assumptions or beliefs may be more realistic and less judgmental.

Assumptions are rules that are learned through experience. They often run in families in one form or another. Many are culturally reinforced, meeting gender or cultural stereotypes which make it difficult for the individual to identify or challenge the beliefs. Unhelpful assumptions can often be fitted into three themes: achievement, acceptance and control (Beck and Emery, 1985). Examples may include, 'In order to be happy, I must be successful in everything'; 'To be happy I must be accepted by all people at all times'; 'If someone disagrees with me, it must mean I'm an awful person'; 'If I am nice and never angry, bad things won't happen'; 'I must be in control all the time'. Assumptions are often quite unconscious. We are not immediately aware of the rules themselves, only the emotional or physical discomfort that may arise from transgressing them. For example, an individual whose rule says, 'I need to be perfect in everything I do in order to be acceptable' will feel excessive anxiety or depression on making a mistake that will strike others as a minor one.

Deeply held beliefs and assumptions exert an ongoing influence on how we perceive and behave in our daily life. An individual who believes, for example, 'I am a failure' may have many examples throughout life to prove that this belief is distorted. However, we have subtle ways of discounting and ignoring information that does not confirm our beliefs while collecting and remembering instances where the belief is confirmed. We will look more at the process of how beliefs are maintained throughout life in Chapter 7. Young and colleagues

(2003) describe a process of 'schema maintenance', whereby our beliefs become self-fulfilling prophecies, and we pay attention to information or behave in a manner that confirms our beliefs and discounts, ignores or alters information that disconfirms the belief. The process has been compared to that of a prejudice (Padesky, 1990): however much the world, our experience or other people disconfirm our rules, we may carry on believing our beliefs, reinforced through selective attention, distorting information to fit the facts, and ignoring contrary information. For example, a room may be filled with 99 people offering praise and encouragement, while one is muttering how badly the job was done. The perfectionist or the individual whose self worth is determined by others' views only pays attention to the one negative voice, hardly noticing the other 99. Safety behaviours inadvertently maintain and reinforce beliefs, because the person is never able to collect or pay attention to information that may disconfirm the beliefs (Bennett-Levy et al., 2004).

CONCEPTUALIZING ASSUMPTIONS

In practice, the stage of identifying and conceptualizing assumptions often runs in parallel with the development of a basic-level conceptualization, but is developed more fully during the later stages of therapy. It involves looking at more general principles and themes involved in the client's problems as well as working with specific examples. Various sources are used to track down assumptions. These include the presenting problems, themes in therapy, diaries of negative automatic thoughts, questionnaires, the client's response to therapy or the therapist, and issues in the therapy process, and the 'downward arrow' described in Chapter 5.

Unhelpful assumptions may be those that the person holds all the time, which lie around waiting to be triggered, or those that are formed and active during times of low moods, but disappear when the person feels well again. If the person's life is going well, particular assumptions may hardly ever be triggered. If there is impending loss of an important person or the prospect of failure, then a significant assumption may well be triggered. At this moment, the person is not only dealing with the emotion that anyone would feel when appearing to fail but is also dealing with the latent negative feeling contained within the assumption. This double effect explains the strength of the resulting feelings. A conceptualization of underlying assumptions can help the client to understand more about these strong feelings and thus be less frightened of them.

As noted previously, drawing out these patterns with pen and paper can help the client face and work with these strong feelings and therefore can move the therapy forward. For example, Sydney had the assumption: 'If I can please people, I might win their respect'. When his colleagues at work showed even minor irritation with him, he had the automatic thoughts: 'They think I'm crap. They hate me'. This triggered his assumption, along with the thought: 'I'll never win their respect'. He then felt overwhelmed by negative feelings to the extent that his work deteriorated and this elicited yet further negative signals from his colleagues. The chain of events was discussed and drawn out on paper, as shown in Figure 2.10.

Figure 2.10 Conceptualizing assumptions

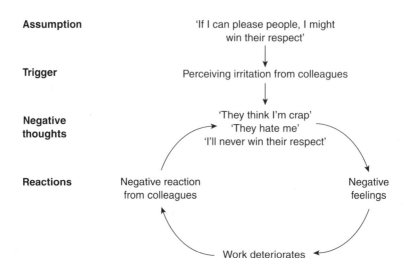

In Sydney's example, the assumption leads to a stream of thoughts whenever activated; it is also clear that the assumption may act as a 'self-fulfilling prophecy' in that trying to please people all the time and trying too hard may well provoke irritation from others, as well as lead to a deterioration of performance.

Some assumptions may be adaptive and socially acceptable and reinforced. For example, high standards and perfectionism may help someone to do well with a career, but may cause problems when the assumptions are not adapted according to changes in the environment or the individual. For people with chronic fatigue syndrome, for example, assumptions about doing well, achievement, not letting others down and being reliable can get in the way of recovering from illness, leading to the person 'pushing through' symptoms of exhaustion rather than allowing time to heal and recover (Burgess and Chalder, 2005). Such assumptions can also underlie irritable bowel syndrome (Toner et al., 2000). Shelley, who sought help with recurrent unexplained bowel symptoms, had extremely high standards for herself and her work and did well with her career, but became very stressed and anxious as she got older, when demands of her family and natural decline in energy levels meant she could not maintain the same high standards in all areas of her life. Her assumptions, 'If I do well at one thing, I need to do well everywhere' and 'If anything needs to give, it's got to be me', were not enabling her to ease off on her work and meant she kept on trying to be the 'perfect career-wife and mother' to the detriment of her health.

CONCEPTUALIZING CORE BELIEFS

Core beliefs and schema are the deepest level of cognition, underlying both automatic thoughts and assumptions. While assumptions are 'if/then' conditional rules, core beliefs are absolute: 'I am bad', 'I'll never find anyone who could love me', 'Nobody can be trusted'. They are so negative and tyrannical that they are very hard to live with. Hence assumptions develop which, while in themselves may not be totally helpful or functional, at least mitigate the effects of the core belief. Core beliefs are not only about the self, but are about wider concerns – about other people and the world. For example, beliefs such as 'People are never to be trusted' and 'The world is a dangerous, unsafe place' may lead the individual to be over-vigilant and have a heightened sense of vulnerability. Beliefs are often more rigid and resistant to change than assumptions, and appear from the outside as extreme, irrational and unreasonable. They are relatively impervious to ordinary experience, and may be treated as a fact rather than as a belief. They may be expressed in very clear, simple, black-and-white language: 'I'm bad', 'I'm weak', 'It's wrong to lose control'. The words may be those of a child, representing primitive and undeveloped meanings that clearly do not reflect the attributes or skills of the individual. They are often unhelpful and not functional, preventing the individual achieving many goals in life (Young et al., 2003).

The conceptualization of core beliefs provides a bridge between cognitive therapy and other forms of therapy that give prominence to the client's early experience. While early forms of cognitive therapy may have reacted against psychoanalytic therapy by developing a suspicion of exploring the past experience of clients, Beck, right from the start of his work, has always reserved an important role for past experience, specifically in the way that clients have drawn certain conclusions about life, other people and themselves based on their experiences (Beck et al., 1979, 2003). Therefore, as part of conceptualizing the client's past experience, when reviewing the client's history, an important question for client and therapist to explore is: 'What conclusions do you think you drew about yourself, others and the world, based on what happened to you at that time?'

THE FULL CONCEPTUAL MODEL

While the above description of the process may sound like putting together pieces of a jigsaw bit by bit, in practice the process is more organic and flexible, conceptualization being a *process* that runs through the whole of therapy. We would usually start with the basic-level conceptualization, putting together the pieces with the client. However, we would do this with the wider model in mind, thinking about what kind of underlying mechanisms might be driving the problem, and the kinds of experience that might have led the client to develop such beliefs about the self, others and the world. The general model of case conceptualization, modified from Fennell (1989) and Judith Beck (1995), is illustrated in Figure 2.11.

These detailed conceptualizations may be developed early on in therapy, or, in the case of clients with more complex, long-standing problems, may evolve over many sessions (see Morrison, 2000). As we have described above, the process of developing a detailed conceptualization may in itself be therapeutic, providing a blame-free understanding of why the client is as she/he is today, and also a workable bridge between the present and the past.

Figure 2.11 Cognitive conceptualization (J. Beck, 1995; Fennell, 1989)

Early Experience
Information about the client's early and other significant experiences which may have shaped core beliefs and assumptions.

Development of Beliefs about the Self, Others and the World
Unconditional, core beliefs developing from early experience, such as 'I am bad', 'I am weak and vulnerable', 'Others will always look after me' or 'The world is a dangerous place'.

Assumptions or Rules for Living
Conditional statements, often phrased as 'if … then' rules, to enable the individual to function despite core beliefs: e.g. 'If I am vigilant about my health at all times, then I'll be safe, despite being vulnerable'; 'If I work hard all the time. I'll be OK, despite being a bad person'.

Critical Incidents which Trigger Problems
Situations or events in which the rules are broken or assumptions are activated.

Problems and Factors Maintaining the Problem
Physical symptoms, thoughts, emotions, behaviours interacting in a 'vicious cycle'.

PRÊT À PORTER FORMULATIONS

Cognitive therapy provides an ever-increasing number of what we might call 'ready-made' conceptualizations, where the problems clients are facing have been seen to fall into familiar patterns, leading to the development of conceptualizations which may well fit a range of people. For example, the model of panic (Figure 2.12) is well known, well researched and familiar (Clark, 1989) and an accurate description of the experience of panic attacks and is therefore relevant and valuable to those who suffer from them.

These conceptualizations guide what sense the therapist is making of the client's problems as well as the specific questions the therapist asks; similarly, being found to fit in with a familiar and well-established pattern can be helpful to the client, in so much as they feel relieved that 'I'm not the only one; if it makes sense, I'm not mad after all'.

A number of conceptual models are referenced throughout the book. New models are continually developed; old models are revised in the light of clinical and research experience, and we will provide resources for keeping up to date at the end of the book.

Figure 2.12   The Vicious Cycle of Panic

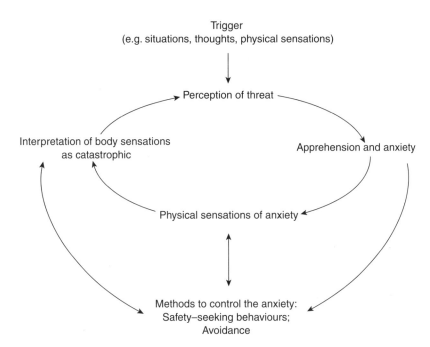

Source: Clark (1986); Wells (1997)

HOW RELIABLE AND VALID ARE FORMULATIONS?

As therapists, we aim to arrive at a working formulation with the client within the first few sessions. However, if another therapist was to see the same client, would this therapist also arrive at the same formulation, or would it be different – how reliable are formulations across therapists? Also, is the formulation valid, in that it is a useful map of the terrain, representing what it is supposed to represent, and increasing the effectiveness of therapy? Persons et al. (1995) found that 46 clinicians working with information from one client achieved good agreement on what kept the client's problems going, and on factors such as family or marital problems and grief, and had moderately good agreement on some of the underlying mechanisms, but there was less agreement about underlying assumptions and beliefs, also replicated by Persons and Bertagnolli (1999). Other studies have also found that therapists agree on the descriptive aspects of problems, such as maintenance factors, but about underlying mechanisms and inferential aspects they have less agreement, for example, on such questions as what the underlying assumptions and beliefs may be, and why the person developed the problems (Bieling and Kuyken, 2003; Eells and Lombart, 2003; Kuyken, in press; Kuyken et al., in press; Mumma and Smith, 2001). There is, at present, limited research evidence linking formulation with outcome – whether having a good formulation improves outcome – but their utility is frequently borne out by clinical experience. The reliability and quality of formulations increases with the practitioner's level of training and experience, suggesting it is a skill that improves with time and practice. Experience also enables therapists to conceptualize more intuitively and effortlessly, having more of a felt sense of what is going on rather than using active reasoning (Kuyken, in press).

CONCEPTUALIZATION AND DIAGNOSIS

Cognitive therapy has relied on diagnostic systems such as the *DSM* (APA, 2000) and the ICD-10 (World Health Organization; see www.who.int/classifications/icd) to categorize the problems people bring to therapy, and as a basis for research. Many of the trials of cognitive therapy, such as those for depression, panic disorder, social anxiety or obsessive-compulsive disorder, have included only people meeting the criteria laid down within diagnostic systems. Diagnostic criteria and labels with which to understand, categorize or offer therapy to clients are a rich resource but may also create a thorny minefield, full of debate and controversy (Beutler and Malik, 2002; Harvey et al., 2004; Sequeira and Van Scoyoc, 2001; Strawbridge and James, 2001). The downside of diagnosis is that it risks seeing the client as a label rather than a whole person. Labels carry the potential for stigmatizing clients, making them feel even more different and potentially distressed. Labels, too, are an oversimplification of the complexities of people. People are more complex than a disorder, and very often, two or more difficulties or 'diagnoses' coexist (Kessler et al., 1994). For example, the break up of a relationship or other life events may lead someone to start to have panic attacks; if they persist for more than six months (panic disorder) that person may well avoid going out (agoraphobia), become socially unconfident and fearful (social phobia), lose many enjoyable things in life, become very low (depression) and start drinking to try and cope (dependency disorder). While many of the trials have chosen relatively 'clean' examples of a problem, in most therapists' experience the people we see are likely to struggle with a number of coexisting difficulties. A finding across many research trials, and clinical experience, is that by focusing on one problem, regardless of how many difficulties the client brings to therapy, the others get better as well, despite not being worked on in therapy (Tsao et al., 2002). For clients experiencing panic attacks, for example, tackling the panic attacks may also dismantle the layers of avoidance of going out, low mood and use of alcohol, without needing to make these difficulties the main focus of therapy.

Formulation, aiming to understand the person in terms of maintenance, predisposing and triggering factors, in theory bypasses the need for diagnosis. However, it is also informed by what we know about specific models developed from specific diagnoses. Specific protocols have arisen from particular diagnoses, such as the original cognitive therapy protocols Beck developed for depression, and protocols for anxiety problems, obsessive-compulsive disorder and phobias (Leahy and Holland, 2000; Steketee, 1999a, 1999b; Wells, 1997) and standard programmes of therapy are effective for a wide range of problems. Diagnostic categories are useful guidelines, but we need to avoid reifying them, treating them as more discrete and real phenomena than they actually are; on the other hand, we know that specific methods and models work well for specific problems, and therefore using the diagnosis to inform the formulation is possibly the most useful strategy.

CAUTIONS ABOUT CONCEPTUALIZATION

Cognitive conceptualization or formulation involves a delicate balance between holding in mind a conceptual model in which to slot the data generated by the client, and being open-minded to the information that the client is actually giving us. Like any therapeutic process, it can be misused. Both therapist and client need to be flexible enough to throw out an initial conceptualization if it does not fit with later evidence. A formulation is a hypothesis to be tested, and if the evidence does not support the formulation, it needs to be revised. Therapists do have influence over clients, and we need to go out of our way to invite them to criticize or refute the formulation. This is particularly true when working at the level of core beliefs, where the views that the client holds about themselves, other people and the world are so firmly ingrained as to seem to be facts. Therefore formulating a client's underlying beliefs may lead them to retort, 'Well, that's just the truth – it's how it is', being so confrontational to them as to lead to a great deal of either emotion or avoidance. Similarly, it can be just as difficult for us as therapists to get rid of our own beliefs about our clients as it is for clients to relinquish their beliefs about themselves. We may develop a perfect, sophisticated and theoretically sound conceptualization that has little empirical or practical value to the client, and, because of our own cognitive distortions, start to see everything in those terms. There is also a danger in attempting to be overinclusive: while one conceptualization may explain a number of problems, it is also possible that a number of different conceptualizations are necessary to work with disparate problems.

There may be times when it is best to simplify and tailor the formulation with elements of the model used as we have done throughout this chapter. We may want to make highly sophisticated, technical conceptualizations that in fact are incomprehensible to the person we are working with, or not fit with their frame of reference. Charlesworth and Greenfield (2004) give examples of simple conceptualization for family carers of people with dementia, where complex models may be less comprehensible to an individual with cognitive impairments, medical problems or overwhelming distress. They suggest that the greater the client's cognitive impairment, the more concrete the formulation should be, with simple, clear links. This fits with the parsimonious nature of cognitive behavioural therapy (CBT), and Beck's call to 'simplify, simplify, simplify' (Beck and Emery, 1985). For older adults, a simplified version of Padesky and Mooney's (1990) 'hot cross bun' may suffice (p. 39), taking two or three elements of a mini-cycle. For example, 'more challenging behaviour in the care recipient, leads the carer to feel less able to cope, leading in turn to hostility from the carer, leading in turn to more challenging behaviour in the care recipient' and so on.

CONCLUSION

Conceptualization is, ideally, a working map, which aims to improve both thera-pists' and clients' understanding of the terrain of the client's problems, to guide the process of therapy, and to predict and deal with problems. Although the words 'conceptualization' and 'formulation' can make it sound complex and mysterious, in fact it is not, and should not be, rocket science, but something that is under-standable to all and explains the person's difficulties. To build a conceptualization, we start with a recent, typical example of the client's problem, and build up a model of how thoughts, feelings, behaviour and biology interact. From this simple model, built collaboratively with the client, we have a snapshot of the problems, and a clear guide for therapy: where, and how, to intervene to break cycles and produce change. Once the 'bottom end', or symptom picture, is clear, and we have worked towards at least some changes, then we move on to conceptualizing under-lying assumptions and beliefs which can be running the show, to answer questions like 'Where have my problems come from?' 'How does the past influence the pres-ent?' 'What might make me vulnerable to relapse?' Working on these underlying issues, particularly core beliefs, is not always part of standard cognitive therapy, and for many people a 'bottom end' formulation, with some clarification of under-lying rules, is enough for effective change. We have stressed in this chapter the way in which our formulations need to be flexible and open to new material and processes as therapy proceeds. While a conceptualization provides a useful map, some of the most valuable journeys involve wandering off the chosen path. We stress, too, the way in which conceptualization is built up within the context of a collaborative relationship, and we turn to the therapeutic relationship in the next chapter.

Further Reading

Bruch, M. & Bond F. W. (1998). *Beyond diagnosis: Case formulation approaches in CBT*. Chichester: Wiley.

Butler, G. (1998). Clinical formulation. In A. S. Bellack & M. Hersen (Eds.), *Comprehensive clinical psychology* (pp. 1–24). Oxford: Pergamon.

Eells, T. D. (1997). *Handbook of psychotherapy case formulation*. New York: Guilford Press.

Tarrier, N. & Calam, R. (2002). New developments in cognitive case formulation. Epidemiological, systemic and social context: An integrative approach. *Behavioural and Cognitive Psychotherapy*, 30(2), 311–328.

Padesky, C. (2004). *Case conceptualization. An in-session collaboration*. Audiotapes. Newport Beach, CA: Center for Cognitive Therapy. www.padesky.com

3 The Therapeutic Relationship in Cognitive Therapy

One of the criticisms of cognitive therapy from other therapeutic perspectives is that cognitive therapists pay little, if any, attention to the cornerstone of other therapies, the therapeutic relationship. Person-centred therapists may view cognitive approaches as being overconcerned with technique and method without taking into account the primacy of the relationship. Psychoanalysts may dismiss cognitive therapy as not using the most important therapeutic tools of their trade, the transference and countertransference in the therapeutic relationship (Persons et al., 1996). Somehow, many older writings on cognitive therapy gave the impression that the therapeutic relationship is a mere container in which to do the real work, viewing difficulties and issues in the relationship as problems to be solved before getting on with the therapy. The therapeutic relationship has been notable by its absence, at times seemingly dismissed.

We are glad to say that these views are anachronistic and the idea that cognitive therapy does not pay attention to the therapeutic relationship is now regarded as a myth (Leahy, 2001; Waddington, 2002). Throughout psychotherapy, regardless of the model or method, clinicians see therapy as an interpersonal and emotional endeavour, a far cry from the idea which some manualized forms of therapy might give of what Norcross (2002a) describes as 'disembodied therapists performing procedures on Axis I disorders'. The development of therapy in general has provided many useful ideas that help us to understand the underlying processes of therapeutic change within the therapeutic relationship, processes that are now being actively integrated into cognitive therapy. As a result, there is a growing cognitive model of the interpersonal process of the therapeutic relationship as well as a substantial focus on how to use the relationship as an active ingredient in therapy. These issues have been particularly developed in the therapy of 'personality disorders' and 'schema-driven problems', where the client's transference, the therapist's countertransference and the experience of impasse in the therapeutic process all provide invaluable information for the facilitation of therapeutic movement. We would argue that relationship issues can also be helpfully used to form a more vibrant and emotionally engaged practice model for all cognitive therapy.

In this chapter, we look at how the therapeutic relationship has been viewed in the past, and how recent work on cognitive therapy has brought the therapeutic relationship to centre stage, particularly for those clients with long-term difficulties, and those for whom relationships are of central concern. We describe how to build and develop a collaborative relationship in cognitive therapy, and the similarities and differences between collaboration and other therapeutic relationships. We look at ways the therapeutic relationship is used in cognitive therapy to conceptualize the client's difficulties and facilitate the therapy process. We also look at problems that can occur in the relationship and ways of repairing therapeutic difficulties or ruptures.

WHAT DOES COGNITIVE THERAPY SAY ABOUT THE THERAPEUTIC RELATIONSHIP?

Traditionally, and in contrast to other therapeutic approaches, the task of cognitive therapy was seen to be to resolve the client's problems, as far as possible, using the tools of cognitive therapy rather than using the therapeutic relationship per se. A good relationship had to be in place in order to do the work, and was seen as necessary but not sufficient for therapeutic change (Beck et al., 1979). Traditionally, the technical aspects of therapy have been felt to be the active ingredients. If the therapeutic relationship were a car, the cognitive therapist would use it to travel from A to B, whereas the psychodynamic or Rogerian therapist would be a collector, spending hours polishing and fine-tuning the vehicle. For many clients, particularly those whose problems are amenable to short-term work, a mode of transport is called for: it may be sufficient for the therapist to be warm, empathic, respectful and collaborative for the therapeutic work to proceed. For clients with long-term difficulties, more complex problems, personality disorders, or interpersonal difficulties, however, the therapeutic relationship becomes more significant. For these clients, particularly those whose core conflicts are interpersonal in nature, it is likely that the therapeutic relationship will prove a rich source of information for understanding them and their difficulties. It is also likely that there will be issues and difficulties in the therapeutic relationship, and the travellers may well have to turn their hand to mechanics and bodywork.

Although the view of the therapeutic relationship as 'necessary but not sufficient' has been central to cognitive therapy, more attention is now being paid to the importance of the therapeutic relationship itself. It comes as no surprise that the research in cognitive therapy supports what our humanistic colleagues have been saying all along: that the quality of the relationship is central. Various studies looking at the relative contribution of non-specific, relationship factors versus technical factors in therapy indicate the importance of both, a positive relationship making a significant contribution to the outcome of cognitive therapy (Hubble et al., 1999; Norcross, 2002a and b). In some research, therapist effects exceed those of the method or treatment used, in others it is at least as important (Hubble et al., 1999; Keijsers et al., 2000; Wampold, 2001). Reviews and meta-analyses of psychotherapy outcome literature have claimed that specific techniques and methods account for around 5–15 per cent of the outcome variance, much of which is attributable to the therapeutic relationship (see for example Luborsky et al., 1999; Wampold, 2001). This is not to say that either method or relationship can work in isolation, but that the combination of both is critical. Meta-analytic evidence is, however, notoriously difficult to evaluate (Lazarus, 1990), some evidence showing that it may downplay significant differences between therapies and conversely overemphasize the influence of 'common factors'.

There is also more attention being paid to ways in which the therapeutic relationship itself can be used as an active ingredient in therapy (Beck et al., 2003; Layden et al., 1993; Safran and Muran, 1998, 2003; Young et al., 2003). For example, the relationship can provide an arena in which people can identify and test out beliefs about relationships, such as practising alternative or new behaviours (Flecknoe and Sanders, 2004) and trying out and learning new ways of relating, as we discuss later in the chapter.

THE CORE CONDITIONS

> The general characteristics of the therapist that facilitate the application of cognitive therapy ... include warmth, accurate empathy and genuineness ... [I]f these attributes are over-emphasised or applied artlessly, they may become disruptive to the therapeutic collaboration ... [W]e believe that these characteristics in themselves are necessary but not sufficient to produce optimum therapeutic effect ... [T]he techniques in this book are intended to be applied in a tactful, therapeutic and human manner by a fallible person – the therapist ... [A] genuine therapist is honest with himself as well as with the client. (Beck et al., 1979: 45–9)

It is an, often unstated, assumption that the core conditions of any therapy, namely empathy, understanding, genuineness, respect, congruence and unconditional, non-possessive positive regard (see Rogers, 1957) have to be in place so that therapeutic work can proceed. If clients do not feel understood or respected, their inner worlds cannot be shared with another and the idea of being able to identify and challenge their strange and illogical thoughts will not get off the ground. Leahy provides a valuable reminder of one of the key components of any therapy, being able to validate what is going on for the client: 'It is this aspect of the human condition, the recognition that we must learn to "weep for the plague, not just cure it", that is an essential component of meaningful therapy and meaningful relationships. When we experience what seems awful and horrible in our lives, we often take solace in knowing that another person understands, or, at least, is attempting to understand, our pain' (2001: 58).

The importance of such core conditions has tended to be implicit rather than explicit in cognitive therapy. For example, in *Cognitive Therapy and the Emotional Disorders*, Beck devotes one line to the subject: 'if the therapist shows the following characteristics, a successful outcome is facilitated: genuine warmth, acceptance, and accurate empathy' (1976: 221). This does not mean that Beck only paid token attention to these qualities. Throughout his work he stresses the importance of showing the client warmth, acceptance and respect, giving an impression that 'This is someone I can trust'. Listening, summarizing, reflecting, empathy, congruence, reflecting feelings, and all those characteristics that make for a warm encounter are vital to cognitive therapy, and these skills are particularly used in building therapeutic collaboration, enabling the client and therapist to work together to identify and resolve the client's difficulties.

The characteristics of the relationship may well influence outcome in cognitive therapy. For example, Burns and Auerbach (1996) focused on whether, and how, therapeutic empathy makes a difference in cognitive therapy, concluding that empathy has a large influence – a warm and trusting relationship can significantly enhance therapy and speed recovery. Keijsers et al. (2000), in a comprehensive review of empirical studies of the therapeutic relationship in cognitive therapy, identified two aspects of interpersonal behaviour clearly associated with a positive outcome. One is the group of variables associated with Rogerian therapy: empathy, unconditional positive regard, warmth and genuineness; the second, the perceived quality of the therapeutic alliance. Keijsers and colleagues point out that there is considerable evidence that cognitive behavioural therapists are just as supportive, perhaps even more so, than therapists using other models: 'There is no empirical evidence for the stereotype of the cognitive behavioural therapist as being more superficial, colder, or more mechanical in their contact with patients than of therapists from other psychotherapy orientations' (2000: 268). They also suggest that the higher degree of directiveness in CBT does not adversely affect the outcome of therapy unless it is overemphasized too early in therapy. Outcome is improved if the client perceives the therapist as being self-confident, skilful and active. Other relationship factors take into account the characteristics of the client and how these impact on therapy, such as the person's willingness and ability to be open about the problems, and whether the person is predisposed to change and accepts therapy as a means to do this (Keijsers et al., 2000). Thus, to consider what works in therapy we are always looking at an interaction between the qualities of the client, the therapist and the therapeutic method – the so called 'common factors' across all the therapies (see Batchelor and Horvath, 1999), which include the therapeutic relationship, the qualities of the client, therapeutic hope and expectation of change, and the technical aspects of therapy (Hubble et al., 1999). If the client perceives the therapist to have positive attributes, this is likely to increase trust and mean that the client is less likely to drop out and more likely to feel satisfied with the therapy, comply with the methods and make gains with therapy (Waddington, 2002). The relationship may promote hope, which is central to effective therapy.

Cognitive therapy also allows adaptation of the core conditions to maximize their helpfulness to the individual client: for example, too much empathy or warmth may be perceived as threatening to, say, a very depressed client, who believes 'I do not deserve such caring' or 'No one understands me, why is she pretending?' Silences may be useful reflection time for many, improving collaboration by allowing the client to take the lead, but could be anxiety producing or threatening to another person, perhaps reminding them of times of 'going blank' when a teacher was waiting for an answer, or not wanting to 'look stupid' by not saying anything. Hence the value of a good conceptualization of the client's needs in being able to modify the core conditions accordingly.

GOING BEYOND THE CORE CONDITIONS: DEVELOPING A COLLABORATIVE RELATIONSHIP

I certainly consider the therapeutic alliance as a common factor shared with other therapies. But I also believe that the shared and explicit focus on changing belief systems, reinforcing and refining reality testing, and developing coping strategies makes for a more robust therapy. (Beck, 1991: 194)

Cognitive therapy uses factors that are common to many other therapies, but is more specific in how such factors are used. Beck has often stated that the active ingredient of many of the 'common factors' among various psychotherapies, including the therapeutic relationship, leads to cognitive change. Cognitive therapy aims to produce the same result but by a more direct route. The way such work is achieved is by means of developing a collaborative relationship and collaborative empiricism (see for example, Beck et al., 1979). In the words of Beck and Emery:

The cognitive therapist implies that there is a team approach to the solution of a patient's problem: that is, a therapeutic alliance where the patient supplies raw data (reports on thoughts and behaviour ...) while the therapist provides structure and expertise on how to solve problems. The emphasis is on working on problems rather than on correcting defects or changing personality. The therapist fosters the attitude 'two heads are better than one' in approaching personal difficulties. (1985: 175)

Collaborative empiricism helps the therapist to 'get alongside' the client, so that the work of 'attacking' the client's problems will not be seen as an attack on the client herself. Again, in the words of Beck:

It is useful to conceive of the patient–therapist relationship as a joint effort. It is not the therapist's function to reform the patient: rather his role is working with the patient against 'it', the patient's problem. Placing emphasis on solving problems, rather than his presumed deficits or bad habits, helps the patient to examine his difficulties with more detachment and makes him less prone to experience shame, a sense of inferiority and defensiveness. (1976: 221)

What does this mean in practice? Beck and Emery (1985) spell out two implications:

- *The relationship develops on a reciprocal basis*. Both therapist and client are working together to observe and comment on the client's way of being, to offer solutions to the problems and difficulties facing the client. When the client is unable to see the way forward, or is unable to see an alternative to their thoughts or beliefs, the therapist may be able to look from a different view and offer this to the client. Similarly, the client can see and offer to the therapist another perspective. There is a feeling in cognitive therapy of both client and therapist rolling up their sleeves and getting on with the work;

- *Avoid hidden agendas.* Cognitive therapy is an explicit therapy. The therapist does not form hypotheses about the client, or interpretations, and keep these to herself. Instead, everything is out on the table. If client and therapist are working to different agendas, then it is unlikely that therapy will proceed smoothly. If the therapist is trying to manoeuvre the client into seeing things from her point of view, or trying to get the client to be more logical, while the client simply wants to feel understood, again therapy will be a rough ride. Instead, the therapist is clear and explicit about what is in his/her mind. This clarity allows both client and therapist to know what the agendas are for therapy as a whole, as well as for individual sessions and moment-to-moment interactions in the session. The therapist admits mistakes, is open to suggestions, and is willing to go where the client wants to go, without colluding with difficulties.

A spirit of collaboration gives a reflective 'ping-pong' quality to sessions: the time that therapist and client are speaking may be about equal; therapists share their thoughts about the client's thoughts, and ask for feedback. While both therapist and client may ask questions, both work together, collaboratively and empirically, to find answers. The client's thoughts, feelings and behaviours are reflected on, not interpreted.

The spirit of collaboration may be clearer when it is absent: when, for example, the therapist tells the client what to do or think; or she comes up with a brilliant suggestion about how the client may view a situation, which leaves the client cold. It is very easy for the therapist to get drawn into this kind of overly directive behaviour. It is not always authoritarian in intent, but often motivated by a genuine desire for the client to get to a better place, and at times can be helpful, but in general collaboration should come before didactic methods. Collaboration may also be absent when there are long silences in the session; when, rather than the silence representing a meaning-laden pause, it leaves the client high and dry, struggling with where to go next. In true collaboration, the therapist is willing to help the client out without being patronizing, condescending or disempowering the client. In developing a good therapeutic collaboration, therapists should be warm, open, empathic, concerned, respectful and non-judgemental.

Throughout cognitive therapy, we aim to work collaboratively, and this is expressed in many of the things we do, discussed in greater detail in Part II of the book. At the first meeting we explain and discuss cognitive therapy and how we are aiming to focus on specific issues and work together. Therapist and client work together to identify goals across therapy, such as 'Being able to go out and see friends', 'Get back to work', and 'Feel much better and able to do things during the day rather than stay in bed'. We aim to define and focus on mutually acceptable problems. Collaboration is built into the structure of sessions. Each session starts with an agenda, where the client and therapist decide what the session will cover today. The process of regular feedback, summaries and reflection also sets a collaborative tone, with both therapist and client thinking about what is going on in therapy. Asking questions such as 'What went well?'; 'What are you taking away with you?'; 'Is there anything we did or talked about today which you did not like, or was difficult?' shows that we are open to feedback and not setting ourselves up as infallible experts. Using Socratic questioning and guided discovery is a collaborative way of working, enabling the client to find answers and different ways of seeing things without the therapist appearing to be the expert or becoming didactic or directive. We aim to encourage the client to be active in therapy, and give the message that the client has a central and equal role in making progress. We share information and skills, aiming for the client to become their own therapist. The kinds of things we might say to improve collaboration are:

- 'What shall we focus on today?'
- 'I was wondering if ...'
- 'From my point of view ... what do you think?'
- 'What question might you ask yourself right now?'
- 'Just to check we're both on the same wavelength, what sense do you make of what we've just been saying?'
- 'Where shall we go next?'
- 'What do you think?'
- 'Let's have a look ...'

Some people find the collaborative relationship a surprise, expecting perhaps that the therapist will take a back seat and listen to whatever the person brings along, or conversely, the therapist is an expert who is there to solve the problems. Therefore it is extremely important to explain explicitly the way cognitive therapy works, and how teamwork is the best and most effective way of using the time, right at the beginning of therapy as part of 'socializing' the person into a cognitive way of working (see Chapter 4). The person's difficulties or reservations about such an approach can be discussed, so the individual feels comfortable with the way of working and is not surprised by it. When working with the more entrenched patterns of people with long-term problems and personality issues, the relationship can become more central, as discussed later. These people may have come from backgrounds where they have not learned skills to help them get through life, evolving unhelpful and self-harmful ways of coping, including inappropriate or unhelpful ways of relating to people. For these clients, we may need to be more directive and educational, against a background of strong support and collaboration (Beck et al., 2003) or take a limited reparenting role (Young et al., 2003).

USING THE THERAPEUTIC RELATIONSHIP IN COGNITIVE THERAPY

The therapeutic relationship is not something that either is or is not in place for the real work of therapy to begin, but rather is a quality that continually fluctuates and which can be actively used in therapy. We have discussed in Chapter 1 how the interpersonal has been brought centre stage in cognitive therapy. Safran and Muran (1998, 2003) see a strong imperative for humans to maintain relatedness that has survival value not only to the infant during the long period of dependency, but also to all people. This means that the core beliefs and assumptions that people hold about life and the world are likely to be interpersonal. Paul Gilbert (2000a, 2000b, 2001) has similarly highlighted interpersonal issues and concerns in his work on depression. In practice, clients may bring their interpersonal style and difficulties into therapy, and these issues can be used. Similarly, we as therapists bring our own beliefs and assumptions, making the relationship an interaction between the client and therapist, both influenced by the environment in which the therapy takes place, as shown in Figure 3.1.

The concepts of transference and countertransference are far from neglected in cognitive therapy, but can and should be used as valuable aids to conceptualization as well as to therapeutic progress. We examine these concepts in turn.

Figure 3.1　The Therapeutic Relationship

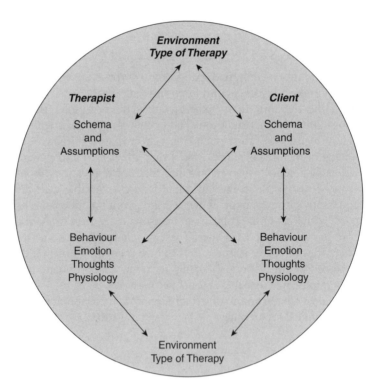

THE USE OF TRANSFERENCE TO AID CONCEPTUALIZATION

The therapeutic relationship is an arena in which people behave according to their beliefs about relationships. If a client's way of being seems surprising or unusual in therapy, perhaps charged with emotions which seem out of context, or if the therapist feels pushed into adopting a particular role with one individual client, it is likely that 'transference' may be an explanation. Translated into cognitive terms, what happens in the therapeutic relationship is very likely to arise from the client's core beliefs and assumptions and the mechanisms by which the client confirms these assumptions (Beck et al., 2003; Safran, 1998; Safran and Muran, 2003; Wright and Davis, 1994). Therefore, what goes on in the relationship can be used as valuable information to help understand and conceptualize the client's difficulties. The client's reactions to the therapist, and the therapy, while not forming the cornerstone of therapy, nor being deliberately provoked in cognitive therapy, provide 'windows into the patient's private world' (Beck et al., 1990) and can be seen, not as obstacles in therapy, but as a rich source of information.

Persons' case formulation approach (1989) assumes that the client's behaviour with and reaction to the therapist may be influenced by their underlying problems, and therefore may be similar to behaviours with others. For example, being late for sessions or not doing homework may be driven by a number of different beliefs, such as those relating to extremely high standards, resulting in problems with being disorganized and chaotic and an inability to get anything done on time; or to core beliefs of 'worthlessness', so that the client does not feel it is worth making the effort for herself to try anything that might help. Another person may not be willing to come to sessions on time, or work on tasks between sessions, which may indicate fear of dependency on the therapist or therapy. People who have a strong need for advice, information and reassurance about how to lead their lives may have evolved specific, and possibly subtle, behaviours, leading the therapist to become a 'friendly expert', giving advice, or doing all the work in sessions. Detecting tell-tale signs of a 'transference' cognition uses the same means as detecting any in-session automatic thought: a sudden change in the client's emotional response or non-verbal behaviour, such as a shift in gaze, or rapid change of topic. While it is important to note these reactions, it may not always be appropriate to work on them there and then, being too threatening for the client and risking closure of affect or risking the therapeutic collaboration. It may well be enough to simply notice what has happened and to 'file it away' for use on another day. This also allows more evidence to accumulate and helps to guard against premature interpretation, always a danger in any therapy (Lomas, 1987). One of the authors (FW) has an internal rule that generally he waits for at least three occurrences of a transferential transaction before raising it with a client. This usually allows a possible intervention to be discussed in supervision before trying it.

The processes of schema maintenance, avoidance and compensation, behaviours that perpetuate our beliefs described by Young et al. (2003) can affect the therapeutic relationship, where clients may test the therapist to check for a good 'fit' with their assumptions and beliefs – a process that the psychodynamic world describes as a 'transference test'. For example, the belief that 'I'm boring' may lead the client to speak or behave in a flat, boring manner, or selectively attend to tiny cues that the therapist is finding them boring, thereby maintaining the belief. Someone with central issues around dependency on others may become very passive or dependent in the therapeutic relationship, possibly evoking a complimentary caring response, which in turn maintains the beliefs about the self. Schema avoidance describes the affective, cognitive and behavioural processes employed to avoid activating our beliefs: for example, the client might change the subject or laugh whenever something painful was being approached; someone else believing that no one can be trusted might find it very difficult to attend sessions when things got 'too close for comfort', or arrive with new crises each week which had to be looked at, thereby avoiding core issues. Schema compensation describes the process of acting in a way opposite to that predicted by the beliefs. For example, a person who tends to become dependent on others, feeling that he cannot trust his own decisions or cannot manage on his own, may refuse to trust the therapist, or prematurely discontinue therapy, saying that he would prefer to carry on alone. Schema maintenance is illustrated in the following example.

> **TONY**
>
> Tony had struggled for years with persistent abdominal pains and believed that 'No one is to be trusted'. He compensated for his belief with an assumption that 'If I search long and hard enough, I'll be able to find the one person who can help me with my problems'. He had spent years consulting doctors, in several different countries, during which time he had also collected numerous examples of medical incompetence, as his frequent tests inevitably had their side effects. From the start of therapy I (DS) would find myself subtly manoeuvred into situations where I did not know the answers, which proved his point. I became, inevitably, frustrated and irritated with him, and found myself feeling incompetent. I wanted to discharge him quickly, thereby confirming his beliefs that no one could help him. He invoked similar feelings in others in the medical profession who had tried to help him, and had been referred on to many different people in an attempt to find someone who could help. I had to work my way through these personal reactions before I could attempt to help him to move on. Tony, in fact, left therapy abruptly and did not allow time for these issues to be examined.

The client's assumptions and beliefs about relationships may force the therapist into a 'damned if I do, damned if I don't' situation (Layden et al., 1993). This feeling can occur when working with people whose experiences and resulting beliefs and behaviours mean that whatever others do can be misconstrued in a negative way, resulting in a 'no win' situation in close relationships. As a response, the therapist can also react in a black and white way, responding to the client's outbursts and irrational demands by eagerness to end therapy and discharge the client, labelling him as 'impossible to help'. Alternatively, at the other extreme, we might find ourselves becoming a rescuer, going to unusual lengths to help the client or offer him unrealistic assurances about our ability to help, inevitably leading the client to feel disillusioned or betrayed. The therapeutic relationship may 'ping-pong' back and forward between the two extremes of overdistancing and overinvolvement, mirroring the client's schema and problems. Layden et al. (1993) give an example of a client who was sexually abused by someone she trusted, who had learned that it was extremely difficult to trust anyone; at the same time, she believed, as borne out by her early experience, that the only way to attain love was to be violated in some way. In therapy, the client both craved the therapist's affection and acceptance, but reacted with horror and distrust when the therapist showed signs of caring. When the therapist, in response to the client's withdrawal, acted in a more reserved way, the client jumped to the opposite extreme, perceiving the therapist as abandoning and neglecting her (Layden et al., 1993). Layden and colleagues (1993), talking about people with borderline personality disorder, stress that if the therapist has powerful, anti-therapeutic reactions to the client, this will feed into the person's propensity for mistrusting the therapist. These people may test out the therapist with a variety of 'schema-driven' behaviours. In contrast, the process of disconfirming assumptions leads to therapeutic progress, so long as the disconfirmation is accepted and integrated by the client, allowing change in beliefs.

The particular response or behaviour can be identified and reflected on in therapy, such as saying to the client, 'It seems like you're quite angry with me right now'; 'I'm feeling like I ought to be sorting this out for you'. Offered in a spirit of empathy and curiosity rather than judgement, such interventions can allow the exploration of what is going on; what the underlying beliefs might be ('My therapist is never going to understand me, no one ever does'; 'I can't do things on my own, I'm not to be trusted') and how they impact on the person's life. The client can also be asked if the feelings experienced in therapy, such as anger, irritation, feeling stupid or needy, come up in other areas of life.

COUNTERTRANSFERENCE AND COGNITIVE THERAPY

Our feelings and responses evoked by clients are known, in classic psychoanalytic theory, as countertransference. Various types of countertransference are described: 'classical', the therapist's transference to the client; 'neurotic', relating to the therapist's unresolved personal issues; 'role', the therapist's response to the role that the client has put him in; or 'complementary', where the therapist begins to experience what is going on for the client and is being unconsciously communicated. In cognitive therapy, countertransference is viewed as a valuable means of gaining a deeper understanding of the therapeutic process and of ourselves (Leahy, 2001, 2003b; Rudd and Joiner, 1997). The following example illustrates how the therapist's response was used to highlight an issue for the client.

ALISON

Alison came across as gloomy and miserable even when she was describing things that she had enjoyed at the time, and would often weep in her sessions. Rather than evoking empathy, I (DS) experienced her as moaning, and felt that what she said was, somehow, lacking substance. It was, for me, an almost intangible feeling of dread before the sessions, when I would find myself feeling very cheerful in contrast to her glumness. She described wanting to have a boyfriend but had difficulties in forming any relationships that lasted more than a few weeks. Inside me, a voice said: 'I'm not surprised people don't stay around. Who would want such a misery guts?' Although my first concern was that I had lost my sympathy, I explored my reactions in supervision and identified Alison's beliefs about relationships. Alison could quickly identify her tactic of having problems to gain people's attention, linked to the assumption 'I can only get love and help from others if I am really miserable, otherwise they are not interested in me'. As soon as the assumption was identified and explored with Alison, the feeling of sessions changed, and she was able to describe a greater variety of feelings, both happy and sad. In this example, my own feelings were an accurate reflection of the client's assumption.

Much of interpersonal communication takes place at a non-verbal level: subtle posture, eye contact, and tone of voice or muscle tension. Therefore it can be hard to define why the therapist is reacting in a certain way. The therapist's bodily reactions, images or metaphors can provide useful clues to the conceptualization. I (DS) nicknamed one of my clients 'Malteser Man', because of my habit of buying Maltesers after our sessions. On reflection, I realized that I perceived him as empty and sapping my energy. He filled his life with consultations to numerous doctors with his aches and pains. Having identified this feeling of emptiness, we could begin to conceptualize some of his problems in terms of beliefs around life being 'hard work'; 'It's too risky to get close to anyone'; and 'The only safe place is work'. Images of myself in the therapeutic relationship have provided important clues as to the client's conceptualization. Feeling like a 'wise owl' has served me well in identifying the client's need for reassurance. If, conversely, the client believes that no one can help, then the client may well treat the therapist with suspicion. A clue to this is if I find myself trying exceptionally hard, and against all odds, to 'sell' the model to the client with my 'estate agent' hat. Supervision is the ideal place to explore these reactions to clients, and therapists often need help and support in working out the most therapeutic responses.

THE THERAPIST'S ROLE IN THE RELATIONSHIP

It is only fairly recently in the history of cognitive therapy that the role of the therapist has been looked at in depth. Cognitive models were originally developed for people with relatively short-term, focused problems, where so long as the core conditions of the relationship were in place, the therapy could proceed without too much attention to the therapist. Some models assume that therapeutic relationship issues are related primarily to the client's underlying difficulties. However, with the advent of models and methods for people with longer-term, more enduring and complex problems, along with an increased openness to the emotional and interpersonal aspects of therapy, greater interest is paid to ourselves as therapists.

While examination of the therapist's own feelings and beliefs has always been explicit in other therapies, and personal therapy is seen as an essential training requirement, cognitive therapy too now pays more attention to explicit means of examining and working with our own psychological make up. Research has suggested that therapists' conceptualizations based on their own feelings are not systematically related to what the client is thinking or feeling (Free et al., 1985; Squier, 1990). For example, there may be significant differences between therapists' own estimates of their level of empathy, compared to how empathic the client experienced the therapist to be (Burns and Auerbach, 1996).

Work on the role of the therapist has developed in two main areas. First, a more explicit focus on therapist beliefs, developed by Jacqueline Persons and Christine Padesky, and second, James Bennett-Levy and others' work on the role of personal therapy and reflection in CBT.

THERAPIST BELIEFS

There are a number of ways in which our beliefs impact on therapy, and may cause recurrent problems in our therapeutic style or process (Persons, 1989). For example, sessions that repeatedly lack structure and focus and overrun may reflect therapist beliefs such as 'If I am structured, I will miss important things that the client has to say', or 'If the client gets very emotional, I have to stay with them until they feel better'. Core beliefs about being a caring person, whereas others are needy and vulnerable, may lead the therapist to focus on empathy and allowing the client to talk uninterruptedly, not allowing time for collaborative work on interventions.

Other therapist beliefs might include 'It is wrong to dislike/disagree with/feel attracted to/be angry with my clients', 'I must not get angry', 'I should not dislike my client', or 'I must cure the patient'. Such rules are likely to interfere with the therapeutic relationship: if therapists have particular feelings or thoughts that contravene their rules, then they may be ignored or put back on to the client, rather than be actively used in therapy. If, for example, the therapist felt annoyed with a client, and also believed she/he must never show or share this annoyance, she/he may be more likely to think: 'The client is being irritating: it is his fault. I won't let it affect me', rather than stopping and thinking what exactly is going on to provoke these feelings of annoyance.

If therapists have difficulty in empathizing with certain feelings of the client, it may be because they cannot accept these in themselves. For example, if the client is describing angry feelings towards a deceased friend, the therapist may find these feelings difficult to accept if they similarly feel rage towards someone for dying but believe that 'I shouldn't be angry'. Any strong thoughts such as 'I hate working with clients who are x' indicates that the therapist may have issues that may need looking at in order to work with that client group. If the therapist is working with a relatively new problem, or if they have just learned more about a problem, the long-suffering client may receive a mini-lecture on this particular disorder. The therapist's thoughts of 'I must be shown to know something about this problem' may lead them to be overprofessional and knowledgeable.

Cognitive therapy itself provides a number of tools that therapists can use to understand their role in the therapeutic relationship. These might include doing thought records to monitor what comes up for us with particular clients, observing and reflecting on work, listening to therapy tapes, conceptualizing ourselves and identifying our own 'schema maintenance' behaviours, and trying out experiments to test out our beliefs, and regular supervision focusing on process issues. Many of the key names in cognitive therapy have stressed the importance of trying things out for ourselves. 'To fully understand the process of therapy, there is no substitute for using cognitive therapy methods on oneself', wrote Christine Padesky (1996: 288). Judith Beck says that 'to gain experience with basic techniques of cognitive therapy by practising them on yourself before doing so with patients … and putting yourself in the patient's role affords the opportunity to identify obstacles that interfere with carrying out assignments' (1995: 312). Christine Padesky has developed training materials to enable therapists to identify and work with our own beliefs and assumptions (see www.padesky.com). All in all, we feel that we should, as Lao-Zu advises in the *Tao Te Ching*, yield to our own fallibility in order to overcome the problems of therapist perfectionism. We should be ready to admit our mistakes, a gesture often appreciated by clients frequently burdened by a sense of their own fallibility.

PERSONAL THERAPY AND COGNITIVE THERAPY

In many counselling and psychotherapy traditions, personal therapy is seen as an essential requirement for training and practising as a therapist (Wilkins, 2006) and therapists rate this as an important aspect of training (Macran and Shapiro, 1998; Orlinsky et al., 2001). Although it is accepted wisdom that personal therapy is useful, there has not been a great deal of research on its effect on subsequent therapeutic practice, nor on what learning mechanisms can explain its effectiveness (Bennett-Levy, 2002). In a review, Macran and Shapiro (1998) found that personal therapy improved empathy, warmth and genuineness, and given the importance of these factors in therapy, such improvements in themselves are likely to have a good impact on outcome.

In contrast, in the world of cognitive and behavioural therapies, personal therapy is not currently seen as an essential, or widely accepted, aspect of training (EABCT, 2001). The British Association for Behavioural and Cognitive Psychotherapies, while not insisting on personal therapy for accreditation, does stipulate that 'Therapists must ensure that they can identify and manage appropriately their personal involvement in the process of cognitive and/or behaviour therapy' and 'Therapists must have developed an ability to recognise when they should seek other professional advice' (BABCP, 2000).

Counsellors and therapists from other traditions have reported being somewhat mystified by such lack of interest in individual therapy. What they have gained from their own therapy – an awareness and understanding of one's own issues and how these might impact on the therapeutic relationship, the experience of being a client, a place to take difficulties that might arise during training or as a result of client work, material with which to conceptualize difficulties in therapy – are all seen as equally valid within cognitive therapy, but have not until recently been explicitly focused on. In addition, we know that reflection is an important aspect of learning, and personal therapy provides the opportunity to reflect on both professional and personal issues. Part of the reason for the lack of focus on personal therapy may be historical: many of the 'old school' practitioners of cognitive therapy came from behavioural traditions and clinical psychology, where it has not always been seen as essential or even relevant. Those seeing cognitive therapy as an educational model, involving the application of appropriate techniques, again might see therapy for therapists as unimportant.

Given the strong belief in the benefits of personal therapy for therapists, it is rather baffling that there is little evidence of its overall effectiveness (Roth and Fonagy, 1996). This may be because of the way it has been implemented as a compulsory element in some training courses. We think that this may not be a good enough reason to undertake therapy, partly because it is important for the 'client' to be able to decide when the time is exactly right for this commitment. We are also aware that undertaking therapy in this way has led to some quite adverse and even abusively exploitative outcomes for some of both the trainees and therapists involved.

We are glad to report that the need for personal experience of therapy is increasingly recognized within cognitive therapy and that our colleague, James Bennett-Levy, has devised a method for facilitating such experience in a way that overcomes some of the difficulties described earlier by formatting it as a safer and more educational experience. Working in Australia and more recently in Oxford, he has developed a training method called Self Practice/Self Reflection (SP/SR), where trainees undergo cognitive therapy with a training partner, and reflect in writing on the process of each session, thinking through the implications of the therapy experience for themselves, for their clients and for their cognitive therapy practice. Bennett-Levy found that SP/SR impacted on therapy in a number of ways. The trainees reported a 'deeper sense of knowing' of cognitive practices. They gained a deeper understanding of therapy, understood themselves better and demonstrated improvement in cognitive therapy skills (Bennett-Levy, 2001; Bennett-Levy et al., 2003). Trainees also noted a re-emphasis on therapeutic relationship skills: 'the experience of being "in the client's shoes" demonstrated starkly some of the anxiety and difficulties in making changes, even as high functioning individuals; and served to emphasize how valuable empathy, understanding, respect, tolerance and guidance of the therapist is' (Bennett-Levy et al., 2003: 150). The study found that SP/SR helped trainees develop self-reflection, enabling them to reflect both during and after sessions. We know that client perception of empathy is correlated with positive outcome; and if SP/SR leads therapists to be more empathic, as judged by our clients, then it is likely to lead to better outcomes. A review of self-reflection and self-practice in CBT training (Laireiter and Willutzki, 2003) confirms Bennett-Levy's findings, showing that trainees report substantial personal and professional gains from using SP/SR. They report improved self-insight and self-awareness, and a better understanding of the role of the therapist and the process of therapeutic change, as well as a better understanding of and skills in CBT methods. As summarized by Laireiter and Willutzki: 'Although empirical evidence is not extensive at present, it supports the notion that most of these goals may be attained by a combination of person- and practice-related self-reflection together with self-practice of CBT methods' (2003: 28).

Personal therapy or SP/SR may take a while to filter through to become incorporated within cognitive therapy training, but is certainly becoming recognized as a means of improving understanding of ourselves and of personal aspects of our clinical practice.

USING THE THERAPEUTIC RELATIONSHIP TO PRODUCE CHANGE

The therapeutic relationship is in itself a powerful way of working on the psychological difficulties which are the basis of the client's problems (Persons, 1989). A good therapeutic relationship can disconfirm negative beliefs about relationships learned early on (Safran and Muran, 2003; Safran and Segal, 1990), and can offer the client a form of limited reparenting, where beliefs can be directly challenged in the relationship with the therapist and the client can learn more appropriate and helpful relationship skills. In this way, the therapeutic relationship can be a corrective experience in itself, particularly for clients with long-term difficulties characteristic of the personality disorders (see for example, Young et al., 2003). Resolving alliance ruptures can provide a model to sort out difficulties in other relationships. Padesky describes how the relationship can be used as a 'laboratory for testing beliefs' (1996: 270). For example, the client who finds it difficult to trust anyone can be encouraged to try trusting the therapist in small ways and observe the results, and use this as a way of both learning new skills and developing new beliefs. A client with difficulties expressing emotion could test out the impact of describing his feelings to the therapist. For clients who believe that people always let them down, the relationship in which the therapist does her best to be trustworthy and reliable can begin the process of challenging beliefs. Other ways of using the therapeutic relationship to experiment with relationship issues are described in Flecknoe and Sanders (2004). Two examples are given below.

SONIKA

Sonika, who had experienced abuse from her stepbrother as a child, had difficulties in trusting another person with personal information, believing that 'If others knew what had happened to me, they would reject me.' She did a mini-experiment in the session revealing some information from the past that she had never told anyone before. We then discussed how we each felt about hearing this story. Sonika predicted that I would feel disgust for her, and she in turn would feel shame, but in fact I told her that I felt extremely moved by her story and deeply sympathetic to her as a child. We then went on to look at general issues of trust, and when it is, or is not, appropriate to disclose such personal information to another person.

JACK

Jack feared rejection if he ever criticized anyone, and if he ever felt unhappy about what someone else had done, he would avoid them or the situation. As a result he tended to 'lose' friends he was not happy with. When he began to miss sessions with no explanation, the therapist wondered if the same mechanism was operating with her. The belief that 'If I tell someone else I'm not happy with them, they'll get really angry and reject me' could be tested in the session: Jack tried out criticizing the therapist for cancelling a session at short notice, and for not immediately understanding what he had said. The therapist reacted by first apologizing, and we then discussed what had happened to make Jack feel misunderstood. Jack discovered that he could let someone else know he was not happy with something, and rather than rejecting them first, could try and sort it out in a constructive way.

Careful self-disclosure from the therapist can offer experimental evidence for clients on the possible impact of their way of being on others in their environment. This is illustrated with Alison, mentioned earlier.

ALISON

Alison would weep in sessions about how difficult everything was and how frightened she was of never being able to cope. For many clients this would evoke empathy and understanding. However, with Alison I (DS) would mentally walk out of the door, and feel impatient and non-empathic with her tears. Once Alison and I had established a good therapeutic relationship and were working well together, I reflected how her crying and calls for help seemed to have the opposite effect to the one she wanted, which in turn made her feel more desperate, and weep more. Her weeping, we conceptualized, was a cry for help rather than an expression of sadness. We then looked at how she might more effectively get the help she wanted, enabling her to test out my reactions to the changes in her in sessions, as well as try out different ways of behaving outside sessions. Gradually, the weeping and wailing was replaced by more genuine expressions of sadness and fear, in turn leading to a more genuine and helpful response from others. For Alison, testing out new interpersonal behaviours within the therapeutic relationship was in itself an important arena for change.

CONCLUSION

The therapeutic relationship in cognitive therapy is now a focus of attention in its own right, with the development of cognitive interpersonal models of the therapeutic process, as well as substantial work on how to use the relationship as an active ingredient in therapy. The cornerstone of cognitive therapy is the collaborative relationship, within which client and therapist work to identify and resolve the client's difficulties. Therapeutic collaboration, we believe, is an empowering model, giving the message that difficulties are resolvable, and enabling the difficulties to be addressed in a parsimonious, and empirical, way. We have described in this chapter ways in which the relationship can be understood and used, discussing concepts such as transference and countertransference within a cognitive framework and within a spirit of collaboration. In line with the empirical philosophy in cognitive therapy, the relationship can in itself be used to test out clients' beliefs, and provide an arena in which clients can practise new ways of being in the world and test deeply held interpersonal beliefs. However, as in all relationships, things do not always run to plan or smoothly, and difficulties can and do occur. In Chapter 8 we look at difficulties arising during therapy, and describe how to assess, conceptualize and work with therapeutic relationship issues. Supervision and high-quality training are crucial to enable us as therapists to work with process issues in cognitive therapy.

Further Reading

Safran, J. (1998). *Widening the scope of cognitive therapy: The therapeutic relationship and the process of change*. Northvale, NJ: Jason Aronson.

Leahy, R. L. (2003). *Roadblocks in cognitive-behavioral therapy: Transforming challenges into opportunities for change*. New York: Guilford Press.

Padesky, C. *Therapist beliefs. Protocols, personalities and guided exercises*. Three-hour clinical workshop (2 audiotapes). Newport Beach, CA: Center for Cognitive Therapy. www.padesky.com

Safran, J. D. & Muran, J. C. (2003). *Negotiating the therapeutic alliance: A relational treatment guide*. New York: Guilford Press.

Waddington, D. (2002). The therapy relationship in cognitive therapy: A review. *Behavioural and Cognitive Psychotherapy, 30*, 179–191.

Part two

Cognitive Therapy in Practice

4 Beginning Therapy: Assessment, Formulation and Engagement

Cognitive therapy is a structured, focused, collaborative and educational form of therapy, and these qualities are present right from the beginning. The initial stages of therapy start with the first contact between therapist and client, and then work through a formal assessment phase, developing the beginnings of a working formulation. These stages involve introducing the client to the cognitive way of working, developing a spirit of collaboration, introducing the ideas of working in a structured and focused way, and gaining feedback. Engagement in therapy is a key issue. The therapist engages the client with a collaborative working style that emphasizes the use of continuous feedback, and gives the client a clear rationale for what the therapist and the therapy are aiming to do. This cognitive style is taken into the assessment process, which aims to appraise not only the client's overall situation but also her capacity and willingness to enter into cognitive work.

After the assessment phase, subsequent sessions follow a structure, which helps clients to become familiar with the therapy and consequently promotes their ability to actively use it. Working in this way, we are laying the foundations for the therapeutic work, and the spirit of cognitive therapy needs to be present throughout. Table 4.1 is an overview of cognitive therapy as a whole, not representing a rigid structure, but illustrating the process of the therapeutic work, from assessment and formulation, to using methods for therapeutic change and endings. In this chapter we focus on first contacts, assessment, formulation and engagement, ending with an overview of the essentials of cognitive therapy: structure, agenda setting, feedback, recording sessions and homework – the themes and nuts and bolts throughout all the work.

INITIAL CONTACTS: WORKING COLLABORATIVELY AND GAINING FEEDBACK

Contact between client and therapist often starts before the first full therapy session. Exactly how the first contact is made will depend on the setting in which the therapist works. The client may call first to make a general enquiry or to refer himself. Either client or therapist may initiate contact after the referral system has put them in touch with each other. As this kind of contact is usually conducted

Table 4.1 Structure of Cognitive Therapy Across Sessions

Session Number	Main Focus
Assessment	Initial Meeting Collect information about current problems, maintenance factors and background. Beginnings of simple formulation. Engaging client in cognitive approach, showing collaboration. Education about Cognitive Therapy. First 'homework' (e.g. reading about CT, diary and so on).
1	Formulation: building up a model. Engagement and socializing about how therapy works. Homework focusing on collecting information, e.g. thought diaries, behavioural methods such as activity diary.
2–4	Continuing formulation, engagement and socialization. Working with information to start change – e.g. identifying negative thoughts and how to change these; activity scheduling in depression.
5–7	Using cognitive and behavioural methods to produce changes – thought challenging, beginning behavioural experiments.
8–9	As above, but beginning to identify and work with assumptions and rules. Testing out rules verbally and through behavioural experiments.
10–11	As above, introducing ideas of ending therapy. Looking at what client is learning and able to do outside sessions. Generalizing learning to other problems and client's life.
12	Ending – blueprint for ending. What client has learned and how to tackle future difficulties. Issues around endings.
Six-month follow up*	Review progress, troubleshoot difficulties and solve future problems.
Yearly Follow up*	As six months. Dealing with final ending.

*Follow up sessions depending on the individual client and/or service setting

Source: Adapted from Wells (1997) and Beck (1995)

on the telephone, it is often relatively brief and geared towards setting up the first face-to-face session. The first session then comprises formal assessment.

During initial contacts between client and therapist, working collaboratively may consist mainly of taking a very open stance towards the client – 'Is there anything about therapy, or about me, that you'd like to ask about or discuss at this stage?' In our experience, many clients opt to wait for face-to-face contact before asking such questions. Nevertheless, the opportunity has been offered and a degree of openness established. Additionally, some clients do raise valuable and important questions at this stage. Despite some growth in public knowledge about therapy in recent years, there are still areas of misunderstanding, raising questions such as 'Can talking really help?' and 'How long will the therapy go on?' Although it is probably best to regard these questions as requests for information, the therapist will also be aware of starting to get glimpses into the windows of the client's world-view. While these glimpses are mainly noted and put aside for another day, there may be some occasions when useful therapeutic work can be done at an early stage. The following example of a telephone conversation between Bill, a man referred for depression, and a counsellor in his GP's practice, illustrates how Bill's secondary appraisal of his problem, feeling stupid for feeling depressed, may interfere with his motivation to even get to the first face-to-face session.

Bill: I don't know if I'd just be wasting your time really. I sometimes think that it's all so trivial …

Therapist: Sometimes it seems hardly worth bothering with?

Bill: I'm just letting things get to me, it's so stupid …

Therapist: Is that what you say to yourself about how you're feeling, it's stupid?

Bill: Yes, it is stupid really.

Therapist: But I'm wondering if part of you *can* imagine not letting things get to you like this?

Bill: … Mmm … Yes, some days I can …

Therapist: So perhaps one thing we could work on might be getting those kinds of days more often …

Bill: … Mmm … Yes [*uncertainly*] … it would be hard, though …

Therapist: Yeah, it may be hard … Worth giving it a go? … What do you think?

Note in this example that, tempting although it might be as a cognitive practitioner to want to explore Bill's thoughts about being 'stupid', the therapist does not dive in, but allows a much more gentle exploration of what might be possible at this stage. During the initial contact, we aim to be as clear and explicit as possible about what is involved in therapy. An information sheet or booklet describing cognitive therapy, individualized to the setting, can answer many questions (Horton, 2006), as well as suggesting questions the client may like to ask the therapist (McMahon, 2006). The BABCP produces a leaflet called 'What Are Behavioural and Cognitive Therapies?' with basic information (see www.babcp.org), which can be adapted to the individual work setting. A clear summary of what to expect is also helpful: 'I'd like to meet up for an hour or an hour and a half and discuss with you what your current problems are. I'll be asking a little about your background and circumstances, and then we'll have a chance to talk over whether cognitive therapy is right for you at the moment. How does that sound to you?'

Beck et al. (1979) stress the importance of gathering ongoing feedback regularly, especially at the end of each session. Feedback is also a good 'marker' to end an initial contact, with questions such as 'How do you feel about the sorts of things we've discussed during our call?' The place of feedback in sessions is discussed in more detail towards the end of this chapter.

ASSESSMENT IN COGNITIVE THERAPY

A RATIONALE FOR ASSESSMENT

It is probably true that therapists from most disciplines begin to assess the client from a relatively early stage, and the tradition within the cognitive approach has been to make assessment a highly structured step. The aim of the assessment is not to 'label' or 'diagnose' the client but to reach some early, and therefore provisional, agreement on the issues to be worked on in therapy and how the work might proceed. It is therefore a two-way process, for the therapist to assess the client, and for him to decide if the therapeutic model, and therapist, is right for him at this time. Some therapists from different disciplines have expressed reservations about formal assessment, being concerned that it can turn into a judgmental process with an implication that the therapist is an expert, which would be out of tune with the concept of therapeutic alliance favoured by many traditions. These objections are obviously valuable, but can be overcome if collaboration, openness, curiosity and feedback are present right from the start. One potentially helpful way out of this logjam might be to distinguish clearly between 'being an expert' and 'having expertise'. In our view, the client will frequently expect that the counsellor or therapist lays claim to some expertise. The therapist can regard their expertise as expertise about people in general but this will prove of little avail unless it can ally itself with the client's expertise about his life, expressed as 'collaborative empiricism': 'The only way for therapists to accept [clients] as the final arbiters of their own reality is to be genuinely open to the possibility that the [client] knows something about reality that the therapist does not' (Safran and Segal, 1990: 9).

AREAS COVERED IN THE ASSESSMENT

The main areas to cover in the initial assessment are:

1. Problem-focused information (Cross-sectional);
2. Broader background information (Historical/Longitudinal);
3. Interpersonal information;
4. Environmental information, the person's circumstances.

To some extent, such areas represent a coming together of three different strands within the cognitive approach: (1) the original model (Beck et al., 1979); (2) the schema-focused approach (Beck et al., 2003; Young et al., 2003); and (3) the cognitive-interpersonal approach (Safran and Muran, 2003). Different therapists are likely to be drawn to different mixes of these models and therefore to somewhat different information-gathering styles. The original cognitive model laid a lot of emphasis on gaining precise data, which, in practice, seems to sit rather more comfortably with psychiatrists and clinical psychologists than with counsellors and therapists: these disciplines may be more attracted to recent, explorative cognitive models which lay greater emphasis on historical and interpersonal information gathering. In practice, we believe that it is important to have a balance between different ways of collecting information. Firing a lot of specific, closed questions at a client is as undesirable as getting lost in endless exploration of past experience.

The key areas of assessment are detailed in Figure 4.1. The overall aim of collecting information is to build up a picture of the client and start to develop

Figure 4.1   Assessment Information (*to adapt to client need*)

1. **Current problem**

What is the problem? Give a recent, detailed example, collecting information on:
  Triggers to problem (external or internal)
  Thoughts
  Feelings
  Physical aspects
  Behaviour
  Environment

2. **What keeps the problem going now?**

What makes it worse? What makes it better?
Safety behaviours and unhelpful coping strategies:
  Avoidance
  Checking of symptoms or checking for danger
  Seeking reassurance from others
  Rituals
  Suppressing thoughts or feelings
  Worrying away at the problem all the time
Hopelessness and lack of belief in change
Other people in the person's life maintaining the difficulties
  Lack of social support or
  Too much support and dependency
Continuing life events and stresses

3. **How did the problem develop?**

History of the problem
What started it in the first place
What was going on in the person's life at that time
Is it lifelong or recurring?
Main life events and stresses
Key themes in the individual's or family's life
Ideas about underlying assumptions and rules

4. **Developmental history**

Early life history, occupational and educational background
Family and relationships
Significant life events
Themes within the family
Medical and psychiatric history
Previous therapy and reactions to this

5. **General health issues**

Medication
Prescribed or non-prescription drugs
Alcohol, smoking
History of dependency

6. **Expectations of therapy and goals**

Ask about hopes or fears for therapy
List key problems to work on
Identify main goals for therapy

a conceptualization. At the assessment stage, an initial conceptualization is used to agree a common understanding about how the client's difficulties arose and what will be the appropriate strategies for working on them. The conceptualization becomes a map for understanding what has happened in the past, is happening now, and, crucially, how future therapeutic work can begin to transcend some of the difficulties.

The outline of assessment is not intended to be a fixed rota for therapists to stick to. Rather it is a series of coat hooks on which to hang information as it is assimilated, and people will use it according to their core training. Counsellors, for example, may be more likely to use it in a less didactic and more 'conversational' (in the sense discussed by Hobson (1985)) style with their clients; psychologists or medical therapists may be more structured, thoroughly covering the questions in a systematic manner; and nurse therapists may integrate such an assessment with a clinical interview or mental state examination (for an adapted version, see McMahon (2006)). Detailed life history questionnaires such as the Multimodal Life History Inventory (MLHI; Lazarus and Lazarus, 1991) can also be used, the client filling these in and bringing them along to the assessment. Questionnaires, however, may be offputting to some people, due to difficulties in reading or writing, or English not being their first language, and should be used only when we are sure that they are appropriate.

Whatever our form or style of assessment, we need to be working in a collaborative way, explaining what we are asking, and why. The assessment session starts with an agenda: 'Today I'd like to ask you about your difficulties, and how they developed. I'd also like to find out more about you, and ask you some things about your past, family, work and so on. We'll then discuss how cognitive therapy works, and whether it is right for you. How does that sound?'. We can then start with an open question such as 'What brings you to therapy?', mindful that, on one occasion, my open question was answered by 'I came on my bike'.

ASSESSING THE SUITABILITY OF COGNITIVE THERAPY FOR THE INDIVIDUAL

As cognitive therapy develops to cover a wide range of clinical problems, and is being adapted for clients who need longer-term therapy, so the number of clients for whom we are able to offer effective cognitive therapy increases. In addition, using formulation or conceptualization as a basis for our work means that we can be adaptable according to individual need. Therefore, the rules are changing as to when cognitive therapy versus another therapeutic approach might be called for. This does not mean, however, that cognitive therapy is appropriate or helpful for everyone. Many of the research trials into its effectiveness have used only carefully selected clients, with a generally 'pure' form of the problem being evaluated, and therefore are not always representative of the range of difficulties our clients present with in clinical practice. However, the developments in cognitive therapy are allowing for greater flexibility in the way we work, and therefore potentially increasing the number of clients who may find cognitive therapy suits them.

Despite our enthusiasm for the effectiveness of cognitive therapy for many of our clients, it is still important to be aware of its limitations and those clients who are unlikely to be able to use the approach. Safran and Segal (1990) and Dryden and Feltham (1992, 1994) published separate short questionnaires for assessing a client's suitability for, respectively, short-term cognitive therapy and brief therapy. Clear indications of suitability are found if the client shows the following characteristics:

- Is able to access automatic thoughts;
- Is able to distinguish different emotions;
- Accepts responsibility for change;
- Understands the rationale for cognitive therapy;
- Can make sense of a formulation approach;
- The methods make sense to the person;
- Is able to form a good enough relationship with the therapist;
- Is able to concentrate enough to focus on issues;
- The person's problems are not too severe or chronic;
- The person's safety behaviours, such as avoidance or excessive intellectualizing, are not going to get in the way of engaging in therapy;
- The client has some optimism regarding therapy.

Such criteria probably apply to most forms of therapy and should therefore be regarded as somewhat ideal. In practice, a client may already be well involved in therapy before it is realized that they do not meet such criteria. Cognitive therapy is continually being adapted for use with many different people, such as those with complex problems, chronic depression or psychoses (Morrison, 2003; Tarrier, in press; Tarrier et al., 1998), some of whom would not meet the above criteria. Therefore, the criteria in the above list are best regarded as positive indicators for standard cognitive therapy rather than as exclusion criteria for any type of cognitive therapy. In order to adapt cognitive therapy to meet the needs of many more client difficulties, it is vital that the practitioner is very familiar with the cognitive model; therefore, the criteria may be particularly appropriate for beginner cognitive therapists to follow closely. (For further information on the selection of clients for cognitive therapy, we recommend Padesky and Greenberger (1995) and Young et al. (2003)).

GIVING A RATIONALE FOR COGNITIVE THERAPY AND MAKING THERAPY RELEVANT

There are several different ways to give a rationale for the therapy, depending on the client and type of problem brought to therapy. The key aim is to make it relevant to the individual, so that he or she can see clearly what cognitive therapy has to offer for their particular issues at this particular time. Rationale giving varies from a didactic explanation of the form and process to more organic explanations as therapy proceeds. In the didactic approach, the therapist explains the principles of cognitive therapy in a direct way – as a teacher might do with an evening class. This is particularly useful where the client has a clear problem and is likely to find the possibility of a standard 'treatment' reassuring. For example, a client suffering from panic attacks may very clearly meet the 'textbook' model for both the problem and the solution. Therefore, the rationale may involve explaining the therapy in terms of aiming to help the client get her fears into perspective, and to work on different segments of the panic vicious cycle. Working with a depressed person, the therapy may be explained in terms of helping the client to break two vicious cycles contributing to the depression: low levels of activities and negative, depressed thinking. For many of these clients with 'diagnosable' problems, where more standard approaches apply, it is helpful for them to know that the problems are both recognizable and soluble using well-known formulas. In contrast, for clients with complex problems, the rationale may need to be highly idiosyncratic and evolve as the therapy proceeds.

The rationale is undoubtedly most effective when it is pitched at situations with which the client is familiar and where the therapy is clearly seen to match his needs. Judith Beck describes the process: 'the therapist explains, illustrates ... the cognitive model with the patient's own examples ... He tries to limit the explanations to just a couple of sentences at a time' (1995: 36). The therapist explores a situation that is characteristic of the client's problems, discussing in detail the specific emotions and thoughts. A common example is to ask clients what they were thinking about in the waiting room or on their way to therapy. These thoughts are often rather anxiety provoking ('Will I perform well?'; 'What if he thinks I'm wasting his time?') and can be easily linked to subsequent anxious feelings and behaviour. The method is demonstrated in the well-known 'Richard' videotape, where Beck begins the session with a discussion of how Richard felt while waiting for the session to start.

The personal example can be used to introduce the client to the basic cognitive model, by asking how thinking such a way might make him feel, and how feeling such a way might make him think. Such an exploration leads on to a discussion of how focusing on the client's patterns of thinking might alter mood or behaviour: for example, asking 'What if you were to think *x* instead of *y* in that situation?'

In the dialogue below, Alan is a 39-year-old man who works for the Health Service. He refers himself because of what he describes as stress at work. The therapist has asked Alan to describe in detail a recent episode of feeling very low.

Therapist: So, think of a recent time when you felt really bad.
Alan: OK, yesterday morning.
Therapist: Was that a typical morning, like you feel when you're low?
Alan: Yes, the same old story for me.
Therapist: Talk me through what happened. What was the first thing you noticed?
Alan: I was trying to get out of bed and get up. I felt, like, leaden. Heavy. I just wasn't going to make it. I felt, what's the point? I was thinking about how weak I'd become, how I used to be able to cope, and look at me now.
Therapist: So, you felt really heavy, leaden, and low? (*Alan:* Yes). And when you felt that, you had a number of thoughts: 'I'm not going to make it, what's the point? I've become weak, I used to be able to cope' [*writes these down*]

Alan: Yeah, really negative.
Therapist: And how did thinking that way make you feel?
Alan: Crap, complete and utter crap. Like lying in bed all day.

We then use this example to illustrate the model. Note how Alan spontaneously goes into sentence-completion mode, showing that he recognizes himself in the description of depression, which in turn encourages the therapist to move quickly into cognitive work.

Therapist: The basic idea of this is that the way we see the world, see what is happening to us, has a big influence on …
Alan: How we feel.
Therapist: Yes. There are probably different ways of seeing things and some seem to help us more than others … If you're depressed, you seem to develop a kind of negative bias (*Alan:* [nodding] Yes) … not see some of the good things (*Alan:* Yes) … and focus on the bad (*Alan:* Yes, that's me) Does that make any sense to you?
Alan: Yes, yes … I would think so … because I feel at one time I could take the knocks a bit more, I suppose … If anyone said I'd done something wrong, I used to be able to shrug it off quite easily.

The therapist recognizes that Alan is very sensitive to criticism, and asks for a specific example of when he felt criticized. Alan describes a meeting at which he had to present a report. He felt very criticized and depressed and this led to taking two days off work. Reviewing the evidence of the comments that were made, however, revealed that these had been 80 per cent neutral, 10 per cent negative and 10 per cent positive.

Therapist: So there were an equal number of positive and negative comments?
Alan: I would say so … but, I don't know, I seem to grasp, take hold of the negative things more.
Therapist: Remember what we said before – that one of the features of depression is that you do over-focus on the …
Alan: Negative.
Therapist: I mean do you think it is possible that happened on this occasion?
Alan: It's possible.
Therapist: [*laughing*] You're looking at me incredibly unbelievingly!
Alan: No, no … it probably is what happened … it seemed though that they made more emphasis on the negative … or at least I thought they did.

In the above example, the therapist is able to bring this opening phase full circle by referring back to the original rationale – 'what we said before'. The client's final comment expresses some doubt about his appraisals – an indication that he is beginning to see them as hypotheses rather than facts. This constitutes an excellent 'base camp' from which the therapeutic exploration can proceed. Although it is only a first session, Alan immediately gains some symptom relief, which helps to engage him in therapy.

By contrast, the next dialogue offers an instance in which a laboured rationale quickly runs into the sand. The client, Beti, is 20-years-old and a regular club goer.

She is feeling suicidal, following a relationship break up that she experienced as humiliating. The therapist tries to offer her a rationale close to her experience:

Therapist: If you were going to a disco with a mate and she thought, 'I've got to get off with someone tonight or it'll be a disaster', how do you think she'd be feeling as she went in?

Beti: Nervous. She'd be worrying if she'd meet someone.

Therapist: Yes, that's right. If you were with her and were thinking, 'I'd like to meet someone tonight … but if I don't, I can enjoy the music, have a laugh, whatever …' How would you feel?

Beti: More relaxed. Not so worried.

Therapist: So can you see then that the way you see things does affect how you feel about them?

Beti: Mmmm …

Therapist: And which of you might enjoy yourself more?

Beti: Depends on which one of us met someone …

Therapist: And which of the two of you might stand the best chance of meeting someone, do you think?

Beti: Well, that would depend on which of us was the best looking.

Beti attended for two more sessions during which she achieved some symptom relief but, in the therapist's estimate, little lasting attitudinal change. In retrospect, the therapist moved on too quickly from the client's uncertain response to his question about the effect of the 'way you see things'. Moving on did not allow Beti's doubts to be properly explored. The client's final comment, though showing an admirable realism, does perhaps indicate other areas that would need to be addressed. The need to address other areas would not rule out a cognitive approach, but would suggest that strongly individualized packaging might be needed. The therapist in this instance was perhaps not able to grasp the need for such individual packaging quickly enough.

There are two important points to remember about giving a rationale. The first is to keep it brief and try to follow the 'three-sentence rule'; the therapist should not say more than three sentences at any point in the dialogue and should be constantly seeking client feedback as she/he proceeds. The second is that the client's queries about and objections to the rationale should be welcomed and openly discussed in an explorative way – we want the client to be convinced within her own frame of reference, not from the power of therapist logic. By asking for and discussing feedback, the therapist starts from a basis of collaboration and empiricism.

USING A PROBLEM LIST AND NEGOTIATING THERAPY GOALS

The 'problem list' is a concept that has been taken into cognitive therapy from behavioural therapy. The list is usually developed in initial sessions as a simple list of the areas that clients feel are problematic in their lives and want to do some therapeutic work on and is kept in written form by both client and therapist. It can therefore be used in reviews of progress during the course of therapy. A list of goals for therapy can also be negotiated at the end of the assessment. While a problem list defines what issues are to be focused on, goals specify where the person would like to be as a result of therapy. It is a good chance for both therapist and client to check that they are working together with the same ends in mind, and that the goals are realistic.

Goals need to be fairly specific, and measurable. If, for example, someone comes into therapy with the goal of 'changing my life' or 'getting out of debt' then we need to specify exactly what goals could be met as part of therapy, and specify manageable and measurable steps such as 'Reducing the frequency of panic attacks so I can get out of the house and start looking for work; stop spending money as the only means I have of comforting myself when I feel low.' Many people we see say that their goal is to 'Feel better'. This can be translated into smaller goals, which can then be measured during the course of therapy, as the following illustrates.

ANN

Ann is a mature student of history. She has battled with anxiety for two years since starting the course, and at times has felt too panicky to get to lectures. She has suffered from anxiety on and off since having leukemia in her early twenties but has always managed to cope on her own, 'waiting for it to pass'. She's sought help from the student counsellor.

Counsellor: [*Summarizing towards the end of the assessment session*] You've told me a lot about yourself today, and about the anxiety you've been 'battling with' for the past two years. We've talked about how it started and what's been keeping it going. It's really helpful to have a clear plan of where we're going in our work together, and what you'd like to get out of coming to see me. Could we spend a few minutes talking about that?

Ann: Sure.

Counsellor: We'll first summarize the problems you're bringing today: panic attacks which you get every week or so.

Ann: Yes, depending on the pressure of my college work.

Counsellor: So, we'll write down 'panic attacks triggered by work pressure'? (Ann nods). And feeling anxious and uneasy a lot of the time? (*Ann*: Yes). And we'll add the consequences of the panic attacks and anxious feelings …

Ann: Not being able to get on with my work when I feel anxious, and not getting to lectures.

Counsellor: Yes. [*Writing them down*] So, we have four main areas: panic attacks; feeling anxious; not getting on with work; and not getting to lectures. [*Shows* Ann *the list*]

Ann: Mmm, sounds a lot.

Counsellor:	It must look daunting. What is really helpful too is to look at where you'd like to be as a result of therapy, what are your goals?
Ann:	I'd like not to have panic attacks, or at least know what to do when I get them, and not feel so anxious all the time … just feel better, I guess.
Counsellor:	So, we can write down 'Not get panic attacks' and 'Know what to do when I do get panicky'. As to 'Not feel so anxious all the time': what would be different for you if you didn't feel so anxious? Can we translate that into a specific goal or two?
Ann:	I'd be able to get on with my work and get it in on time, at least most of the time, and I'd get to lectures rather than staying at home when I'm anxious.
Counsellor:	Our goals, therefore, are: 'Get on with work better'; 'Get my work in on time'; 'Get to more lectures' [*Writes them down*]. What about 'Feeling better': how would I know if you were feeling better? What would you be doing?
Ann:	I'd spend less time worrying about work and be able to go out and see friends more, and not have to agonize over work all weekend.
Counsellor:	A goal might be 'Going out and seeing friends at weekends'. More play time, perhaps? (*Ann:* Definitely!). Anything in particular you'd like to be able to do, that you're not doing because of the anxiety?
Ann:	I used to go to a salsa dancing class. I've not done that for ages. That would be a good goal for me, I guess.

Ann's problem list and goals are shown in Table 4.2.

Goals need to be manageable and measurable, and ones that can be met in or as a consequence of therapy. They need to be achievable within the time frame of therapy, given service or other constraints, and given the history and issues of the particular client. People with long-term problems who have received different

Table 4.2 Ann's Problem List and Goals

Problem	Goal
Panic attacks	Reduce frequency of panic attacks
Feeling anxious all the time Not being able to go out when feeling panicky	Know what to do when I get panicky.

Not being able to work
Not getting work in on time
Avoiding lectures
	Not feel so anxious:
	  Get on with work
	  Get my work in on time
	  Go to lectures

	Feel better:
	  Not work at weekends
	  Go out more with friends
	  Re-start salsa dancing

forms of treatment and perhaps many types of therapy may have either very ambitious goals, believing cognitive therapy to be an opportunity for a miracle ('I'm hoping you'll be the one person who can sort me out') or extremely small or negligible goals ('I don't know, really, I just came along because my GP told me to. I don't really expect anything to work'), reflecting hopelessness that anything can change. We therefore need to be realistic in what is possible, raising hope without being overambitious.

The great strength of a list of problems and goals is that, in keeping with the parsimony of cognitive therapy, both client and therapist are clear as to the direction in which therapy is headed, and can therefore work towards those goals rather than being side-tracked by issues which later prove to be less relevant to the matter at hand. Goals can be frequently reviewed, and measured to see how much they have been met, or whether they need revising or breaking down into smaller sub-goals. The downside of the problem list is that it may exclude exploration of those issues that later prove to be essential. Therefore, it is important to note that the list is not cast in stone, but is regarded as provisional and can be added to and subtracted from.

In practice, therapists and counsellors from different disciplines use a problem list and goals in different ways. Those with a leaning towards behavioural work may well use the problem list frequently. Others may get the feeling articulated in a Paul Simon song: 'The nearer your destination, the more you keep slip-sliding away'. Those from some other therapy traditions have expressed discomfort at overfocusing on 'problems' and failing to identify client strengths. Overfocusing on 'problems' may also hold the danger that one might be unable to pick up new themes and issues. Where a therapist feels a strong ideological resistance to focusing on problems, it may often be useful to examine what that discomfort is about. Equally, where there is a strong tendency to focus on problems at the expense of being open to new ideas or material, it may be useful to try to detect in oneself any strong sense of discomfort with spontaneity. Thus, working with a problem list and goals requires a balance between maintaining a structured focus and being flexible enough to move away from the defined issues into uncharted territory as and when the therapy requires. A rule of thumb is that, if the therapy seems to be moving off the defined client issues, it is important to check out with clients whether they wish to continue in this direction, or get back to the previously defined goals.

USING MEASURES

Once we have defined where we are going, it is very helpful also to have a clear idea about how we will know when we have got there. Obviously what our clients tell us and what they are doing is one of the most important measures, but in addition, a more formal measurement process can help both parties to evaluate progress. Measures can also be a useful shorthand to gain vital information at different stages of therapy. They keep us on track and check whether therapy is useful or not. Most clients will happily go along with filling out an inventory form that takes only three or four minutes to complete. For some, it is actually helpful to have their depression contained or defined. It may help to inure them from blaming themselves for having symptoms if these symptoms are in some way legitimized. Measures can help people to communicate things that they might otherwise find difficult to say face to face, such as having suicidal thoughts or unacceptable physical symptoms.

The Beck Depression Inventory (BDI) was devised by Beck in 1961 and revised in 1978 and more recently as the BDI-II . The BDI is a 21-item self-report inventory that assesses emotional, cognitive and physiological aspects of depression. The BDI can be found in Beck et al. (1979), and a self-scoring version is in Burns (1999a, 1999b). A manual giving guidelines on its use can be found in Beck and Steer (1987). The BDI has been extensively tested for both its internal and external validity and has been found to correlate strongly with severe depression (Carson, 1986) and suicidal wishes (Weishaar and Beck, 1992). The BDI-II has varied some of the items, looking at loss of energy, increases and decreases in weight and energy, and is somewhat more sensitive than the BDI (Beck et al., 1996). Both measures are available for purchase from www.psychcorp.com or www.harcourtassessment.com.

The BDI is useful to cognitive therapists in a number of ways. First, it gives an overall score that can be taken as a guideline to the degree of depression. Second, highly specific pieces of information can be quickly gleaned from it. For example, one question asks about suicidal thoughts. This question offers a fairly easy way into a dialogue about self-harm and suicide, valuable for some therapists who find it difficult to initiate such discussion. There are also questions about specific cognitions such as guilt, and physiological features such as sleep disturbance. Many cognitive therapists would use the BDI at the start of every or most sessions with clients where depression is part of the picture. The development of the scores – usually in a downward direction, towards less severe symptoms – gives an indication of how the overall intervention is developing and can enhance motivation as things start to improve.

There are a number of measures for other problem areas such as anxiety (Beck et al., 1988; Burns, 1999a, 1999b), hopelessness (Beck et al., 1974a, 1974b), agoraphobia (Chambless et al., 1984), self-esteem (Robson, 1989) and obsessive-compulsive disorder (Clark and Beck, 2002). Measures such as the Hospital Anxiety and Depression Scale are widely used and easy to complete. The metacognitions questionnaire (Wells, 1997; Wells and Cartwright-Hatton, 2004) is useful in highlighting beliefs about thinking, particularly where worry and rumination are part of the person's difficulties. Wells (1997, 2000) also covers several rating scales, including those for panic attacks, social phobia, health anxiety, general anxiety and worry.

Later on in therapy, measures can be used to assess assumptions and beliefs. For example the Dysfunctional Attitudes Scale (Beck et al., 1991) is a 40-item scale with attitudes such as 'It is best to give up my own interests in order to please other people'; 'It is shameful for a person to display weaknesses'; 'I should be able to please everybody'; and 'If you cannot do something well, there is little point in doing it at all'. The attitudes measured fall into the categories of Approval, Love, Achievement, Perfectionism, Entitlement, Omnipotence and Autonomy. Jeffrey Young has devised a number of schema questionnaires to measure core beliefs (Young et al., 2003). We have noticed that some clients can become quite disturbed after filling out these long schema questionnaires, especially where they seem to have a number of underlying beliefs. Young and Klosko (1994) contains a much shorter version and this can often serve as a useful starting point for clients for whom schema-focused issues are evident.

We stress that such measures of assumptions and beliefs may be more appropriate later on in therapy once a client is fully engaged in the process, and can understand and make sense of where assumptions and beliefs fit as part of their therapeutic picture.

In addition to using formal measures, simpler methods are invaluable, such as asking a client to do a simple weekly rating out of 10 on problem areas. Similarly, we can develop our own measures. For example, I (FW) wished to have a record of how a client was trying to increase her assertiveness at work. The client and I devised an Assertiveness at Work Scale from a number of scaling questions about the sort of situations she often found herself in. Giving it to the client to fill out every week showed how well she was succeeding over the period of the intervention. Another client, Tracy, found it very difficult to say just how she was feeling, and found filling in questionnaires difficult. She devised a 'global yeuch' measure, a 0–10 scale that she called her 'yeuchometer', which gave us both useful feedback as to how she was. Other measures can be the number of panic attacks and the number of times going out was avoided, such as for Ann earlier, or measures of time someone is able to stay in a room without checking for the presence of spiders, the number of obsessional thoughts, the number of episodes of bingeing and vomiting, and so on. Some therapy sessions may include very specific, on-the-spot measures. For example, during therapy for phobias, the client repeatedly gives an anxiety rating during a series of experiments to test out what happens when in contact with their phobic object. In therapeutic work with people with post-traumatic stress disorder (PTSD), 'subjective units of distress', measured from 0 to 10, or 0 to 100, enable us to identify and work with 'hot spots' in trauma reliving. The list of measures is as long as the number of clients we see, and clients can be very creative in coming up with their own ratings.

Another important way of using measures is in rating the degree of belief held in specific thoughts or assumptions, which we discuss further in Chapters 5 and 6. We can also measure the success with which a client has met specific goals, such as using a simple 0–10 measure of meeting the goal 'Engaging in previously enjoyed activities' (Grant et al., 2004), or for Ann, who was described earlier, we could keep a record of the number of times she has gone out with friends, handed in an essay on time, or gone to lectures despite feeling anxious.

CAUTIONS ABOUT MEASURES

When using measures, it is important to be aware of both client's and therapist's expectations. Most measures have some 'demand characteristics': there may be a subtle subtext that implies that they should show reducing scores over time. They can therefore lead people to feel temporarily unsettled or worse, particularly if presenting them with difficulties they have tried to avoid, or if a high score on the measure means that the individual is not doing as well as thought. When measures become a regular weekly feature of therapy, clients come to understand more about their nature and purpose. They may therefore be tempted to reduce their scores to convince either the therapist or themselves that they are getting better. Clients may sometimes exaggerate their scores in order to stay in the 'patient role' or avoid ending therapy. Sometimes there can be misunderstanding about what exactly is being measured, as the following examples illustrate.

BEN

Ben had a deep and regular concern that he would go mad. After months of therapy during which his BDI score plummeted, he confessed that he had been deliberately underscoring his BDI and BAI (Anxiety) because he couldn't stand the idea that he might not be getting rapidly better.

LORNA

Lorna had been regularly filling out Depression and Anxiety inventories. Much of the work was centred on her concerns at work. Several weeks passed before it emerged that she considered that she was filling out the inventory with the view that it was about her mood at work, rather than her general mood, as her therapist had assumed.

Both of these examples show that a degree of caution is warranted in the inter-pretation of symptom measures. Regular review of the purpose and meaning of using scores is therefore recommended.

We do come across clients who really do not like using measures. If there seems no reasonable resolution to this difference, it is usually most helpful to either resort to a simple measure ('How do you feel out of 10?') or put the whole idea to one side. Some therapists, as they do about the general notion of assessment, may find the notion of using any measuring procedures foreign or objectionable, wondering initially if it is legitimate to use such measures outside the psychiatric domain to which they seem to belong. Some clients may refuse to fill out a BDI, perhaps because they fear what it will uncover (Persons, 1989). The measures may be off-putting or too challenging to some, or the questions may seem irrelevant to their problems. Others report a degree of dislike of the BDI – as a symbol of 'science' or of 'homework' – possibly linked to a degree of avoidance of unpleasant emotion. In practice, however, measures do have a real place in therapy when they are used sensitively and collaboratively, and their limitations are accepted.

KEEPING NOTES AND AUDIO-RECORDING SESSIONS

In line with the principles of structuring therapy and collaboration, recording sessions is an important ingredient of cognitive therapy. Keeping detailed notes, particularly at the assessment stage, is valuable for both client and therapist, helping clients to feel that their concerns are being noted and understood. Making photocopies of notes of salient points after sessions is useful, allowing the therapists to give simultaneous *aide memoires* to the client and to themselves. Alternatively, carbon copies could be used. Therapy notebooks enable the client to keep notes and helps prevent the common scenario of key information becoming lost on scraps of paper (Beck, 1995). We almost always encourage clients to bring notebooks or notes along to each session, to review where therapy has got to so far and to serve as a reminder. In addition, it is very helpful to have a white board to use during the session to illustrate the conceptualization.

A further record is for therapists to tape or digitally record sessions and give the recording to the client to listen to for homework. We have found tapes invaluable to the process of therapy, improving what is remembered from the session (even if it does include all the bits and pieces we wish we had not said). The records allow the opportunity for repeated listening and reflection, essential to making sense of and learning from therapy, as well as giving the client useful feedback. For example, a client who believed she presented a very muddled account of her difficulties was surprised at how clearly she was able to describe them; another client may learn that while she states that she really wants the therapist to help, she never really listens to what the therapist is saying.

Occasionally, and in our experience the exception rather than the rule, recording sessions may not be easily accepted. Since our voices sound very different to us when we hear them externally, as opposed to when we listen to ourselves speaking, the sound of our own voice can come as an actual or predicted shock, and feed into a negative self-concept.

TRACY

Tracy was initially very reluctant to say anything when the tape recorder was running. She predicted: 'I know if I hear myself speak, I'll sound horrible and it will be embarrassing.' She knew she would then use it to 'beat myself up'. We used this in therapy in two ways. First, what she predicted about the tape fitted in with her general tendency to make negative predictions and, by taping a short part of the session and listening to it again, we could test her prediction. Second, we formulated her response to the tape as potentially valuable information for therapy, telling us more about her beliefs about herself. During the experiment of listening to the tape, Tracy also recorded her negative thoughts listening to herself, which we then wove into the formulation. During the following session Tracy reported that she initially thought: 'God, I sound rubbish, I hate my voice', but then found she got absorbed in the content of the tape, and listening to it made her realize how she only ever said negative things about herself.

SESSION STRUCTURING AND AGENDA-SETTING

'Would you tell me, please, which way I ought to go from here?'
'That depends a good deal on where you want to get to', said the Cat.
'I don't much care where ...', said Alice.
'Then it doesn't matter which way you go', said the Cat.
'... so long as I get somewhere', Alice added as an explanation.
'Oh, you're sure to do that', said the Cat, 'if you only walk long enough'.
(Lewis Carroll, *Alice's Adventures in Wonderland*)

One of the characteristic features of cognitive therapy is the structured, focused approach running throughout each session as well as for therapy as a whole. Figure 4.2 illustrates a typical session structure (Blackburn and Davidson, 1995).

Figure 4.2   Structure of Cognitive Therapy Within Sessions

1. Review of client's mood – e.g. brief report and quickly review measures;
2. Agenda for today – work with client to decide on what to cover during the session;
3. Feedback on last week's session, listening to the tape;
4. Last week's homework and measures;
5. Main session items;
6. Today's homework;
7. Feedback on session.

Although such structuring may smack of anally retentive quirks, it may be justified by the finding that a business-like attitude is very useful in therapy and indeed correlates with a positive outcome. Such an attitude is especially helpful in making the best use of frequently limited time. In practice, most clients seem to like the structure, especially because they are able to learn it, follow it and understand its purpose. It is easy for therapists to forget what an uncommon experience therapy is for most clients. While it can sometimes be useful for therapy and therapists to be unpredictable, predictability can be a virtue for clients already struggling with unfamiliar problems and changes.

When working in a structured way, it is very important that the client also agrees with the structure. Therefore, initial stages involve negotiating the structure and being clear with the client exactly what session format we are following. Suddenly introducing agendas and homework later on in therapy can leave the client puzzled. Giving a rationale and explaining the therapy is often called 'socializing' the client into therapy. While the term hints of behaviourism, such socializing may be seen as a two-way collaborative process, with therapist and client learning how each other works and how each can adapt to work well with the other. As therapy proceeds, there is less need for so much stress on overt structure: the therapy begins to 'run itself'.

The usual prelude to a review of the client's mood is for the client to complete a measure such as the BDI or the BAI or other relevant measures as discussed earlier before each therapy session. Scores need to be interpreted with care and should generally be matched with a client self-report, asking the client: 'That's what the scores suggest. How has the last week seemed to you?' Usually the client's self-report will match the score closely but sometimes not: 'Well, I know the scores have come down but I still feel lousy, it doesn't feel better'. This material is often therapeutically valuable. One client, for example, reported that the day on which I (FW) saw him, a Monday, was always his worst day. As we were exploring work-related issues, this led quite nicely to a useful agenda item: how to start the working week.

SETTING AN AGENDA

Although the structure of the session may be varied, agenda setting is generally considered essential. The purposes of setting an agenda are to maximize the use of time in the session and to make sure certain items are covered. Agenda setting also aids the client's memory of the session. We know that memories about specific sessions are often quite limited, and will no doubt be aggravated by therapeutic 'clutter'. An agenda should help the session to begin collaboratively and maintain such collaboration throughout the session.

The content of the agenda will most probably include both therapist items and client items and there can be useful dialogue on what to cover and when to cover it. One deficit of the Rogerian model is that it may lead some client-centred counsellors to conclude that they have no right to raise things in sessions. This seems to us to deny the use of therapist skills to both therapist and client. Equally, however, therapists must ensure that they do not impose too many issues that they would like to talk about. To do so would be bad cognitive therapy – it would not be collaborative and would not facilitate the process of the generalization of therapy, that is, the client gradually learning to be their own therapist. Over the course of therapy, the client gradually takes more and more responsibility for agenda setting. In the beginning phases we may say, for example, 'It would be useful today to talk about how you've been during the week, and I've got some things I wanted to ask so we can get a better understanding of your difficulties. I'd like to find out how you got on with the diary as well. Is that OK, and is there anything in particular you'd like to cover today?'. Later sessions may start with a joint understanding of agendas: 'What shall we put on the agenda today?' We have, at times, to negotiate what is most important to cover if someone brings along a number of issues (Grant et al., 2004).

REVIEW OF PREVIOUS HOMEWORK AND THE SETTING OF NEW HOMEWORK

Doing therapeutic tasks between sessions, known in the jargon as 'homework', is an essential part of cognitive therapy and related to good outcome, as discussed earlier. However, the idea of setting 'homework' is sometimes difficult for therapists and clients alike, having overtones of being an authoritarian teacher and school child. This sensitivity can be regarded as useful because it is just how certain clients will experience being set homework. The very word may awaken old memories of bad experiences in schools and/or in other authority situations. This possibility should lead the therapist to undertake an exploratory discussion with the client about why homework may be useful.

Clients' reactions to homework and the factors that prevent them from doing it can also be helpfully reviewed. It can be very demotivating for clients when they have gone to the trouble of doing the homework and the therapist either fails to follow it up or gives little time to it. This is why checking on the previous week's homework is included as an item on the session structure list. Equally, its inclusion later is a reminder to the therapist to discuss homework while there is reasonable time remaining in the session. This prevents homework becoming an appendage, thrown in as the client leaves the room. We have stressed the central importance of homework in cognitive therapy several times so far and will continue to do so as we progress through the process of therapy as homework can begin to take on different aspects at different stages of therapy.

When considering what might be appropriate homework, the general rule is 'the simpler the better'. The client can, after all, ask for something more complex if the homework proves to be too simple. One regular homework task is to listen to the tape of the session. Reading one of the many self-help cognitive therapy books or a handout specific to the client's difficulties can also be valuable homework. Care should always be taken to read written material before it is given out, thinking about the client's frame of reference – sometimes a book or pamphlet may unwittingly refer to some aspect of the client's situation which may be disturbing to them. Devising a homework sheet is also valuable, influenced by the 'reformulation letter' concept of cognitive analytic therapy (Ryle and Kerr, 2003). Figure 4.3 gives an example of a homework sheet, which includes the client's conceptualization, goals and homework.

SESSION TARGETS

The targets for the session ('What do you want to talk about today?') constitute the main part of the session and will generally take up the majority of the time. The items that are worked on will be those already identified during the agenda-setting stage or issues that have arisen during the actual course of the session. It is not unusual for homework to become a central focus of the session. Working on the session targets is where the main skills and techniques of cognitive therapy will be brought to bear on the identified issues. As has already been described, the direction of cognitive therapy tends to start at the symptom level ('bottom end') and works towards the underlying issues (the 'top end') as becomes necessary. Often the symptom-level focus will begin with behaviourally oriented work, such as graded task assignments, and then move on to identifying and challenging negative automatic thoughts. These techniques will be described

Figure 4.3   Example of an individualized homework sheet

Mike:

Reminder of the sessions: When you were a little boy, your dad was a difficult man who drank a lot. He was violent and abusive towards your mum and your brothers and sister. Your mum tried to look after you, but the situation was so bad that you got 'passed around' a lot to be looked after by others.

You came to believe 'I don't belong anywhere'. You didn't have consistent care, and didn't learn how to look after yourself properly or how you feel about things.

Aims for therapy: To learn how to stand on your own two feet more, instead of relying so much on your wife. Another aim is to learn to take critical comments less personally, and not to strike out, especially at your wife.

The homework for this week:

1. Spot how you feel when you are being criticized: Write it down in your notebook.
2. Try counting to five before reacting to criticism. Write down how it went – how you felt, any difficulties, etc.
3. Listen to the tape and write down important points in your notebook.
4. Remember to bring the notebook to the next session.

---

further in Chapter 5. At a later stage in therapy, the work may tackle underlying issues by evaluating dysfunctional assumptions and modifying core beliefs via methods such as continuum work and positive data logs. These techniques and skills will be described further in Chapter 9.

SESSION FEEDBACK

Feedback is an essential part of collaborative and open work, enabling us to focus and gear our work to the specific needs of each client session by session. Open questions at the end such as 'How have you found the session today?'; 'Is there anything that was particularly useful?'; 'Is there anything that was difficult or you didn't like?' encourage both positive and negative feedback. We also start each session with feedback on the last week's session, particularly relevant when the tapes have been listened to and reflected on.

Most of us can accept positive feedback more than readily, but we may have to do more work on ourselves to really want to know what our clients do not like about our therapeutic style and us. Yet it is crucial that we are aware of negative as well as positive reactions because negative client reactions can easily bring therapy to an abrupt halt. Therapists may often need to look at their own negative automatic thoughts ('Ungrateful sod!'), dysfunctional assumptions ('If I work hard at therapy, I will be recognized as a good therapist and wonderful human being') and maladaptive core beliefs ('I must be the perfect therapist'), as discussed in Chapter 3.

Continuous feedback should help the therapy to stay as close as possible to the client's needs so that a kind of 'rolling contract' (Wills, 1997) between therapist and client develops. Continuous feedback and the therapist's attempts to explain what she is doing by giving rationales for each move mean that the therapeutic contract will be negotiated regularly on an ongoing basis.

CONCLUSION

The early stages of cognitive therapy set the scene for the process of therapy, with the therapist actively involving the client right from the start. The therapist explains both the overall aim and structure of the therapy, and the aim and structure of each technique. Each stage of the therapy is thereby properly introduced and negotiated with the client, by asking for feedback from the client about what they have experienced and learned as well as on what may have 'jarred' with them. Thus, we keep on track with the client, aiming to use the therapy in the most effective fashion. This focus is facilitated by the structuring of each session around key activities, a structure that can also be varied when flexibility is required.

Further Reading

Horton, I. (2006). Structuring work with clients. In C. Feltham & I. Horton (Eds.), *Handbook of counselling and psychotherapy* (2nd ed.) (pp. 118–126). London: Sage Publications.

McMahon, G. (2006). Assessment and case formulation. In C. Feltham & I. Horton (Eds.), *Handbook of counselling and psychotherapy* (2nd ed.) (pp. 109–118). London: Sage Publications.

Grant, A., Mills, J., Mulhern, R. & Short, N. (2004). *Cognitive behavioural therapy in mental health care*. London: Sage Publications. (**Chapter 3.**)

Wells, A. (1997). *Cognitive therapy of anxiety disorders*. New York: Wiley. (**Useful first section on assessment and measures.**)

5 Tools and Techniques of Cognitive Therapy: Working with Cognitive Content and Processes

Cognitive therapy is, by reputation, characterized by methods and techniques. As well as the essential psychotherapy tools of two comfy chairs and a box of tissues, the cognitive therapist is armed with tape recorders, pens and paper, thought diaries, activity schedules, questionnaires, and, in the case of the client with phobias, esoteric items in pots such as spiders or wasps. Perhaps the more technical aspects of cognitive therapy have led to some of the criticisms of it: that it is mechanistic, stressing tricks and techniques at the expense of emotions, concentrating on what methods to use in therapy rather than on the process.

While it has been acknowledged that some of the early models of cognitive therapy stressed the verbal and rational over the role of emotion (Safran and Muran, 2003; Safran and Segal, 1990), this does not mean that the more rational, verbal and behavioural techniques of cognitive therapy should be rejected. The use of case conceptualization in cognitive therapy, as well as more recent developments looking at the therapeutic relationship and the role of emotion, allow for a far more sophisticated approach, using a range of powerful tools of proven value to enable the client to understand and tackle their particular difficulties. In addition, we have greater understanding of which methods work and why, integrating both rational and emotional aspects in order to produce change, enabling people to feel differently as well as think differently. A careful conceptualization, within a collaborative therapeutic relationship, allows for the more mindful selection of which approaches may be of value to the particular client. The selection bears in mind both the evidence for problems in general, and the client's specific needs. In addition, cognitive therapy aims for the client to learn a set of new skills that can be applied to different problems, and therefore cope better with such difficulties in future. In other words, the therapy aims to provide people with a toolkit for life:

> The goal of cognitive therapy is not simply to make our clients think differently or feel better today. Our goal as cognitive therapists is to teach our clients a process of evaluating their goals, thoughts, behaviours, and moods so that they can learn methods for improving their lives for many years to come ... [W]e are not simply fixing problems but also teaching ways of finding solutions. (Padesky, 1993: 12)

In this first of three chapters on methods used in cognitive therapy, we will be focusing on interventions that are aimed at explicit cognitive change to automatic thoughts and to thinking processes. The second of the three methods chapters will focus on the use of behavioural methods to enhance cognitive change, what we have called the 'B' in 'CBT'. The third methods chapter will focus on deeper cognitive change through working with assumptions, core beliefs and schemas. We discuss how to choose specific approaches according to the client's conceptualization, and how technical and experiential approaches are used in practice. In order to set the scene for using methods in cognitive therapy, we start with a discussion of how different techniques work to produce change in beliefs.

HOW AND WHY DO COGNITIVE THERAPY METHODS WORK?

Tell me and I will forget. Show me and I will remember. Involve me and I will understand. Aristotle

Beck has always stressed that the end result of cognitive therapy, the means for people to feel better, is cognitive change. Reading early texts, cognitive therapy seemed to achieve this by a method of identifying thinking biases, and empirically putting these views to the test, often by verbal and rational means. As behavioural methods were integrated into cognitive therapy, these seemed to work by also producing cognitive change. More recent models of how we process information and make sense of our worlds, combined with adult education theory, have given us greater understanding of how such methods work, and how to use them to greater effect (see Bennett-Levy et al. (2004) for a useful summary). Such models include Teasdale's Interacting Cognitive Subsystems approach (Teasdale, 1996), Brewin's duel representation theory (Brewin et al., 1996), Epstein's theories of the cognitive-experiential self (Epstein, 2002), as well as models of metacognition (Wells, 1997) and the integration of methods of mindfulness (Segal et al., 2002).

These theories propose, in brief, that we have different ways of processing information roughly corresponding to 'head' and 'heart'. Teasdale's model describes different modes of meaning, the specific, propositional mode and the more general, implicational mode. The specific mode of meaning is activated when an event, such as failing to get a job, leads to a specific, verbal interpretation: 'I've failed, I'm hopeless, no one will ever want to employ me'. The meaning appraisal in this mode can be easily articulated – failure, hopelessness, and a belief that one is unemployable – and these are seen as 'facts' that can be assessed and tested out against the reality of the situation. The client, in having the thought 'I've failed, I'm hopeless, no one will ever want to employ me' might be asked to assess, rationally, empirically, the truth of the meaning he is giving the rejection letter. True, he has failed to get the job, but does this mean he is a failure at everything? He can be asked to list those things he has done successfully: brought up two children;

worked for all of his life until he was made redundant due to the company going bust thanks to a crash in the stock market and so on. But he may not feel any different.

We therefore need to understand how he is processing 'heart' or 'felt' information in the second, implicational mode, which is more general, reflecting pervasive themes, a felt sense of something being wrong, a overwhelming feeling of failure, hopelessness. It is difficult for clients to put these meanings into language: 'I just feel awful'; 'I just know I'm a failure'. It is a holistic, sensory experience. Information from the body will both convey the feelings and be used as evidence for the meaning; thus the client will be hunched over, slumped, sad looking, and these bodily reactions will both convey the emotion, and be used as evidence to support it ('I feel bad, this confirms I am bad'). The implicational meanings relate, broadly, to core beliefs and schema, such as Young's schema of abandonment or deprivation (Young et al., 2003). This model clarifies our experiences, and those of our clients, of intellectual and emotional belief. It explains why in cognitive therapy we can get so far with verbally working to change patterns of thinking but may then meet a 'brick wall', often articulated in the client statement: 'I know my thoughts aren't true, but I still feel bad'. In short, holistic, intuitive meanings may be less amenable to change by purely verbal interventions.

Seymour Epstein's (2002) theory of different tracks – the experiential and the rational – in the mind is also valuable in understanding how psychotherapeutic methods work. The dual track concept can inform the ways in which we need to move between different minds in order to change (Epstein, 1994, 1998, 2002). Our minds are both experiential and rational (Padesky and Mooney, 2000). The experiential mind is based on emotion and intuition, reacts to and learns quickly from direct experience rather than from 'facts'. The experiential mind is also associated with the realm of images, metaphors and memories. It tends to be particularly active when emotion is high: the mind that leads the person to react regardless of the logic: 'I just knew I had to get out, I had to run, I felt like something bad was going to happen'. The 'ah ha' experience, when things fall into place, involves learning at the experiential level. The rational mind, in comparison, is more slow and deliberate, working on cause and effect, and is active and conscious. The rational mind is swayed by sense and logic. In order to produce change, we need to work with and integrate both minds.

Many cognitive methods can be seen as helping to give the client more access to their rational mind at a time when they are driven by negative feelings. This does not imply that the rational mind should overrule the experiential mind, but rather that they can work alongside each other to achieve more balanced and functional responses. The harmonious working of the rational mind in conjunction with the experiential mind allows reflection and observation, as seen in experiential, reflective learning theories such as those of Lewin (1951) and Kolb (1984), which have exerted much influence in the field of adult education (Honey and Mumford, 1992; Schon, 1983). In contrast, behavioural experiments and experiential methods described in the next chapter, allow change at an experiential level.

The link between rational and experiential minds can be strongly reinforced by writing things down, for example, using thought records. The written steps of the thought record replicate the actions of a reflective mind when it is working well. Cognitive therapy may well work because it enables us to move between these two ways of being, a more rational thinking self, and an experiencing, emoting self. We think, and we feel, and both are essential to therapeutic change.

MATCHING THE TECHNIQUE TO THE CLIENT'S CONCEPTUALIZATION

The whole of any system of psychotherapy is more than the sum of the parts. (Beck, 1991: 196)

In order to produce change at both the rational and emotional levels, cognitive therapy has evolved specific methods, such as Socratic questions and guided discovery, 'thought records', weekly activity schedules and behavioural experiments. Cognitive therapy also uses methods from other therapeutic disciplines, such as imagery and metaphor, Gestalt techniques of role plays and two-chair dialogues, and methods of mindfulness using aspects of meditation practice. Beck (1991) clarifies the principles of cognitive therapy and stresses that cognitive therapists can choose from a variety of therapeutic techniques as long as the basic principles of cognitive therapy are kept: the techniques should fit with the model of therapeutic change and be based within the individual conceptualization; and the principles of collaborative empiricism and guided discovery should be used within a structured session format.

The wide range of approaches leads to many questions about what to use at what point in therapy, and which approaches are likely to be helpful. Judith Beck suggests that as therapists ask themselves what they are trying to accomplish with the specific problem, they should be 'cognisant of the objectives in the current portion of the session, in the session as a whole, in the current stage of therapy, and in therapy as a whole' (1995: 284).

Much of the development of cognitive therapy techniques has evolved in response to particular clinical problems, for example, the use of activity scheduling and thought records has proved to be valuable in depression; the hyperventilation provocation test has evolved to help disconfirm clients' fears in the treatment of panic disorder. However effective the techniques may be for particular problems in general, the approaches always need to be allied with the client's experience in particular. It is all too easy for the novice (and more experienced) cognitive therapist to systematically work through the repertoire of approaches, or throw techniques at a problem in the hope that one or the other will work. A common observation of trainee cognitive therapists is that the approaches used in a particular session are based on the approaches learned the previous week. Thus, before introducing any 'trick of the trade' the therapist needs to ask:

- 'What is the problem here?'
- 'What kinds of things are likely to help?'

- 'How does using this approach fit with this person's individual conceptualization'
- 'Am I just using this because I don't know what to do next or it's a new approach I've just learned?'

This is not to say that the therapist cannot use general approaches for particular problems. For example, working through well-tried, well-recognized methods that have been shown to work with particular problems is reassuring to clients, giving the message that their problems are manageable and that a set of effective solutions are available. In addition, protocols developed for particular problems (see Chapters 10 and 11) have proven effectiveness. But the introduction and use of techniques have to be matched to the individual, and 'sold' to the individual in terms of their conceptualization.

Using techniques in cognitive therapy raises questions like, 'What happens if they don't work? Won't this make the client feel even more hopeless and put them off cognitive therapy for life?' Although this can sometimes be the case, the risk of engendering hopelessness in both client and therapist highlights the importance of client–technique matching. The very depressed individual may be only too aware of negative thoughts, but be unable to even begin to look for alternatives; production of a thought record too early in therapy risks exacerbating the person's low mood, and we therefore start with behavioural methods, aiming to help the person become more active. When working with people with somatic problems, it is not unusual for them to report that they have no negative thoughts, just symptoms (Sanders, 2006), in which case, the introduction of thought records may put the client off what the therapist has to offer. The introduction of techniques needs, at all times, to be a 'no lose' experiment.

Information about how the client approaches different therapeutic tasks can be valuable to the conceptualization, aiding the identification of underlying assumptions and beliefs. For example, if a client consistently agrees that filling in thought records would be useful but somehow never gets around to doing them, both client and therapist can collaboratively work together to identify what is going on. Does it reflect the client's fear of 'failing' at homework tasks or their belief that 'Nothing will help so why bother?' Is the client agreeing with the therapist in a passive way to prove that the therapy is rubbish? In another example, a client not attempting activity scheduling, having agreed in the session that it would be useful to her, led to recognition of her belief that 'I don't do things that I should do', and discussion about her hopelessness that her life seemed to be full of things she should do but resented doing. Such feelings and beliefs highlighted by the client's reactions to cognitive techniques then become the focus of therapy.

IDENTIFYING FEELINGS AND THOUGHTS: THE BEDROCK OF COGNITIVE THERAPY

One of the most commonly used, and best-known, approaches in cognitive therapy is helping the client to identify emotions and accompanying thoughts, to look for ways in which biased or unhelpful thinking relates to particular emotions and learn to appraise thoughts differently. The classic cognitive method is the Thought Record, a diary of feelings and thoughts triggered in particular situations. The final steps of the Thought Record act as a tool to come up with more helpful, rational perspectives. The thought record has a number of functions, summarized by Grant et al. (2004) as:

- It enables emotions to be identified and labelled as they occur;
- Thoughts accompanying particular emotions can be identified;
- The person can see how emotions and thoughts arise in particular circumstances;
- It enables patterns of thoughts, emotions and behaviour to be identified, seeing how these interact;
- Thought records enable a different perspective to be taken on thoughts, by re-evaluating and challenging them, and to come up with more helpful alternatives;
- Identifying thoughts gives the 'meta-message' that thoughts are mental events to be observed, identified and evaluated rather than absolute truths, thereby changing the relationship of the self to the thoughts;
- Using records helps generalize the skill of identifying and re-evaluating thoughts and predictions to other events, situations or life circumstances.

The model of identifying emotions and thoughts, as described in Chapter 2, provides the basis for the simple-level conceptualization. Additionally, recognition of these cycles can sometimes offer the client some initial relief, lessening negative feelings and thereby increasing motivation for therapy. Much of the assessment and initial stages of cognitive therapy involves engaging and 'socializing' the client with the cognitive model, introducing the idea that feelings, behaviour or physiology are interrelated and change as a result of working at the level of thoughts. How this is done in practice involves two stages. The first is to verbalize what the client is feeling at a particular point, and what is going through their mind. The second stage involves encouraging the client to keep a diary of thoughts and feelings, which may then be used to discover alternative ways of thinking.

IDENTIFYING EMOTIONS

A number of people come into therapy not really sure what they might be feeling. Some may be aware of feeling bad, but cannot say more about the fine details. Others, particularly those with anxiety or panic problems, will be feeling all sorts of physical sensations, but might be less aware of the emotions. One of the first steps, therefore, is to encourage the client to label feelings. Greenberger and Padesky (1995) stress that feelings can most often be described in one word: at its simplest, 'mad, bad, sad or glad'; in reality as a range of feelings: upset, shaky, scared, terrified, worried, hopeless, sad, panicky, furious, and so on. These might be thought of as 'primary emotions'. People with an undeveloped vocabulary of emotion can be encouraged to think about the use of different words to describe different intensities of feeling. Greenberger and Padesky suggest that the client keeps a diary for a week or two, noting down changes in mood, and identifying specific emotions, described, as far as possible, in one word. A simple two-column diary may help to target and label key emotions and specific triggers (Figure 5.1).

Figure 5.1   Diary of Emotions

Situation	How Did I Feel?
Example: Met friend in the street. She didn't stop to talk to me.	Rejected (90%) Awful (80%) Anxious (70%)

Keeping a simple diary of moods enables the gradual introduction of the thought record, described below, and begins the process of 'distancing' from emotions in order to allow for change. Asking the client to identify feelings may well lead to thoughts. For example, asking the client who has panic attacks 'How did you feel?' may lead to the answer, 'I felt like I was going to lose control', which is more likely to be a thought – 'I'm going to lose control' – than a feeling. Helping the client to distinguish between the two, and identify each accurately, is an important first step.

IDENTIFYING THOUGHTS

The next step is to help the client to identify thoughts, particularly those associated with specific emotions such as those identified earlier. There are a number of ways of identifying negative thoughts, as summarized in Figure 5.2.

While we all have some thoughts most of the time, they are often far from easy to identify. People often mix up thoughts and feelings, and find it very difficult to put their thoughts into words. We have seen how the question 'How did you feel about that?' may elicit thoughts; similarly asking for thoughts may lead to an expression of emotions. It is more helpful to ask: 'What went through your mind' or 'Did you get an image or picture in your mind?' rather than 'What did you think?'

The use of certain types of questions can help the client to clarify thoughts. Questions beginning with 'What', 'How', 'When', 'Why' and 'How' are useful. If the client's thoughts are expressed as questions, such as 'What if I couldn't cope?';

Figure 5.2 Identifying Thoughts

Key steps in identifying thoughts:

Pick a specific example of a problem situation;
Identify how you were feeling:

- And when you felt that, what was going through your mind – either thoughts, or images;
- Aim to be as specific as possible, e.g. if the thought was 'I felt as though something bad might happen' make it into a specific prediction: 'I knew that if I went into that room, I'd feel terrible, shaky and unwell and have to rush out of the room, everyone would point and stare and think I'm mad'; or 'There's no point, I can't be bothered' might be the thought 'If I try and do anything today, I won't feel any better';
- Turn questions into statements, e.g. 'What do other people think?' becomes 'They think I'm really stupid'; 'What if x should happen?' becomes 'If x happens, it would be a complete disaster'.

Sources of thoughts:

- Shifts of mood during the client's day. Write down thoughts and feelings in the thought diary;
- When mood changes during sessions, e.g. the client suddenly looks upset and tearful ask: 'What went through your mind just then?'
- Make predictions, e.g. 'What if you were to go to that job interview, what might happen?'; 'What would it be like to get up rather than stay in bed?'
- Role play a particular situation in the session;
- Ask the client to imagine themselves in the situation, identifying thoughts and images.

'What if I lost my job?'; 'Is there any point in anything?', try and rephrase these as statements which hold the key emotion: 'If I didn't cope, it would be a complete disaster and I'd make a real fool of myself'; 'If I lost my job, it would show how useless I am at everything – a failure'; 'My life has no point anymore'. A recent, concrete example of when the client noticed a change in moods can be used to identify specific thoughts connected to the emotion, such as a change of mood during the session. The therapist reflects: 'Right now you look upset and tearful. What is going through your mind?'. The client can also be asked about mental images or pictures to identify their thoughts: 'Did you get a picture in your mind of that happening?' 'What is going on in the picture?' Similarly, role playing particular situations or conversations can help the client to identify negative thoughts.

A key point in identifying thoughts is to separate out which thoughts are most salient and connected to emotion from the numerous thoughts buzzing around – the so called hot cognitions (Greenberger and Padesky, 1995) or 'Spiky Thoughts' (Holdaway and Conolly, 2004). While an anxious thought to target might be

'Something bad may happen', the more relevant, underlying thought is 'I feel like something awful is about to happen'. The latter thought, like anxious thoughts typically do, makes a negative prediction about the future and explains the raw power of anxiety more completely. Hot thoughts are likely to carry far more meaning to the individual than those that are not connected to emotion, and themes of the thoughts may often be extreme or unhelpful. For both client and therapist to target specific, emotionally laden thoughts is a skill which needs practice on both sides. The feeling of reaching a dead end, of not being where the action is, indicates that the process of identifying thoughts is not on course and we need to change direction to follow the emotion more directly.

Once the client is able to begin to distinguish and identify thoughts and feelings, the thought diary can be introduced. In its full form (see Figure 5.7) the diary can appear intimidating and induce further feelings of panic and hopelessness. For some clients, particularly those struggling with low mood, low energy or feeling overwhelmed, we have found it more helpful to introduce the record in stages, as described by Greenberger and Padesky (1995). The two-column diary can be extended to three (Figure 5.3), identifying the situation, feelings and thoughts.

Figure 5.3   Diary of Emotions and Thoughts

Situation	How did I feel? (Rate 0–100 per cent)	What went through my mind? (Rate belief 0–100 per cent)
Met friend in the street. She didn't stop to talk to me.	Rejected (90%) Awful (80%) Anxious (70%)	What have I done to offend her? I must have upset her last time we met. What did I say? I just know she must hate me (80%). I don't have any friends left (90%). I'm useless at friendships (100%).

Alternatively, for people who tend to respond with emotions expressed in bodily sensations, or think more in images than words, an elaborated thought diary is shown in Figure 5.4. The diary also includes a column for behaviour – 'What did you do in response to your feelings and thoughts?' – which helps identify coping mechanisms or safety behaviours (James Bennett-Levy, personal communication, 2004).

Figure 5.4   Elaborated Thought Diary

Date Situation	Emotions	Body Sensations	Thoughts	Memories	Behaviour

The client can initially be encouraged to keep a record of all thoughts and then underline or highlight particular 'hot thoughts' accompanied by emotion. Here is where ratings come in very useful. The client keeps a record not only of thoughts and emotions but of the relative strength of each, usually on a 0–100 scale. For example, in a crowded situation, an agoraphobic person may experience terror (95) and the thought 'I'm going to faint and make a fool of myself', which they believe 100 per cent. In the safety of home, the client may become annoyed with their partner (20) and think 'What an unhelpful old fool!', believed 60 per cent. For the purpose of helping the client to look at alternatives, the first, stronger, set of emotions and thoughts would be more useful to target, in light of the relative strength of the emotion (95, not 20) and the client's goal for therapy: to be able to go out without panicking. Belief ratings can also give the helpful meta-message that thoughts and feelings are not true or false in a black and white way, thus beginning the process of distancing from negative or unhelpful thoughts or thinking processes.

Written records help the client to pinpoint specific thoughts more accurately, and create distance between emotions and thoughts, particularly when emotions are riding high. Thought records also enable us to pinpoint specific predictions, such as 'They'll think I'm stupid', or 'It'll be a disaster', in order to test out the predictions more accurately. We have found in practice that some people are reluctant to write down their thoughts, believing that the act of recording what is going on will make the feelings worse, or preferring to avoid rather than focus on the thoughts. In this case, the client can be encouraged to try an experiment to test out whether keeping records does in fact make them feel worse, or whether, as is more common, writing down thoughts is a way to get them into perspective.

Once proficient at identifying and writing down thoughts, in order to begin the process of evaluating them, it can be useful to introduce the idea of 'thought biases' (sometimes known as 'thinking errors'). Common patterns of biased thinking were shown in Figure 1.2. Reading these biases, and seeing common themes from the thought diaries, enables people to begin to see patterns in their ways of thinking, how such biases relate to emotions (for example, 'Always labeling myself, whatever I do, makes me feel worthless'), and introduces the idea that such biases are not facts. Burns (1999a, 1999b) points out that people tend to have characteristic cognitive biases. By identifying these, people can develop a helpful thinking heuristic such as 'Oh, here I go – personalizing things again!'

MODIFYING NEGATIVE THOUGHTS BY DISCOVERING ALTERNATIVES

Once specific negative thoughts are identified, the next step is to test out the validity of this way of thinking, treating the thoughts or negative predictions as hypotheses to be tested rather than facts. Such an approach is named 'collaborative empiricism', using guided discovery and experiments to test out thoughts and beliefs and explore alternatives. Exploring the link between events and our interpretation of them must be done in a friendly and understanding way, and not give the message that there is a 'right' or 'wrong' way of seeing things, just that there are many alternatives which may influence our reactions.

It is vital to be empathic and non-judgmental; putting the thoughts into context is particularly important: 'Given your experience, it makes sense that you keep saying that to yourself'. We are asking penetrating questions of our clients, and we need to maintain collaboration and empathy: 'The danger is that the question is asked in the wrong tone or the wrong spirit, and comes across as "smart"' (Davies, 1998: 41). Davies, focusing on guided discovery with angry clients, gives the example of working with a man who reacted very aggressively when someone jogged his elbow in a pub, causing him to spill his beer. The man interpreted this nudge as having been done intentionally and deliberately and threatened to smash the beer mug into the other's face. When questioned whether the jog had been deliberate, asking 'So, the only reason he jogged your elbow is because he had it in for you?' could potentially sound patronizing or dismissive. But asking, collaboratively, carefully, 'Lets have a look … could there be another reason …. exactly what happened? What would someone see if they were looking in from outside?' may be less threatening, more inclusive and curious, and allows the client to think through the situation rather than feeling put on the spot.

Regular summaries can help to check that the client and therapist are on the same wavelength. The overall message in challenging the client's way of thinking is to enable the client to take their thoughts to court, enabling information and evidence to be collected for the defence and the prosecution, rather than automatically jumping to conclusions based on one way of seeing things.

GUIDED DISCOVERY AND SOCRATIC QUESTIONS

Guided discovery is an investigative process whereby client and therapist work together in a collaborative way to see if there is a different way of seeing things. It involves asking questions in order to understand the client's point of view and help the client to discover alternatives. A key method of guided discovery arises from the Socratic tradition. Socrates was a fifth-century Athenian philosopher and teacher whose most famous pupil was Plato. Socrates had an unwavering commitment to truth, arrived at through systematic questioning and inductive reasoning.

> Socrates (469–399 C.E.) was famously ugly, seeming to recall facially the half-human, half-animal satyrs who in Greek myth were the lewd attendants and drunken companions of the wind god Dionysus. But in a dialogue written by his less famous pupil Xenophon, Socrates is said to have joked that his bug eyes, although aesthetically unpleasing, were functionally superior to normal eyes, since they enabled him to see side-ways as well as straight in front ... When told that the Delphic oracle had replied to a questioner that Socrates was the wisest man on earth, he reportedly said, 'Ah yes, but that is only because I know that I know nothing for certain' ... Such a stance may plausibly be interpreted as marking the beginning of wisdom. (Cartledge, 2001: 126–37)

Socratic questioning does not mean we all need to be famously ugly, but being able to look sideways might be an advantage. It defines a way of using primarily a question and answer format, to look at things not only from the side of the head, but from all different angles, understanding that the way we think about things is only one way among other possibilities. Anxiety, for example, makes our minds work towards exaggerating the seriousness and likelihood of feared consequences, and undermining our abilities to cope. When depressed, we see everything, past, present and future, in a negative light. By using guided discovery and Socratic questioning, we aim to guide the client to explore alternatives and come up with more measured ways of thinking (Padesky, 1993, 2004a, 2004b). It is not about positive thinking – many human fears are real and need to be taken seriously – but working with thoughts aims to find a more helpful and realistic balance.

Reading the cognitive therapy vignettes of early texts can give the impression that the therapist knows the answer to a particular issue, and is asking questions that lead the client to this answer. However,

In the best cognitive therapy, there is no answer. There are only good questions that guide discovery of a million different individual answers. ... [W]e can ask questions which either imply there is one truth the client is missing or which capture the excitement of true discovery. (Padesky, 1993: 11)

The Socratic method is not a case of the therapist trying to persuade the client to see things from his point of view. One common mistake is to ask too many leading questions, too soon, without taking time to explore why the client thinks the way he does. Questions such as 'Don't you think it would be more helpful if you did x?' or 'Do you think this way because of ... [guesses]?' may well close down the process of discovery, imposing the therapist's way of seeing before discovering the client's viewpoint. Instead, therapists need to be curious, cultivating a question mark over our heads. We cannot assume we know the answers, and very often other people's way of thinking is surprising and unexpected, as though we are all Alice in Wonderland. Open questions, in a gentle and friendly manner, enable issues to be explored collaboratively. A useful question when wanting to clarify meanings is to ask: 'What do you mean when you say x?' This helps to define more clearly the meaning of a thought, which may be very idiosyncratic. Other useful questions are shown in Figure 5.5.

Padesky (Padesky, 2004b, 2004c; Padesky and Greenberger, 1995) has identified that there are four unfolding stages in the Socratic technique:

- Asking informational questions to uncover information outside the client's current awareness;
- Accurate listening and empathic reflection;
- A summary of information discovered;
- Asking synthesising questions which help apply the new information discussed to the client's original thought or belief.

Good *informational questions* are those to which the client has the knowledge to answer, but may not be able to see on their own. When in a state of raised negative emotion, our awareness becomes narrowed, for example by negative attentional bias in depression, hyper-vigilance in anxiety, or preoccupation with violation when very angry. High emotion also affects the memory, so in the affect-laden moment, people are unable to easily recall information that might be contrary to the activated beliefs. Informational Socratic questioning draws the client's attention to relevant information that may be outside the client's focus, asking questions to increase the range of attention and memory.

For example, the therapist might ask a client who is afraid of collapsing during a panic attack, 'When you say you're terrified that you might faint when you feel so panicky, have you ever felt really faint but not actually fainted?' The question can help the client think about the realities of fainting, moving from a vague fear to remembering information that may be useful. They may answer, 'I've felt really awful lots of times, but I've never actually collapsed ...'. The questions can then move to discovering why this might be so: 'How might you

Figure 5.5   Guided Discovery Questions (with thanks to Adrian Wells)

- What do you mean when you say x?
- What is the evidence that x is true? What is the evidence against x being true?
- What might be the worst that could happen?
- What leads you to think that might happen?
- And if that happened, what then?
- If it did happen, what would you do? How would you cope?
- Have you been in similar situations in the past? How did you cope then?
- How does thinking that make you feel?
- Are you thinking in a biased way? (See Figure 1.2) e.g. are you predicting the future or mind reading?
- Are you paying attention only to one aspect? What if you looked at it from a different angle?
- What would you say to a friend who kept on saying x to herself (e.g. 'I'm stupid'; 'I'm terrible')?
- How would that work in your body?
- Is there an alternative explanation?
- Is there any other way of seeing the situation?
- What are the advantages and disadvantages of thinking that?
- Is it helpful, or unhelpful?
- What would it mean to you to see things differently?
- Are you making decisions based on your feelings, or is reality telling you something different?
- What might you tell a friend to do in this situation?
- What would your friend say to you?
- Is there something else you could say to yourself that might be more helpful?
- What do you think you could change to make things better for you?
- How would you like things to be different?
- What would you like to do instead?
- What would have to happen to make that possible?

have stopped yourself fainting?'; 'If you feel faint, but don't actually collapse, what does this tell you?'. Many writers about therapy have suggested the wisdom of using 'why' questions sparingly (Egan, 2002). Asking 'Why do you think that way?' is likely to elicit 'I don't know, I just do'. 'What might be the consequences of thinking x to yourself? is more likely to elicit a useful answer, such as 'It makes me feel bad, it stops me getting on with my work'.

The following example illustrates how drawing the client's attention to information outside her awareness enables her to evaluate a thought.

CAROL

Carol had written down a recurrent thought – 'I don't have any real friends' – in response to her regular feelings of loneliness. When feeling down, she was unable to remember any good contacts with people. Her thoughts seemed real. In the session, she was asked to think over the past year and remember as specifically as possible what other people had said to her, or things that people had done for her. She remembered her birthday two months ago, when the women in her office surprised her with a cake and a card; she recalled a neighbour coming round one evening to bring her a parcel that the postman left on her doorstep, which the neighbour had rescued knowing she would be out all day; she remembered a young woman in her Italian class asking her to a party. Tearfully, she realized that there were people in her world who had been friendly and warm to her, and who would like to be her friends. When she felt bad, however, she would dismiss this information as somehow irrelevant, or would even find it hard to remember, the feeling of loneliness resulting in 'selective memories' and 'discounting the positive'. Carol realized that the problem was not in fact that she did not have any real friends, but that she did not know how to move in slowly escalating steps from friendly overtures to deeper friendship. This could then become the focus of therapy, as discussed in the section on Behavioural Experiments in Chapter 6.

When asking questions to explore alternatives, these should be peppered with *reflection and summaries*, in order to allow reflection time and to check that we are going in the right direction. The dialogue moves from a series of questions and answers to an overall statement of summary, either by the therapist – 'So, what we are saying here is …' – or by the client, invited by the therapist – 'What are we saying so far? What sense are you making of it?'

The final phase of Socratic Questioning is to move from the concrete to the more abstract, asking *synthesizing questions* to enable the client to generalize from the discussion and therefore apply new information to either re-evaluate a previous idea or construct a new belief. If the client reports being 'bad', what does this mean? Initial questions focus on specific, concrete examples or areas where the client believes they are 'bad', such as bad at a job, bad to be so angry and so on. Guided discovery will initially aim to explore the meaning and relevance of 'badness' to these examples. For example, the client may discover that they are not particularly good at some aspects of their job, but that they generally do a good job; while being angry all the time is not particularly helpful, being angry sometimes does not make the client a bad person. The discussion then aims to help the client move from concrete examples to the more abstract general and, in this case, questionable concept of 'badness'. Padesky (2004b, 2004c) and Mooney and Padesky (2000) stress the importance of asking synthesizing questions to help the client to draw conclusions. Synthesizing questions include:

- 'How does this fit with what we're saying about you being a bad person?'
- 'What do you make of this?'
- 'How might these ideas make a difference to you?'
- 'Given these experiences, what do you think will help?'
- 'What would your close friends say if they knew all this?'

In the above example, the client is asked to think about how the information that they are good at some parts of their job and is not angry all the time can fit with their general belief – 'I am a bad person'.

Some kinds of guided discovery questions focus on possibilities rather than on problems (Mooney and Padesky, 2000). In the above examples, we are looking at ways that a negative construction of events can be viewed in a more helpful light. For some people who feel very stuck with long-term, entrenched, problems, where problems are poorly defined, or where environmental factors continually reinforce a negative perspective, asking 'How would you like things to be?' and 'If things were getting better for you, what would be happening in your life?' helps to define where the person would like changes to occur. Therapy can then look at ways to achieve movement towards the possibility, via constructing new underlying assumptions and testing out ways of living life according to these (Mooney and Padesky, 2000). Questions that aim to conjure up 'possibilities' are also used during the process of goal setting described in Chapter 4, and parallel the dialogues used in coaching (Neenan and Dryden, 2002).

The aim of guided discovery is for clients to learn how to question thoughts and beliefs for themselves. Rather than just asking questions in sessions, the therapist can teach the client the kinds of question to ask in order to look for alternatives. When the client has the automatic thought 'I'm bad', they learn to ask instead, 'What does bad mean?'; 'What is the evidence I'm bad?'; 'Is there anything in myself that is not all bad? And why am I ignoring this at the moment?', and other questions to reduce the potency of the negative thought. By listening to tapes of therapy sessions, people are able to identify key questions and learn to ask them of themselves when thoughts and assumptions are activated.

Although cognitive therapy has integrated Socratic questioning as one of its cornerstones, not everyone sees Socrates himself as the best model for the practice of Socratic Dialogue (Neighbour, 2004). Socrates frequently used irony and other tricks in his arguments, and the dialogues described in Plato usually end in confusion. This confusion has, however, been linked to the philosophic concept of *Aporia*, which refers to a sense of cognitive dissonance, a gap in knowledge, which can lead to the motivation to close the gap. Therapists may equally find that their attempts at Socratic Dialogue end up producing not so much insight as *Aporia*, a gap in knowledge that may be the necessary forerunner of insight and a sign of progress. Therapists should therefore develop tolerance for confusion and aporia, seeing them as necessary stages in therapeutic work (Wills, 2005a).

USING PIE CHARTS TO LOOK AT ALTERNATIVE EXPLANATIONS

Where thoughts centre on particular explanations of events, a 'pie chart' of explanations can help gather in other relevant factors and draw the person's attention to different reasons why something may occur. For example, clients who are very anxious about health issues may be able to see only one, catastrophic, interpretation, such as a headache meaning a brain tumour, for body symptoms. Such a client may be asked to brainstorm all possible causes of headaches and each is given a probability rating. Often, the cause seen as the most likely when the client is anxious ends up being given a low probability, as illustrated in Figure 5.6. A pie chart can be useful where self blame or blaming others is an issue (e.g. 'It is all my fault my marriage broke up'; 'I was responsible for the car crash'): brainstorming all the possible explanations, and assigning responsibility appropriately draws attention to the range of factors leading to any particular event. The method can also be used for reassigning responsibility for negative events, for people with excessive concern about responsibility and guilt, featured strongly in obsessive-compulsive problems (see Wells, 1997).

Figure 5.6   Pie Chart of Causes of Headaches

- Ask Client to brainstorm causes (e.g. stress and tension, eye strain, tiredness, 'flu, alcohol and so on);
- Give each cause a probability rating;
- Draw up a 'pie' to show causes.

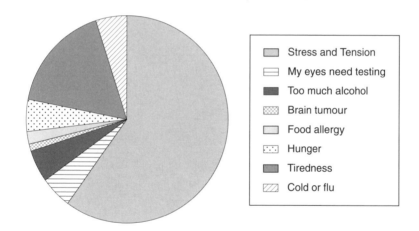

Stress and Tension
My eyes need testing
Too much alcohol
Brain tumour
Food allergy
Hunger
Tiredness
Cold or flu

DIARY OF NEGATIVE THOUGHTS AND ALTERNATIVES

Once the client has become proficient in recording emotions and thoughts, and is able to begin to question some of the thoughts, we introduce the full diary as shown in Figure 5.7 (originally from Beck et al., 1979), using it to work through examples in the session before giving it as a homework task.

Padesky and Greenberger (1995) have suggested that clients may not be convinced by the alternative thought generated by the type of thought diary shown in Figure 5.7. We agree with the view that the credibility of the alternate or balanced thought seems to be enhanced by considering the evidence for and against the negative thought, by using a diary as shown in Figure 5.8.

Given that people can have compelling reasons for believing certain thoughts, it is particularly important to review the evidence in favour of the negative thoughts

Figure 5.7 Thought Diary

Date	Situation	Emotion: How did you feel? How bad was it (0–100)?	Automatic Thoughts: What went through your mind? How much did you believe each thought (0–100)?	Alternatives to Automatic Thoughts: How much do you believe each alternative thought?	Results: 1. How much do you now believe ATs? 2. How do you feel? 3. What can you do?
	Met friend in the street. She didn't stop to talk to me.	Rejected (90%) Awful (80%) Anxious (70%)	What have I done to offend her? I must have upset her last time we met. What did I say? I just know she must hate me (80%). I don't have any friends left (90%). I'm useless at friendships (100%).	Just because she didn't stop does not mean I have no friends. There may have been other reasons for her not to stop. She looked in a hurry. Chris and Ann both came over to talk to me in the coffee break today. I do have friends (60%).	1. 30% 2. I feel better: less rejected, although it still hurt. 3. Say hello to her and find out if she is OK. Concentrate on people who are my friends.

Figure 5.8 Thought Diary-Reviewing Evidence

Date	Situation and Feelings	Thoughts and Images. Identify and Rate the Negative Thoughts	Evidence for My Negative Thoughts	Evidence Against My Negative Thoughts	Alternative, More Helpful and Realistic Thoughts. Rate the New Thoughts	Action: What can I do to test my new thoughts? What do I need to do to feel better?
	Met friend in the street. She didn't stop to talk to me. Felt awful – rejected, useless.	I don't have any friends left (90%). I'm useless at friendships (100%). Everyone has abandoned me (95%). Image of standing alone in the playground watching everyone else playing but not asking me to join in.	I did not have many friends at school. I was often alone. I don't make friends easily. Two of my close friends moved away and left a gap.	It was not my fault that I found it difficult to make friends. We kept on moving due to dad's job and I had to keep changing schools. I did make friends then had to leave them. Now, I had Eleni and Nadine, but they had to move. Jo is quite a new friend and I know she is scatty sometimes. Maybe I don't know enough about how to make friends, and need to practice.	I do have friends (70%) and need to practise making more friends (95%). There are other reasons why Jo might have ignored me (70%).	Find out why Jo did not say hi to me. Make a list of my friends, past and present. Try and meet new people – I need to work out how to do this.

Source: adapted from Greenberger and Padesky, 1995

before reviewing the evidence against them. Going straight to the evidence against the negative thoughts often seems to result in the client resisting what may seem to them as the therapist coming on too positively. For example, a socially phobic man may frequently think, 'People think I'm odd, I cannot make friends', reflecting underlying beliefs about being a misfit and strange. He may have, in fact, lots of evidence to suggest that he gets a strange response from other people, in that he has evolved ways of coping with his anxiety such as staring at the floor when talking to people, saying only a few words then trying to leave, or maintaining too much eye contact to stop other people noticing how anxious he is. This evidence needs to be taken into account. Guided discovery can, however, enable him then to review the evidence against the thought 'People think I'm odd', for example, times when he is with a very old friend with whom he can be at ease; times when another person has been kind and involved him in a conversation despite his awkwardness, and so on. After seeing the evidence for the negative thoughts first, the client seems naturally more receptive to 'hearing' the evidence against.

In practice, we have found that different people prefer different types of diary. Reviewing evidence for and against thoughts might be very difficult for people who struggle to identify any evidence against thinking a particular way, due to strong negative self beliefs, or when working with people with adverse life circumstances such as serious illness where negative or frightening thoughts may in some cases be true (see Moorey and Greer, 2002). For these people, looking at helpful versus unhelpful ways of thinking might be more appropriate than trying to find evidence against thoughts.

Ideally, thoughts should be recorded as soon as they occur, but carrying around a thought diary can be offputting or inconvenient and people forget to take it with them. Using a notebook with the columns drawn up, or recording forms on the computer may be more convenient. It is a sobering lesson for all trainee cognitive therapists to use a diary themselves for a period of weeks. Our experience of this activity was a sense of amazement at the sheer magnitude of the negative dross we found had passed through our minds! We also encountered problems such as forgetting to do the diary, not wanting to identify thoughts, not being able to see alternatives, or the frequent excuse of the diary being lost or thrown away. These problems are exactly those faced by our clients, who also have the additional challenge of wrestling with anxiety or depression. The key to successful work with diaries, therefore, is sensitive use, offering a good rationale for doing them and spending time on the client's difficulties. Identifying and challenging thoughts eventually becomes an automatic process, with less need for writing everything down but, for a period at least, keeping a written diary helps to reinforce the process.

WORKING WITH THE PROCESSES OF NEGATIVE THINKING

As well as focusing on the content of thoughts, enabling people to identify biased thinking and come up with more helpful, rational alternatives, there are times when we need also to be focusing on thinking processes. Common types of unhelpful thinking processes include recurrent, repetitive thinking – rumination and worry – thought suppression, and the processes resulting from metacognition (beliefs and thoughts about thinking). These are characteristic of problems such as generalized anxiety and worry, obsessive-compulsive disorder, post-traumatic stress disorder and chronic relapsing depression, but can also be part of other problems (Harvey et al., 2004; Wells, 2000; Wells and Sembi, 2004). For further information, we recommend Harvey et al. (2004), Wells (2000) and Wells and Papageorgiou (2003). These approaches are summarized briefly below.

Rumination – relentlessly repetitive thinking without any resolution – may arise from a misconception that eventually, if thinking continues long enough, an 'answer' will emerge. Rumination may therefore be viewed as positive or necessary. Rumination or worry may also be a way of avoiding problems: worrying about surface issues prevents the person looking at the seemingly more difficult, underlying problems. People also may have metacognitive beliefs about thoughts, symptoms or worry, for example, the concern that worry is uncontrollable and harmful; or worry means I am going mad. For these processes, the following strategies can help:

- Finding out what beliefs the person has about their thoughts, worry or rumination. Does the person believe they are helpful or unhelpful? How does this work in practice?
- Looking at 'positive' (e.g. 'I need to worry to prevent bad things happening') and negative ('Worry will kill me') beliefs about worry and rumination, using verbal challenging and behavioural experiments to test the validity of such beliefs;
- Exploring the advantages and disadvantages of worry;
- Giving the message that thoughts are just thoughts, mindfully watching them or counting them. The message can be backed up by being written as a 'cue card' that the client can keep with them, or written as bars on a notebook. Wells and Matthews (1994) describe 'detached mindfulness', where thoughts are simply watched in a detached manner. The client is given the instructions to acknowledge what is happening ('Here is a thought; Here is a feeling'), remind themselves that engaging with thoughts or symptoms is unhelpful, and learn to watch the thoughts without dipping into them or following the stream of thought. Wells and Sembi (2004) use analogies of the 'recalcitrant child' – where we stay with the child but do not engage in his/her demands; or 'pushing clouds' – we cannot push clouds away, we can only observe the weather;
- Emphasizing that not engaging with thoughts is not the same as avoiding them – beware of the person using thought-control strategies rather than detached mindfulness;
- Planning worry time, postponing worries until a set time of 10 or 15 minutes later on in the day to help worries seem more manageable and controllable;
- Using imagery to put worries into detailed pictures that can then be worked with and resolved;

- Shifting from an abstract level to a more concrete level, working out exactly what is going on and what the person can do – e.g. find realistic and manageable answers to 'what if …' worries, and problem solve alternatives. Butler and Hope's (1995) Worry Decision Tree specifies questions that can be asked to decide what to do about a worry:

  1. *What am I worried about?*
     Be specific about the worry, spell it out in so many words;
  2. *Is there anything I can do?*
     If *Yes*, work out what needs to be done and do it rather than worrying;
     If *No*, accept that it is out of our hands, or unsolvable, or unpredictable, and use distraction or other techniques to stop worrying;
  3. *Is there anything I can do now?*
     If *Yes*, do it;
     If *No*, make plans to do it later then stop worrying by distraction or other techniques.

- Asking 'How' and 'What' type questions instead of 'Why': the musicians in the band Travis, for example, could be invited to respond constructively to their questions in the song 'Why does it always rain on me? Why is it raining so?' by working out first whether they are the only ones being rained on, and whether an umbrella or raincoat might help. Similarly those ruminating over 'Why me?' questions can be invited to consider whether it is helpful to ask this question, what to do and how to respond.

- Decreasing avoidance of underlying issues by helping the person to look at the worries, using writing (Pennebaker, 2004) or talking, to 'process' underlying affect.

- Normalizing certain thoughts that may appear antisocial to the client but are in fact relatively common. Some clients have obsessive thoughts about harming people but are extremely unlikely to act on them (Wells, 1997).

Trying to suppress negative or unpleasant thoughts is a common way of dealing with them, but is not always helpful. People who habitually try and 'shut out' bad thoughts, for fear of what they might mean or being overwhelmed by them, may not realize that trying to suppress thoughts can have a paradoxical effect of increasing the very thoughts we are trying not to think (Purdon and Clark, 2000; Wenzlaff and Wegner, 2000). The 'white bear/green giraffe/purple hippo' example shown in Box 5.1 illustrates a means of demonstrating this point.

BOX 5.1: THE 'WHITE BEAR' SUPPRESSION TEST

Sheila strongly believed that all her worrying, frightening thoughts about bad things happening to her family, meant that she either, unconsciously, wanted these things to happen, or that if the thoughts came into her head, it meant they were more likely to happen: 'It puts bad karma out and makes bad things happen'. She tried hard to stop the thoughts when they arrived, humming to herself, saying 'Stop' and desperately trying to think of something else. At times she felt plagued by thoughts.

Therapist:	It is possible, just a hunch at this stage, that the thoughts are getting worse because you are trying to stop them, not in spite of trying to stop them. Would you like to try a little experiment to test this out?
Sheila:	Um … not sure. OK then.
Therapist:	All I'd like you to do is to try not to think about a purple hippo. It's a big hippo, bright purple – but don't think about it – wearing a tutu. A pink tutu, but don't think about that either. It's drinking by a big lake, and along comes a green giraffe, wearing an orange beanie. Again, don't think about it. Whatever you do, don't think about that purple hippo and green giraffe.
Sheila [smiling]:	I'm trying not to, really, but …
Therapist:	But?
Sheila:	But they keep on coming into my head. I can't help it [laughing].
Therapist:	So, what do you make of that?
Sheila:	The more I try and stop myself thinking of them, the more I keep seeing them. They're dancing together now! I can't stop thoughts, can I?
Therapist:	So, if you were to try and push the thoughts away, get rid of those dancing animals in the way you try and push away your frightening thoughts …
Shelia:	I wouldn't be able to. It just makes them worse.
Therapist:	So, trying to stop your thoughts …
Sheila:	… Isn't a good strategy. No!

Instead of thought suppression, a more positive, constructive method is what might be called mindful distraction, moving the mind gently on to alternative, positive thoughts or images, then watching any intrusions as clouds across the field of vision, or other imagery, akin to detached mindfulness. In the example above, clearly Shelia also has metacognitive beliefs about her thoughts ('If I think this way, it means it will happen'; 'Bad thoughts puts bad energy out') which need considering (Wells, 2000).

Attention training has been developed by Adrian Wells and Costas Papageorgiou as a means of decreasing self-focus, and enabling the person to become more flexible in what is attended to (Wells, 1990). In worry and rumination, the focus of attention is almost exclusively on thinking, and people report being 'lost in thought' and out of touch with what else is going on. Attention training involves explaining the rationale for the therapy, that dwelling on negative thoughts and feelings does not help the person to feel better, and attention training involves learning to focus elsewhere. Having discussed the rationale and any concerns the client might raise, including concerns about the credibility of the treatment, the therapist introduces at least three competing sounds, such as the therapist's voice, a clock ticking, slow tapping noises or the radio, as well as sounds outside the therapy room. The client is asked to pay attention, in turn, to the different sounds, and practise the method as homework until she is able to focus on whatever is the current sound, rather than on competing noises, or the pull of ruminatory thoughts (see Papageorgiou and Wells, 2003). Single case studies have shown that attention-control training is helpful for a number of problems including health anxiety (Papageorgiou and Wells, 1998) and major depression (Papageorgiou and Wells, 2000).

CONCLUSION

In the opening chapters of the book, we emphasized the reciprocal nature of the relationship between thoughts, feelings and behaviours. In this chapter, we have reviewed the main methods for working with unhelpful thoughts and thinking processes. These include methods for identifying feelings and thoughts, then verbal means of looking for alternative ways of seeing events and situations. We also describe means of working with the processes of thinking, including worry, rumination, thought stopping or avoidance. Good therapeutic outcomes often result in the client's behaviour as well as thinking changing towards more helpful directions. In the next chapter, we will turn the tables and describe ways of facilitating change towards helpful behaviours that nearly always result in positive cognitive change.

Further Reading

Christine Padesky and Kathleen Mooney produce a series of audio- and videotapes, *The fundamentals of cognitive therapy*, relevant to learning key skills, including Guided Discovery, Socratic Questioning and Behavioural Experiments. See www.padesky.com

Beck, J. (1995). *Cognitive therapy: Basics and beyond*. New York: Guilford Press.

Grant A., Mills, J., Mulhern, R. & Short, N. (2004). *Cognitive behavioural therapy in mental health care*. London: Sage Publications. (**Chapter 4.**)

Greenberger, D. & Padesky, C. (1995). *Mind over mood: A cognitive therapy treatment manual for clients*. New York: Guilford Press.

Wells, A. (1997). *Cognitive therapy of anxiety disorders*. Chichester: Wiley. (**Chapter 4.**)

Wells, A. & Sembi, S. (2006). Metacognitive therapy for PTSD: A core treatment manual. *Cognitive and Behavioural Practice*, 11, 365–377.

6 Tools and Techniques of Cognitive Therapy: Behavioural Experiments, Behavioural Methods and Mindfulness

At the start of the last chapter we identified how Epstein's (1998) experiential model of the self informs our understanding of how cognitive therapy works. We suggested that optimal mental health rests on a sense of balance between the cognitive and the experiential mind. In the last chapter we described a number of approaches based on the idea that activating the cognitive system can sometimes lead to a better balance between this and the experiential system. In this chapter, we look at methods that work on the other side of that coin: how might the experiential mind be activated to promote positive cognitive change, remembering as we do Beck's dictum that the most elegant and enduring changes in therapy are those that lead to enduring changes in cognition, especially in self concept.

First, we will examine the role of behavioural experiments. Such experiments have always had an implicit place in cognitive therapy. More recent developments have, however, emphasized their importance. James Bennett-Levy and the therapists based in Oxford (Bennett-Levy, 2003; Bennett Levy et al., 2004) have been particularly influential in this regard. Second, we consider other behavioural methods including physical techniques to directly target unhelpful ways of behaving, such as behavioural activation in depression, distraction and relaxation. Third, we describe how mindfulness is being incorporated into cognitive therapy (Segal et al., 2002). All these methods are based on doing things differently and aim to promote a different, more positive and harmonious relationship between the client and their experience of themselves.

BEHAVIOURAL EXPERIMENTS

Despite its close association with behaviour therapy, Beck's cognitive therapy developed as a separate therapy yet was also more than happy to integrate methods from other therapies, including behaviour therapy, where appropriate. The formal integration of behavioural methods forms 'Cognitive Behavioural Therapy' or CBT. However, as we discussed in Chapter 1, we believe that all good cognitive therapists will be using a range of behavioural methods both to help clients feel better and to promote cognitive change. Therefore, in practice, the actual distinction between cognitive therapy and CBT is more historical and semantic than practical. Although for a behaviour therapist, changing behaviour is the end result of therapy, for a cognitive therapist, changing behaviour can also be used in the service of cognitive change (Beck, 1970b; Beck et al., 1979). Thus, the idea of behavioural experiments was born, where a range of tasks are used to test out beliefs. Behavioural experiments have a particular focus on making changes within the experiential mind as well as the rational, enabling the individual to test out their beliefs and have different experiences, and so develop a different 'felt sense' of the self or the problem. (Epstein, 1998; Mooney and Padesky, 2000; Padesky and Mooney, 1998). No amount of logic and rationality can replace a very real human experience of doing things differently and learning at a gut level.

In a study of using self-practice and self-reflection during cognitive therapy training, trainees reported a clear 'head' versus 'heart' distinction between thought records and behavioural experiments (Bennett-Levy, 2003). Thought records enabled them to be aware of their thought processes, gain clarity and see new perspectives, but were also described as 'a tedious but logical process'; 'They helped me slow down and put things into perspective' (Bennett-Levy, 2003). In contrast, behavioural experiments were emotionally driven, and achieved more of an emotional outcome: 'The evidence provided by the behavioural experiment is much more convincing'; 'I am starting to modify my negative belief on a different level and feeling good about it' (Bennett-Levy, 2003). Although such research has not yet been conducted with actual clients, from experience such changes reported by trainees are also those experienced in clinical practice (Bennett-Levy et al., 2004). For example Rouf et al. (2004: 58) report client's views of experiments:

> 'When you get into the nitty-gritty of it, you become a pioneer and you're off'
> 'It's proper feedback, that's the best you can get'
> 'I don't think they would work without all the theory behind it, but on the whole I would say they are the most important part of CBT'

Asking clients to test their beliefs and predictions can be compared to finding out the depth of an area of water in front of them. The anxiety and fear makes the water seem a bottomless, cavernous pool. By jumping in though, the client learns that it is a splashy, shallow puddle.

CAROL (II)

Through guided discovery, Carol (pp. 110–111) was able to 'discover' the idea that maybe she was not so alone in the world. Having worked out, rationally, the possibility that maybe people did want to be friends with her, she reported: 'Yes, I know that … but I still feel all alone, I feel no one wants to know me'. The next step was to develop and build on a new idea – 'People do want to be friends with me' – by experimenting with making friends. Carol dropped a note through her neighbour's door and asked her to come for coffee on Saturday morning. Her neighbour popped in to say that she was busy that morning, but would Carol like to come to lunch on Sunday. Carol identified that her old belief – 'I don't have any real friends' – was immediately activated when her neighbour told her she was busy, so that she could hardly hear the lunch invitation. But, through this experiment, then trying out asking a colleague at work to come for a drink, and keeping a diary of all the 'friendly' overtures other people made to her, Carol did begin to feel differently about herself in relation to friendships.

Two further examples are given in Box 6.1.

BOX 6.1:   BEHAVIOURAL EXPERIMENTS

- *Alice* believed that if she was to say anything positive about herself, she would become conceited, selfish, full of herself and 'puffed up like a self-satisfied chicken'. This view was firmly entrenched in both Alice and her family, who never gave praise and whose motto was. 'Spare the rod and spoil the child'. Alice and I (DS) worked out an experiment for her to do over one week. Every time something went right, or she was pleased with herself (a response that she successfully repressed), or someone praised her, she had to write it down in a diary and repeat it to herself. Her hypothesis was that, by the end of the week, she would have turned into the 'self-satisfied, puffed-up chicken' that she most feared. She did her best to try to praise herself, not an easy task, and came back to the session the next week to report that she had not felt self-satisfied, more that she could begin to feel a bit better about herself, as well as better about other people. She had begun to praise other people, and noticed how they 'lit up': no one became self-satisfied, only a bit more self-accepting. It was clear to both of us, too, that she had not turned into a chicken.
- *Matthew* had very high standards for himself, believing that he had to show his best side all the time, and appear confident and in control. A lot of the time, however, he felt a 'nervous wreck' and believed everyone else could see this as well. In particular, when nervous, he started sweating, and went to great lengths to hide it, wearing only thin shirts with baggy short sleeves even in winter, not cycling to work even though he lived within cycling distance and would arrive in less time by cycling and, on occasions, strapping tissues to his underarms to prevent sweat showing. We tested three beliefs in a series of experiments. First, he believed that signs of sweating were signs of anxiety, and anxiety was judged badly by others, which we tested by

(Continued)

BOX 6.1:   (Continued)

surveying friends and colleagues with the question: 'If you see someone sweating, what would you think was the problem?'. The majority of answers said, 'The person is hot', some said, 'Concentrating hard, unwell' and only a few said, 'Nervous'. The next question was: 'If you saw someone was nervous, what would you think of them?' Although Matthew predicted that everyone would think badly of the nervous person, all the answers were sympathetic. In the second experiment, Matthew tested his belief 'I'm the only person who sweats visibly' by doing a 'sweaty armpit' survey, looking closely at people's armpits and recording how many had damp shirts. To his surprise, when he looked as closely as possible without being caught, Matthew noticed quite a few sweaty patches, even on people he saw as calm and competent. The last experiment involved Matthew not doing anything to control his sweating, cycling to work and not changing his shirt or washing. He did have visible damp patches under his arms, but no one treated him any differently, he felt more relaxed being able to let go of all his control methods, and he got his sweaty armpits into proportion.

FUNCTION OF BEHAVIOURAL EXPERIMENTS

Behavioural experiments have three main functions (Bennett-Levy et al., 2004). First, they can provide information that is used in the formulation. For example, a man with health anxiety who checks a lump on his arm by prodding it several times a day can be invited to repeatedly prod his and the therapist's arm in the session to see what happens. He observes that doing this makes his own lump painful and red, which then confirms his belief 'there is something seriously wrong', causing further checking and so on. By repeatedly prodding the therapist's arm, this also turns red and uncomfortable. Second, experiments are used to test out negative thoughts, assumptions and beliefs, and third, experimenting with new forms of behaviour and trying things out differently is a means of constructing and reinforcing new beliefs (Greenberger and Padesky, 1995; Mooney and Padesky, 2000). Carol, for example, by practising behaving in a friendly way towards others, is able to collect evidence to support a new belief: 'People do want to make friends with me if I go about it in the right way'.

TYPES OF BEHAVIOURAL EXPERIMENTS

Behavioural experiments can be as many and as varied as our clients, and as our imagination and creativity. Experiments can be divided into, first, those that aim to test out predictions by *testing different hypotheses*, and second, those that enable us to *discover* some new information likely to promote therapeutic change (Bennett-Levy et al., 2004). Hypothesis-testing experiments are those where we identify one hypothesis and test this out, or test two alternative hypotheses against each other.

KATRINA

When Katrina, a client with low mood and a low opinion of herself, looked at the list of thinking biases, she thought: 'I'm really stupid to think this way. No one else has such stupid thoughts'. Both Katrina and the therapist tested out her hypothesis – 'Katrina is the only person who thinks this way' – by asking ten other people (not cognitive therapists) whether they ever had these thoughts. Everyone, as well as the therapist reported that they thought like that a lot of the time, but the thoughts only seemed real if they were feeling down.

Another example of hypothesis testing is to test whether it is possible to faint during a panic attack by using the hyperventilation provocation test to induce panic feelings (see Box 6.2).

BOX 6.2:   THE HYPERVENTILATION PROVOCATION TEST

Used to induce sensations of panic, and demonstrate that these sensations are benign and do not lead to fainting or other adverse outcomes.

1. Client and therapist stand up and over-breathe for up to five minutes. Give the instruction: 'Breathe as though you were feeling anxious, like you do in a panic attack. Then exaggerate the breathing, deeper and deeper'. Encourage the client to keep going;
2. When they start to get symptoms, encourage the client not to do anything to control the symptoms, and not use any safety behaviours;
3. Try and disconfirm specific beliefs about panic ('I'll faint or fall over or stagger or mumble') by standing on one leg or walk in a straight line or read text;
4. Time how long it takes for the body and breathing to return to normal without doing anything to control the symptoms.

The hyperventilation test is safe for most people but should not be used for people with cardiac problems, asthma, high blood pressure or for pregnant women, so check before introducing the test.

People with blood injury phobia can faint when exposed to blood due to a sudden drop in blood pressure, but for everyone else, anxiety and panic do not induce fainting due to raised blood pressure.

Source: Wells, 1997

We may also compare two different hypotheses to see which is more correct or helpful. For example, a classic 'two hypotheses' test for health anxiety (Salkovskis and Bass, 1997) is to compare hypothesis A 'My problem is that there is something seriously wrong with my health' with hypothesis B 'My problem is that I am seriously worried that there is something wrong with my health', and collect evidence for and against both hypotheses. Experiments can then be designed to support the new hypothesis.

The second category of experiments are *discovery experiments* to enable us to discover something new, where we are not quite sure what is keeping a problem going, or where an alternative hypothesis is not available. The following is a 'very Oxford' example.

JULIAN

Julian, who was socially anxious, believed: 'I must appear interesting and knowledgeable at all times, otherwise people will think I'm boring'. Working in an academic environment he assumed that everyone else was more knowledgeable than him, and therefore tended to keep quiet in social situations. He tried out an experiment during a college dinner of initiating a conversation with a colleague whom he did not know very well, to find out what happened if he said 'I don't know very much about your area of work'. Instead of looking shocked, the colleague looked pleased and explained his research at great length, clearly enjoying the conversation. Julian discovered that it can be socially useful to 'confess ignorance'. He also admitted that after a 20-minute 'lecture' on his colleague's work, Julian began to feel slightly bored himself. He was interested to discover, rather naughtily, he felt, a new belief: 'People who know everything and tell all can be a bit boring'.

These experiments can lead to new 'rules of living' or assumptions, an important aspect of maintaining change, as we will see later in the next chapter.

Experiments can involve inviting a client to drop safety-seeking behaviours to test out, or discover, what happens. For example, people who panic may believe that if they do not sit down, relax, breathe deeply and otherwise try to control the panic, they would faint, pass out or make a fool of themselves (Salkovskis, 1991). Therapy involves working with such clients to disconfirm what they most fear, such as going into a public place and deliberately hyperventilating in order to induce panic, and then not sitting down. Socially phobic people have many safety behaviours, some of which can make the person seem quite odd, such as avoiding or having too much eye contact, talking quietly, trying to blend into the background, or only talking to known people. By dropping safety behaviours, the client can find out that these behaviours are in fact redundant, or directly contribute to the problem. Other experiments involve actively trying something out, such as going into a previously avoided situation, and intentionally acting or thinking differently.

Experiments can also be observational, where therapist or client find out information by observing others or particular situations, such as observing how other people behave in social situations before trying out something different. Conducting surveys is a useful means of gaining information relevant to the client's beliefs, such as asking people: 'What would you think if you were at a talk and you noticed that the lecturer's voice was shaking?' or 'How often do you clean your house/wash your hands?' Experiments may also involve collecting factual information, such as how many people in the country are single, or how many are involved in road traffic accidents. From our own clinical experience, we have accompanied clients into shops where they have tried to have a panic attack and faint; asked our clients who worry about their thoughts being true to worry for a week that their therapist has won the lottery in order to test out whether their thoughts do indeed have magical powers; and asked clients to conduct a survey of their friends to find out if the client is the only person who ever gets anxious in social situations. Behavioural experiments involve creativity on the part of both therapist and client. Bennett-Levy and colleagues (2004) offer a treasure chest full of best practice ideas on behavioural experiments.

CONSTRUCTING BEHAVIOURAL EXPERIMENTS

Behavioural experiments must be collaboratively devised, no-lose experiments, aimed at both gathering information and testing out alternatives. Whatever the outcome, something has been learned. The stages involved in devising experiments are as follows (see Rouf et al. (2004) for further details):

1. Collaboratively agree the purpose of the experiment so it is a shared enterprise;
2. Find out the exact prediction in so many words, or the exact hypothesis to be tested with a rating of how much the prediction is believed to be true;
3. Use guided discovery to discuss the nature of the unhelpful belief. For example, what are the pros and cons of the belief?
4. What evidence is there that it is true or untrue?
5. Use guided discovery to construct a different belief or what an experiment might discover and rate the alternative belief;
6. Collaboratively devise an experiment to test the belief(s) or discover alternatives. Think about when and how to do it, and make sure it is a 'no-lose' experiment – if beliefs turn out to be true, allow for problem solving to learn something helpful. Anticipate potential problems and work out what to do;
7. Conduct the experiment;
8. Record the results and reflect on them: what does it say about the original belief and the new belief?
9. Re-rate the original and new beliefs, and strength of emotion;
10. What do I need to do now? Practise reinforcing new beliefs.

A behavioural experiment worksheet, using information from Bennett-Levy et al. (2004), is shown in Figure 6.1.

Figure 6.1   Behavioural Experiments Diary

Date	Situation	Prediction: How will I know if my prediction comes true?	Experiment to test prediction	Outcome?	What I learned
Monday	Standing outside the supermarket	I'm feeling so bad I am going to pass out. Unless I get out of here fast then I may be very ill (90%).	Stay in the supermarket. Stop trying to do anything to control the anxiety and see what happens.	I felt quite uncomfortable but I did not pass out, or even need to sit down. I stayed there and was pleased with myself. The bad feelings went away after a few minutes. Found some nice new ice cream!	Stay with it, things are not as bad as they feel. Anxiety won't make me pass out. I enjoy things and feel good if I don't avoid and run away. Buy this ice cream again!

BEHAVIOURAL METHODS IN COGNITIVE THERAPY

Cognitive therapy uses a range of what might be described as behavioural approaches, many of which have evolved from the behavioural roots of cognitive therapy. We described earlier how behavioural methods can be used as experiments to test out specific beliefs. But also, behavioural methods in themselves are extremely valuable, helping to relieve symptoms of depression and anxiety, helping to manage emotions, and give the client a means of coping with problems. The methods can also be used in the service of cognitive change as behavioural experiments, for example using activity scheduling, relaxation and slow controlled breathing or problem solving to test out specific beliefs, as described below. When using behavioural methods, careful matching of specific approaches to a specific understanding of the client's formulation enables them to be used as powerful methods of change.

WEEKLY ACTIVITY DIARY AND BEHAVIOURAL ACTIVATION

The weekly activity diary is a central part of cognitive therapy for depression, helping the depressed person to become more active and increase the level of enjoyable activities (Beck et al., 1979; Fennell, 1989). It can be used either to record what the client has been doing each day in order to review how they are spending time, or filled in prospectively to plan for the next day's or week's activities (Table 6.1). We ask the client to rate how enjoyable each activity was, and how much it gave them a sense of achievement, in order to look for a good balance between enjoyable activities and those that give the person a sense of fulfilment and value, both being necessary for good mental health. Planning activities in advance is a powerful means of overcoming the inertia and lack of motivation associated with depression. The weekly activity diary can also be used as a means of testing out clients' beliefs. For example, the ratings of achievement and enjoyment enable clients to see how much of a sense of achievement they feel in their life; how they predict not enjoying anything but find out that they did gain some enjoyment after all.

DISTRACTION

When the going gets tough, the tough get shopping

Distraction is a means of taking the mind off problems or symptoms, and paying attention to something else. It can involve physical activity, focusing on a mental image and mental 'chewing gum', such as arithmetic or remembering names of capital cities. Distraction can be very helpful to clients who are depressed, encouraging them to stop focusing on how bad they feel and focus, instead, on a practical task or activity. It can help clients to stop paying attention to anxiety, which helps the physical symptoms to reduce. For obsessional clients who ruminate about their thoughts, distraction is a means of helping

Table 6.1   Weekly Activity Diary

	Monday	Tuesday	Wednesday	Thursday	Friday	Saturday	Sunday
6–7							
7–8							
8–9							
9–10							
10–11							
11–12							
12–1							
1–2							
2–3							
3–4							
4–5							
5–6							
6–7							
7–8							
8–12							

*Rate activities for E – Enjoyment; A – Achievement
Source: Fennell (1989)

them to pay attention to something other than what is going through their minds. It is also useful for clients who find it difficult to tolerate strong emotions, giving them a first aid measure, for use within sessions or in daily life, to reduce emotion when it threatens to overwhelm them.

While it sounds a very simple thing to do, in practice not focusing on what might feel like overwhelming problems, emotions or issues can be very difficult. Asking the client to distract from their worries may imply that the therapist is not taking the client's problems seriously. Therefore it is important that the client really understands the rationale behind distraction. For people who ruminate on their worries, not focusing on thoughts can initially be very anxiety provoking. Again, conceptualizing the problems and solutions is important.

There may be occasions when distraction is counterproductive or helps to reinforce unhelpful beliefs, particularly when used as a 'safety behaviour' related to the belief: 'If I don't think about it, it won't happen and so catastrophe will be averted'. For example, people who are anxious may believe that if they paid attention to their anxious feelings, these would overwhelm them, and therefore use distraction as a means of preventing catastrophe. In this case, it is more helpful for the individual to learn that anxious feelings, while extremely unpleasant, are not catastrophic (Salkovskis et al., 1996). Distraction can be a means of suppressing thoughts, which, as explained earlier, may make the thoughts worse, or may be a means of avoiding emotion or issues that need to be faced. In our view, people need different options and strategies to be able to respond flexibly when their problems arise. Distraction can be a useful short-term aid to getting through a situation, and no doubt one all of us use to help with difficult times, but needs to be supplemented by longer-term strategies.

PROBLEM SOLVING

Problem solving is a means of identifying problems and looking for feasible solutions. It has been shown to be helpful for people with depression, enabling them to look for solutions to the issues which may underlie and maintain depression (Gath and Mynors-Wallis, 1997). It can be valuable for people with general anxiety disorder, whose worries may relate to an intolerance of uncertainty and lacking confidence in their ability to solve problems, or to a lack of problem-solving skills (Dugas, 2002). Problem solving encourages the client to work out practical and psychological ways of dealing with problems, using her own skills and resources as well as help from others. It can be particularly valuable when life stresses are contributing to problems, and where the individual is either finding it difficult to address or solve these problems or is avoiding tackling the problems. Problem solving can be used to test specific beliefs about problems being unmanageable or unsolvable, for example by doing an experiment to try and find solutions to a seemingly impossible problem. Alternatively, people who worry excessively may spend a lot of time worrying about insoluble, global, problems, such as natural catastrophes or terrorism, and by trying to actually solve them rather than worrying about them, we can find out what it is possible to do (e.g. avoid going to high-risk countries), and what is not possible to do (prevent any disasters ever happening). The stages of problem solving are shown in Figure 6.2.

WAYS OF WORKING WITH PHYSICAL SYMPTOMS

Various techniques are used to manage the physical component of psychological problems, or for people whose problems are primarily physical. Such methods include relaxation techniques, controlled breathing, graded activity and exercise.

Relaxation, including methods such as progressive muscular relaxation, controlled breathing, biofeedback and hypnosis, used to be the first port of call for people with anxiety problems, and still plays a large part in anxiety management and stress-control programmes (see Kennerley, 1997; White, 2000). With the introduction of concepts of safety behaviours, relaxation techniques are being used with more caution, and rather than being widely advocated, relaxation methods are strategically used depending on individual client conceptualization. Padesky (1995) claims that the inclusion of relaxation in therapy for panic may slow or even reverse the effectiveness of therapy, and some, for example Wells (1997), have argued that a purely 'cognitive' approach should not include

Figure 6.2 Problem Solving Worksheet

What is the problem?

Define exactly what the problem is. Make sure it is concrete, and if necessary break it down into smaller parts.

1. Set Clear Goals

What do I want to achieve?

When do I want to achieve it?

2. Brainstorm Solutions

Write down all possible solutions to the problem, however unlikely they seem. Do not censor anything at this stage.

1.	4.
2.	5.
3.	6.

3. Work out Pros and Cons

For each potential solution, work out advantages and disadvantages, then choose the best option.

Solution	Pros	Cons
1.		
2.		
3.		
4.		
5.		
6.		

My best solution is:

4. Work out a plan for action:

How am I going to do it?

When and where am I going to do it?

Do I need help from someone else?

5. Put the plan into action and write down what happens

If this does not work, or the results are not satisfactory, go back to Step 4 and pick another solution.

Source: adapted from White et al., 2000

relaxation at all with any of the anxiety disorders. Some people who experience panic attacks find that relaxation actually triggers their attacks (Leahy and Holland, 2000), possibly because actively trying to relax involves becoming more aware of bodily reactions such as breathing or muscle tension, and such awareness sets off catastrophic interpretations characteristic of a panic attack. Some people find relaxation extremely difficult and frightening, perhaps relating to the need to be vigilant at all times due to early abuse, and therefore find powerful emotions arising when relaxed and off guard.

Another disadvantage of relaxation techniques is where they are used as safety behaviours and avoidance, preventing disconfirmation of anxious predictions. For example, a client may use relaxation methods to cope with a situation that has previously triggered feelings of panic. Where this is successful, it may lead this person to conclude that they have now developed a skill which could help them with a truly dangerous situation, whereas in fact using relaxation prevents them from disconfirming fearful beliefs about anxiety. For these people, we start with decatastrophizing their fears of anxiety, rather than trying to reduce anxious symptoms. Learning to control the symptoms has to be secondary to cognitive changes, helping the client to more realistically appraise how dangerous anxiety really is, and discover that these situations are very frequently much less dangerous than imagined. Following cognitive restructuring of the danger of situations, the client can drop their safety behaviours, including using relaxation.

Relaxation methods can be used most powerfully as a behavioural experiment, for example to test out beliefs about having to keep going at all costs: 'If I relaxed then I'd never get anything done'. The client can try their normal strategy, then learn relaxation methods to see whether being more relaxed during the day and having time off means that they actually work more efficiently and productively. Slow, controlled breathing can be a useful first aid, and used as behavioural experiments for clients to learn that something as simple as changing breathing can make them feel better, thus showing them that their original fears were out of proportion. For example, clients with benign chest pains can be very anxious about the possibility of heart disease. The pain can be increased or reduced by changing their pattern of breathing, enabling the client to discover that their symptoms were not of heart disease but of more benign physiological changes arising from something as simple as breathing (Sanders, 1996). In our clinical and personal experience, many clients find relaxation methods useful in increasing comfort and a means of getting rid of unpleasant anxious and stress feelings following the core cognitive work to decatastrophize the symptoms. Relaxation may be a positive element of therapy if it is seen as a way of helping the client to cope with his own reactions to a situation that may not be as dangerous as he has imagined in the past. As with distraction, relaxation can be one option for the client's repertoire of coping responses, but needs to be supplemented with longer-term strategies.

Graded activity and exercise are used during cognitive therapy for a number of problems, including chronic fatigue syndrome (see for example Burgess and Chalder, 2005), chronic pain (White, 2000) and as part of activity scheduling for depression. Where the person has been inactive for a long period of time, very small increments in exercise need to be built into a long-term plan. Powell and colleagues (2001) have devised a graded exercise programme as part of a cognitive behavioural and educational programme for people with chronic fatigue, which starts with two or three turns of the pedals on an exercise bicycle, working up to five or ten minutes a day. The key in using graded activity and exercise is in tiny, manageable steps, working well within the person's abilities and using pacing to alternate activity and rest. Increasing exercise can itself have a beneficial psychological effect, and can be used as behavioural experiments to test out, for example, fears of movement and exercise for people with pain or physical disability (see Silver et al., 2004).

MINDFULNESS AND COGNITIVE THERAPY

We hesitate to include mindfulness in a chapter that looks at tools and techniques, since it is more a philosophy of being rather than a method to deal with problems. Mindfulness is both age-old, within the philosophies and spirituality of Zen and Buddhism, and recently borrowed and adapted to the service of cognitive therapy.

Cognitive therapy is concerned with the relationship we have to our thoughts, physical sensations, feelings, shifts in mood, or intrusions of thoughts or images. Much of the focus is on the meaning of such experiences, identifying and re-evaluating them. Newer models of cognitive therapy are concerned with the meanings we attach to cognitive phenomena as experiences in our lives, focusing on how we see the process of such thinking rather than the content of the thought itself (Wells, 2000). Teasdale (1999) has incorporated mindfulness into cognitive models of emotional disorder. He describes different modes of being:

- Mindless emoting, where the individual is immersed in their emotional reactions and unable to evaluate them in any way;
- Focusing on the self or emotions in a detached way;
- Mindful experiencing, or 'being there', where one is aware of thoughts, feelings and felt senses in a non-evaluative manner, enabling us to use these as a guide to self understanding and problem solving.

Being aware of thoughts and feelings is very central to cognitive therapy, and a level of non-judgmental awareness is integral to being able to label and identify thinking, and evaluate it in a helpful manner. Being mindful and non-judgmental can help people to stay with bad feelings, being aware of and to 'notice' them rather than having to leap automatically to control or try and get rid of emotional pain. Rather than taking experience literally, and fighting against it in an attempt to change it, mindfulness enables us to observe experience for what it is (just a thought, just a feeling) rather than what it says it is ('My thoughts and feelings tell me I'm bad'), which in turn leads to acceptance and can begin the process of change. By learning that thoughts are just thoughts, the cycle of rumination, frustration and depression is interrupted.

Mindfulness means paying attention in a particular way: on purpose, in the present moment, and non-judgmentally … the simple act of recognising your thoughts (simply) as thoughts can allow for more clear-sightedness and a greater sense of manageability in your life. (Jon Kabat-Zinn, quoted in Segal et al., 2002: 40–1)

The practice of mindfulness meditation is a means to stay focused on the here and now, learning to be aware and observe what is going on rather than getting involved in automatic patterns of reaction. It enables us to observe modes of mind, and let them change of their own accord, rather than getting caught up in them. For example, learning to be with bad feelings rather than making them worse by ruminating on them, enables the process of recovery to occur by itself. Kabat-Zinn (2004, 2005) describes the methods of mindfulness mediation, and how these are successfully used to help people with pain, physical illness and psychological difficulties. The daily practice of mindfulness meditation, taught in a group format called 'mindfulness-based stress reduction' (MBSR) which includes psycho-educational elements, yoga and meditation methods, has been shown to be helpful for people with a range of physical and psychological problems (Baer, 2003; Kabat-Zinn, 2003; Surawy et al., 2005). Mindfulness forms a key component of 'dialectical behaviour therapy', helping people with long-term personality issues and self harm (Linehan, 1993a, 1993b). An adaptation of mindfulness-based stress reduction, mindfulness-based cognitive therapy (MBCT) has been shown to reduce relapse in those with repeated episodes of depression (Segal et al., 2002; Teasdale et al., 2000). Segal and colleagues (2002) subjected MBCT to a clinical trial with 145 patients who had suffered from depression on three sites in Canada, Wales and England. A group of patients receiving MBCT was compared with a group receiving 'treatment as usual'. The MBCT group had significantly lower relapse rates, and MBCT seemed particularly effective for the most vulnerable people – those who had had three or more previous episodes of depression.

As well as applying mindfulness within formal relapse-prevention treatment such as MBCT, mindfulness and metacognitive awareness can be integrated throughout therapy, as described by Fennell (2004) for people with low self esteem, where depression may not be a one-off episode or time-limited experience, but a pervasive sense of low mood and low self worth. The statement 'I am worthless' is not so much part of depression, changed once the person feels better, but a long-standing theme, perhaps activated and exacerbated by depression, but there all the time. Fennell reviews the methods by which the statement 'I am worthless' can change to a more helpful belief such as 'I am a normal human being, but I believe I am worthless', i.e. changing the statement to a hypothesis rather than a fact. Many standard methods, including questionnaires, thought diaries, formulation, written materials and methods such as Padesky's Prejudice Model (Padesky, 1990) and developing a 'compassionate mind' (Gilbert, 2000b) enable the client to begin to entertain the notion that thoughts and beliefs are not facts.

The application of mindfulness within cognitive therapy is developing quickly, proving helpful to people whose feelings are difficult for them to tolerate, and where learning to stay with bad feelings and observe them rather than react automatically can begin the process of change. There may be occasions where the method is less helpful, for example for people whose difficulties relate to being too self conscious, using their 'felt sense' as a basis for decisions and behaviour rather than checking external reality, for example socially phobic individuals using their feelings as basis for reality (Wells, 2000). For further details, we recommend Kabat-Zinn (2004, 2005), Kabat-Zinn and Brantley (2003), Teasdale (1999) and Segal et al. (2002). Another useful source is Gendlin's (1981) writing on focusing.

CONCLUSION

In this chapter we describe some of the older and newer cognitive therapy approaches that help clients to do something different and that will make a difference. The basic behavioural techniques such as using activity schedules sometimes seem straightforward activation procedures but they also crucially impact on clients' self concepts, for example, by helping them to think of themselves as 'someone who can be active' as opposed to 'a deadbeat, a failure'. In short, such experiences exert an impact on clients' cognitions regarding their very nature. Behavioural experiments are more explicitly Socratic because they aim, like Socrates, to stimulate enquiry that leads to movement in the learning cycle as described in the last chapter. Finally, mindfulness interventions present the client with a series of life choice options about how they live their lives at the level of life's most basic units: moment-by-moment experience. These mindful interventions can range from being relatively discrete strategies for handling things like worry and other intrusive thoughts through to a programme of interventions such as MBCT. All the interventions described in this chapter may impact at any level of the type of formulation discussed in Chapter 2 and elsewhere. Mostly they impact on immediate experience and thus their impact may or may not be felt at the level of the more enduring levels of cognition – assumptions and core beliefs – discussed in Chapters 1 and 2. It is therefore necessary to have a separate discussion on cognitive therapy tools and techniques that are designed to do that. It is to that subject matter that we now turn in our next chapter.

Further Reading

Bennett-Levy, J., Butler, G., Fennell, M., Hackmann, A., Mueller, M. & Westbrook, D. (2004). *The Oxford guide to behavioural experiments in cognitive therapy*. Oxford: Oxford University Press.

Segal, Z. V., Williams, J. M. G. & Teasdale, J. D. (2002). *Mindfulness-based cognitive therapy for depression: A new approach to preventing relapse*. New York: Guilford Press.

7 Tools and Techniques of Cognitive Therapy: Working with Assumptions and Core Beliefs – Getting to the Heart of the Problems

The cognitive model makes a distinction between automatic thoughts, conditional beliefs such as underlying assumptions and rules, and unconditional core beliefs and schemas. In this chapter we look in greater detail at how cognitive therapy tackles these deeper rules and beliefs that determine how we are in the world, which may be adaptive, or contribute to ongoing difficulties. Although cognitive therapy guidelines recommend starting at the automatic thought level and working down to assumptions, then progressing to core beliefs, in practice working with thoughts and assumptions often proceeds hand in hand, thoughts being the embodiment of the assumptions, sometimes in shorthand form, sometimes word for word. Therefore, the same therapeutic interventions may well be working on different levels of cognition simultaneously, and working with assumptions often forms the part of therapy focused on maintaining change after the end of therapy and preventing relapse.

In contrast to conditional assumptions, core beliefs, so called 'early maladaptive schema', are long-standing, enduring beliefs about the self, others and the world, often formed from early experience, and often unhelpful. When entering the territory of core beliefs, we are to some extent entering less-charted waters. Schema-focused cognitive therapy, while not new, is still developing and has less research evidence to back it up. It is also an area to enter once proficient in basic and standard methods of cognitive therapy, and is by no means necessary for many of the people we see in routine clinical practice.

This chapter on assumptions and beliefs is divided into two parts. In the first section, we describe some of the tried and tested ways of working with assumptions, in order to help the client re-evaluate some of their less helpful rules for living and mitigate against relapse. In the second section, we go on to describe schema-focused cognitive therapy with people with long-term and maladaptive personality issues.

WORKING WITH ASSUMPTIONS AND BELIEFS

KEY ISSUES AND SKILLS

Identifying and working with clients' assumptions and conditional beliefs is helpful for a number of reasons. As we have described in Chapter 2, the cognitive model specifies the centrality of assumptions and beliefs in the development and maintenance of psychological difficulties, hence directly targeting these is vital to enable the client to change. Unhelpful assumptions leave clients vulnerable to the risk of relapse: although therapy may help them deal with and work through the present episode of the problem, unless the rules underlying the problem are also worked through, clients may experience similar problems in future. Working with assumptions helps the client to develop skills to deal with future problems (Fennell, 1989).

Work that focuses on assumptions and beliefs requires a number of key skills and approaches. Therapist and client are explicit and collaborative: the client's rules are openly described, verbalized and examined as though they are hypotheses about the world rather than absolute rules (Beck et al., 2003a; Young and Klosko, 1994; Young et al., 2003). Despite all the drawbacks and difficulties our set of rules may pose, our assumptions and beliefs are very central to our frame of reference, fitting like a comfortable pair of old slippers. They feel right, and to act or think against them may seem dangerous and anxiety provoking. It can, therefore, be very threatening to have these beliefs exposed or challenged, and can imply to the client that they have 'got it wrong', sometimes for many years. Therefore therapists need to proceed with empathy and sensitivity and work with, not against, the client. There should be no sense that some beliefs are 'right' and others are 'wrong', or a sense of getting into an argument: the therapist's task is to understand the client's viewpoint, however much we may disagree with it or see it as irrational. We need to be aware of cultural differences in assumptions: Padesky and Greenberger (1995) quote examples of how easily therapists from one culture can misinterpret and misdiagnose those from other cultures, for example by accepting the therapist's cultural norms as healthy, and diagnosing other standards as evidence of emotional problems or personality disorders. The therapist must work at the client's pace, within his or her frame of reference, and be sensitive to cues, spoken or unspoken, that he or she is uncomfortable with the process.

IDENTIFYING ASSUMPTIONS AND BELIEFS

The information for identifying a client's beliefs and assumptions comes from many sources (Fennell, 1989):

- Themes that emerge during therapy;
- Patterns in the client's way of thinking;
- Labelling the self or others;

- Highs or lows of mood;
- The client's response to therapy.

When there is something the client avoids, it may be because a particular rule is operating (Padesky and Mooney, 1998). For example, someone who always keeps quiet at work and avoids talking in meetings may have rules about the meaning of looking anxious: 'If I speak out in a meeting, then my voice will shake and everyone will think I'm stupid; if people see I look anxious, then they will reject me. The only way to be acceptable is to be seen to be strong and coping at all times'. Similarly, if someone is overly rigid in their way of life, an underlying rule may operate: 'If I keep everything tidy and in order, I'll feel in control. If I feel in control, nothing bad will happen'. Someone who is always nice and helpful to everyone else, possibly to their irritation, may assume 'If I am nice, people will like me and won't reject me; If they reject me, I'll be alone for ever'.

The process of guided discovery is a key way in which a client's assumptions are clarified. Asking questions, being curious, finding out how the client thinks and what makes them think that way enables rules to be made explicit. Rather than accepting the client's thoughts at face value, guided discovery enables probing to understand the underlying mechanisms. For example, instead of saying, with empathy, 'Yes, that would be terrible' or 'It sounds like you're very scared of that happening' when a client is talking about the fear of fainting when feeling anxious, the therapist's mode of enquiry is along the lines of 'What if that did happen … what would that mean?' The therapist pursues this form of questioning until it is clear that a rule is being reached, a process called the downward arrow technique (Greenberger and Padesky,1995). The downward arrow involves peeling away the layers of meaning to identify what is beneath the client's specific fears, the questions being repeated several times until a 'bottom line' is reached. The aim is to arrive at a statement which makes sense of the client's fears so that the therapist is able to respond with an empathic statement such as 'If I believed x, then I would feel the same way'. The process is illustrated with Claudia, an adult education tutor, describing her terror of having a panic attack in front of her class.

CLAUDIA

Claudia: [Describing a recent attack] I felt really faint. I just knew I was going to pass out.

Therapist: Suppose that really happened, that you did faint … what would be bad about that for you?

Claudia: Well, I'd fall over in front of all these people.

Therapist: And suppose you did fall over: what next? What is the worst that could happen?

Claudia: Well, I'd just be lying there like a complete fool …

Therapist:	Suppose what you say did happen. What would that mean to you?
Claudia:	It would mean I'm really out of control, just not as good as others. I can't even stand up and do my job without completely messing up.
Therapist:	And if that were true, what would that mean?
Claudia:	It would just show what a fake I am.
Therapist:	Is this something that keeps coming back to you, some form of rule?
Claudia:	I guess I have to be in control. If I'm not in control, people will see me for what I am – a fake.

USING IMAGERY AND METAPHOR TO IDENTIFY ASSUMPTIONS AND BELIEFS

Verbal discussion cannot always reach assumptions or rules, particularly when the assumptions are charged with emotion, or if the individual has an intellectualizing style or avoids emotion by excessive talking. Working with the client's images can be a powerful way of identifying meanings to the individual (Hackmann, 1997, 2004). Images are often far more charged with meaning than are words, and therefore give more clues as to underlying assumptions. Similarly when meaning is hard to identify, or during times of high emotion when unpacking the meaning of events or memories is more difficult, finding metaphors for the experience can be helpful. These might include common sayings or fairy stories or folk tales reflecting themes of goodness and badness (Blenkiron, 2005). A woman describing her black and white views of men in relationships talked about looking for a 'Knight in shining armour' which I (DS) unfortunately one day accidentally 'spoonerized' into 'A Shite in Knining Armour'. Although we both initially laughed at my mistake, it led to an enlightening exploration of how one mistake could in her mind turn her knights into shites, and whether it is fair to judge someone totally on one aspect alone. Another person, finding it hard to express why he felt so burnt out all the time, was talking about his need to be prepared for anything and his need to look after other people, sometimes to his detriment: 'If there's going to be a bridge, I have to cross it several times before I need to cross it' and 'I look out for, not only my own bridges, but everyone else's as well'. We frequently talked about the bridges metaphor, looking at the underlying rules ('Always be prepared, always be helpful, otherwise you'll be found out'), and how he could decide which bridges were worth crossing, and when to cross them. Another person with similar rules about needing to be needed by others had a metaphor, accompanied by a strong visual image, of 'the world on my chest', made up of 'continents' of other people's problems, and 'seas' of their misery, causing episodes of chest pain and panic symptoms. By metaphorically deciding which parts of the world she wanted to live in and travel through, and those that could be left to sort themselves out, she could begin to shrink the world and make it happier and more manageable for her.

Ways of getting in touch with images include asking: 'Did you have a picture in your mind just then?' Once the individual has come up with an image, the client can be asked to describe it in greater detail. Questions such as, 'What is happening? Who else is in the image? What are they doing or saying?' can help the client to be more specific about the image. Once the image is identified, the types of questions below can be used to help the client to unpack the image and explore its personal meaning, implications and origins.

- What is bad about the events in the image?
- What does that mean about you, others or the world?
- What is the worst that could happen?
- How do you feel, now and in the image? Identify body sensations and emotions.
- What is going through your mind in the image?
- Does the image remind you of something earlier on in life?
- If so, when? How old were you? What was happening? What does it say about you now?

MODIFYING AND REVISING ASSUMPTIONS AND BELIEFS

Simply identifying the rules enables some people to begin to change: once the assumption is articulated, the client may well be able to see that it is not realistic or helpful to hold such extreme black and white views. The therapist can then encourage the client to look at the grey area between the black and white extremes posed by the assumption, which may be seen as an ideal or preference, rather than an absolute necessity. For example, articulating the rule 'I have to do a perfect job at all times' might change to 'It's good to aim high, but if its not possible, then I'll lower my expectations'. The process of working with assumptions is, in many ways, similar to the approaches described earlier to challenge thoughts: the overall aim is for the client to empirically test the assumptions, to find out the relative 'truth', helpfulness or unhelpfulness of the rules, and, if found not to measure up, to come up with alternatives (Padesky, 2004a). Guided discovery, Socratic questions, diaries of negative thoughts and behavioural experiments all enable information to be gathered about the client's assumptions in order to test out their validity. Some key questions that can help to guide the client towards alternatives are shown in Figure 7.1, a version of which can be built into a cue card to work on when assumptions are activated.

Padesky (2004a) makes a distinction between trying to disprove old rules by looking at the evidence for and against, or its pros and cons, versus constructing new, more helpful or adaptive assumptions. Key questions include: 'How would you like it to be?'; 'In an ideal world, what would work better for you?'; 'What rule would fit better?' (Mooney and Padesky, 2000).

Challenging assumptions: taking risks

One powerful way of testing out rules is to devise behavioural experiments in which the individual does not act in accordance with the rule, but behaves as though a different rule is in operation, and tests out the consequences (Bennett-Levy et al., 2004). For example, Claudia's belief 'I must be in control all the time.

Figure 7.1   Questions to help the client discover alternative assumptions

- What is the assumption? What are my exact words to describe the rule, possibly stated as If ... Then.
- In what way has this rule affected me? What areas of life has it affected? For example, studying, work, relationships, leisure, domestic life?
- Where did the rule come from? What experiences contributed to its development? Rules make a lot of sense when first developed, but may need revision in the light of subsequent, or adult, experience.
- What are its advantages – In what ways has it helped me? What would I risk if I gave it up?
- What are its disadvantages – In what ways has it hindered me? What would I gain if I gave it up?
- In what ways is the rule unreasonable? In what ways is it a distortion of reality?
- What would be a more helpful and realistic alternative that would give me the pay off and avoid the disadvantages? Is there another way of seeing things, which is more flexible, more realistic and more helpful, giving me the advantages of the assumption without the costs.
- What do I need to do to change the rule?
- How can I test out whether this is a better rule to live my life?

Source: Beck et al. (1979, 1985) and Burns, (1996)

If I'm not it'll prove I'm a fake' could be tested with a series of experiments where she practises being slightly less 'in control' at work, occasionally preparing her lessons slightly less thoroughly than usual, leaving something in the staff room and having to go and get it during a class, or feeling ill in class and having to sit down, to test out whether this proved that she was 'a fake'. She could also practise being more honest with colleagues about how she was feeling, or being more spontaneous in her life, not planning every evening and weekend, and leaving things to chance.

Whatever the outcome of the experiment, the client must be able to learn something useful, and therefore experiments need to be no-lose situations. Taking risks is, by definition, threatening, and the client needs to be supported in the decision to try something new, with a good outcome whatever happens. Before doing an experiment for real, it can be helpful to go through the process using imagery, predicting possible difficulties and practising how these might be handled, thereby giving the client more of a sense of being in control and facilitating a good outcome. When revising rules which may have been in operation for a long time, experiments need to be repeated many times, and in different ways, to reinforce the learning of new rules, also allowing adequate time for reflecting on results (Rouf et al., 2004).

Using images to modify assumptions

Clients who are able to 'think in pictures' and who are able to work with such images may find it helpful to use imagery to modify their assumptions. Although several texts on visualization suggest that substituting a positive ending is a means of changing images, in cognitive terms this may be counterproductive since merely looking at a 'happy ending' enables the client to avoid looking at the feared catastrophes or consequences of the image, and may actually prevent them from re-evaluating the image and coming up with a more appropriate alternative. Very often people freeze the image in time and do not look beyond. A negative event that had negative meaning then stays frozen in time, continuing to hold the same meaning and to 'invade' the client by intruding itself into their mind. It can be like a video player permanently on still-frame. The client may need to experience what came next as usually this will lead to the image receding and perhaps even 'healing'. If the client is able to hold and examine the image, this may help to modify it, especially if they can move on from still-frame by projecting the image forward in time, or can re-evaluate the reality of the image. The image can help the client to experience and work with the salient emotions, facilitating cognitive and emotional processing (Smucker and Dancu, 1999). Ways of working with images are described by Hackmann (1997). In the example of Claudia, she could only see catastrophe arising from her fainting in front of the class: being out of control and seen as a fake. Once she looked at her image and projected it forward in time, she could see that people would see that she was unwell and help her, and that they would not think she was 'out of control', or judge her, for fainting, and most people would have forgotten all about it in a few days.

SCHEMA THERAPY AND WORKING WITH CORE BELIEFS

STANDARD COGNITIVE THERAPY AND CLIENTS WITH PERSONALITY PROBLEMS

There has been some question as to whether the standard cognitive therapy approaches described in these three methods chapters can help those people who also have long-term personality issues and complex problems. What use is it trying to identify and challenge negative views of the self if the client has a life-long overriding theme of the self as bad, and cannot even begin to see that there may be an alternative? In order to consider this question more deeply we need to deconstruct some commonly held views about personality disorders and problems.

PERSONALITY DISORDER: MAD, BAD AND BEYOND HELP?

Peoples' initial reaction to the term 'personality disorder' (PD) often seems to come in the form of images of 'craziness', sometimes in the mould of a Gothic novel. Something, in other words, rare, sick, dangerous and probably very difficult to work with. A review of each of these descriptions in turn will take us far in our attempt to come to terms with the concept.

Rare

Attempts to assess the exact prevalence of personality disorders as defined by criteria specified in *DSM* and *ICD* classifications are made difficult by the relatively poor degree to which even expert diagnosticians can agree on their presence in particular clients. This difficulty is further aggravated by the fact that the disorders themselves are co-morbid; they almost always come as partners of emotional disorders and, frequently, with other personality disorders as well. This does not, however, argue against either their existence or considerable effects. De Girolamo and Reich review international evidence on the prevalence of PDs across many cultures and conclude:

> Firstly, as shown by most recent epidemiological surveys, PDs are common and have been found in different countries and socio-cultural settings; secondly, PDs can be very detrimental to the life of the affected individual and highly disruptive to societies, communities and families ... (1993: 1)

It is also important to remember that the surveys have been conducted using, by and large, *DSM* and *ICD* criteria and that it is our belief that many people, including therapists, show significant PD clusters at sub-*DSM* diagnostic level. When we have shown the criteria to other therapists, they have been only too able to recognize particular personality problem areas in themselves. Jeffrey Young suggests in his workshops that therapists often seem to have what he calls 'self-sacrifice schema', characterized by an 'excessive focus on voluntarily meeting the needs of others in daily situations, at the expense of one's own gratification' (McGinn and Young, 1996: 203). The fact that therapists can see these traits in themselves leads to the ironical possibility that, while labels are often viewed as oppressive, the identification of labels in ourselves could be a liberating and democratizing influence in therapy. It may well be that we are all on a continuum of personality disorders and this could help the therapist to take a 'normalizing' attitude when dealing with clients with significant PD clusters.

'Sick'

The stereotyping tag of sickness, major breakdown and/or psychotic behaviour is inaccurate because, by definition, PDs are specifically non-psychotic. The personality disorder most suggestive of mental illness, 'Schizoid Personality Disorder', actually excludes schizophrenia. Personality disorders do not preclude 'good' or 'normal' social functioning and may even enhance certain types of role functioning. For example, a dependent personality may be very well suited to life in the lower ranks of the military (Fiedler et al., 2004). Histrionic traits may assist in some sorts of drama performance. Some people have even had the cheek to suggest that an obsessive-compulsive personality might make a good cognitive therapist!

While it could be argued that such personality traits would be unlikely to lead to any real sense of happiness and fulfilment in the long run, clients with personality disorders can function quite well over long periods. Problems may only arise when the dysfunctional beliefs and schema underlying the PD become activated or exposed by events – for example, when a client with strong dependent features, believing 'I need someone close at hand at all times', loses the person designated to hold that role for them.

Dangerous

The view of the personality-disordered client as dangerous, running amok and causing random damage and injury probably only relates to one specific personality disorder: Antisocial Personality Disorder.[1] Antisocial Personality Disorder has the smallest prevalence for any PD (De Girolamo and Reich, 1993). However, as a result of their occasional or potential antisocial actions, these people are likely to attract attention to themselves. They are more dangerous than average clients, holding beliefs such as 'People will get me if I don't get them first' (Beck et al., 1990). However, such 'antisocial' personalities do not usually act in an uncontrolled way, in fact, planning is a feature of their behaviour. The real question, though, is whether the identification of the label of Antisocial Personality Disorder might help the therapist. While there may be some danger of a 'self-fulfilling prophecy', there is also the countervailing benefit that early recognition could help the therapist to be more understanding of the client and thus more able to make more accurate predictions about the client, thereby helping him or her to be less dangerous.

Impossible to Treat

The perception that PDs are impossible to work with is held fairly widely within the helping professions. It may well have operated as a negative label that has denied these people access to treatment services. This situation is now hopefully beginning to change, alongside the recent, and significant, growth of interest in helping people with personality disorders, across different therapeutic schools, and with additional funding for services (Beck et al., 2003; Gunderson and Gabbard, 2000; Layden et al., 1993; Linehan, 1993a, 1993b). No therapists working with PD issues would argue that the work is easy, but they would want to change the word 'impossible' to 'difficult but possible'. Beck et al. (2003) and Perry et al. (1999) review therapy for people with personality disorders and conclude that cognitive therapy can be helpful and effective.

SCHEMA ISSUES – A MORE CONSTRUCTIVE APPROACH

At the end of this plea for therapists to look for what might be useful in the concept of 'personality disorder', we are still unhappy with the actual term itself. If it is consistently misunderstood and stereotyped among professionals, the term is likely to be similarly perceived among clients. Interestingly, therapists and clients in the USA appear more ready to adopt the term than in the UK. Fortunately, a more user-friendly term is emerging in cognitively oriented work – schema-focused therapy (Young et al., 2003).

The schema concept has a considerable history in psychology, for such a young science at least. The concept was probably first used by Piaget (1952) and Bartlett (1932). The term 'schema' referred then, as it does in Beck's work, to enduring, deep cognitive structures or 'templates' which are particularly important in structuring perceptions and building up 'rule-giving' behaviours. In Beck's initial work, there was a distinction between surface cognitions – automatic thoughts – and underlying cognitive structures – assumptions and schema.

As we descend into the deeper levels of belief, the broader and more 'primitive' cognitions move from the surface thoughts through to core beliefs and schema, as the following illustrates:

1. *Negative automatic thought*: 'These people don't respect me'. The thought states that the people in this specific situation do not respect me. Despite the discomfort of this specific situation, however, it may be that in many other situations most people do in fact appear to respect me.
2. *Dysfunctional assumption*: 'If I work very hard, even though many people appear not to respect me, it may be possible to get some of them to respect me'.
3. *Core belief*: 'Nobody really respects me'. No matter what I do, however hard I try to please people by working hard, no matter how much I search, I can't seem to find any people who respect me.
4. *Early maladaptive schema*: A 'felt sense' of 'shame' in relationships, that one counts for little or nothing. A consistent perception of indifference or violation from close significant others, most likely from parents, resulting in a profound sense of worthlessness which colours most situations one finds oneself in.

Core beliefs are therefore the central foundation of self-concept. Some writers use the terms 'schema' and 'core belief' interchangeably, but Beck (1996) distinguishes between schemas as cognitive structures or modes, such as an 'unworthiness' schema, and core beliefs as specific content of the schema, such as 'I am unworthy'; 'I don't measure up'; or 'Others are better than me'.

JEFFREY YOUNG'S EARLY MALADAPTIVE SCHEMAS (EMS) AND 'LIFETRAPS'

Young was an early associate of Beck's and the director of training at the Cognitive Therapy Center in Philadelphia in the early 1980s. Towards the end of the 1980s he began to develop a form of cognitive therapy that was suitable for clients with personality disorders. The work evolved as he began to realize that clients with personality issues did not always respond well to standard cognitive therapy. For example, a clinically significant feature of Avoidant Personality Disorder would be the client's lack of close confiding relationships. The avoidance of intimacy might influence the therapeutic relationship, such as when the client does not trust the therapist's feedback (Beck et al., 1990). Another example would be the overcompliant trait of dependent personality behaviour, which could influence the client to give the therapist 'welcome news' of favourable evidence rather than developing what the therapy requires – the ability to identify, sift and present evidence of all kinds. Young (1994) was aware of the difficulties surrounding the label of personality disorder and began to develop the 'schema-focused approach'. Rather than use the labels provided by the *DSM* classifications, he identified 18 Early Maladaptive Schema (EMS) patterns in five general domains: Disconnection and Rejection; Autonomy and Performance; Impaired Limits; Other-Directedness; Overvigilance and Inhibition. These schema patterns might operate multiply. Young's book carries an addendum with a self-rated inventory to help one identify which schema issues might be active in a client's or one's own life. Each domain has a number of schema within it – for example, Abandonment/Instability and Mistrust/Abuse are schema within the Disconnection and Rejection domain. The characteristics of schemas are shown in Figure 7.2.

Figure 7.2   The characteristics of schema

A schema is a relatively enduring, deep cognitive structure that organizes the principles of giving appraisal and meaning to experiences, especially in relation to rules of living, with regard to self, others and the world.

Schema are:

- unconditional;
- usually not immediately available to consciousness;
- latent and can be active or dormant according to the presence or absence of triggering events;
- neither 'good' nor 'bad' but may be considered functional or dysfunctional in how well they fit the client's actual life experiences, and cherished life goals;
- compelling or non-compelling in the extent to which they are active and influential in the client's life;
- pervasive or narrow in the extent to which they influence the client's life, especially the number of areas in which they are active.

Young and Klosko note that:

schemas are central to our sense of self. To give up our belief in the validity of a schema would be to surrender the security of knowing who we are and what the world is like; therefore we cling to it, even when it hurts us. These early beliefs provide us with a sense of predictability and certainty; they are comfortable and familiar. In an odd sense, they make us feel at home. (1994: 6)

In *Reinventing Your Life*, designed as a self-help book for clients, Young and Klosko (1994) use the perhaps more friendly term 'life traps' to describe schemas. The book also contains a simplified questionnaire to help clients identify which of the 11 specified life traps may play a role in their difficulties. It seems that

Young changed the number of schematic patterns for a popularized version of his concepts rather than for theoretical reasons. Young, with various colleagues at the New York Cognitive Therapy Center has continued to develop and research the model. *Schema Focused Therapy: A Practitioner's Guide* (Young et al., 2003) represents the fullest attempt yet to spell out in more detail how the evolving schema-focused model might actually work in practice.

Young also clearly spells out the concept of schema maintenance. Early Maladaptive Schema may be particularly rigid and resistant to change. This resistance will be reinforced by particular behaviours, thoughts and beliefs. For example, a client with a mistrust schema may well create almost impossible conditions of trust for others to comply with. The other person's inevitable lack of compliance with these impossible conditions will then of course reconfirm the client's original belief that other people simply cannot be trusted. Padesky (1990) uses the metaphorical term 'prejudice' to describe the operation of schemas. Like prejudices, schemas are not easily open to evidence that contradicts their assumptions. The prejudice model can be a useful analogy for clients who are unfailingly guided by their maladaptive schema, posing a question such as: 'How much faith could a woman looking for personal advice have in a misogynistic adviser?'

THE DEVELOPMENT OF SCHEMAS

Schemas develop from the particular way in which life events are evaluated and translated into ways of seeing self, others and the world at particular stages of development. Difficult or traumatic early experience is likely to be particularly influential, depending on the developmental stages the child is going through. For example, very early experiences, between birth and two years of age, can be conceptualized against Erikson's (1997) psychosexual stage of 'trust versus mistrust'. A bad experience of untrustworthy care giving during this period might result in the development of a 'mistrust schema'. Without some kind of resolution, this schema could result in long-term difficulties in trusting others. A mistrust schema, as has been referred to several times in this book, is a frequently met interpersonal difficulty with clients. It is highly likely that this schema will be replayed within therapy itself.

Mary Ann Layden and colleagues (1993) have given cognitive therapy the valuable concept of 'The Cloud'. When children are very young, being either pre-verbal or with only very limited verbal development, they cannot encode and store experience in ways that they will be able to later on in life, lacking sophisticated verbal processing and memory retention. Piaget (1952) describes early child thinking styles as 'pre-operational' (that is, lacking the logical operations characteristic of later stages) and 'magical' (that is, over-personalized causal thinking). These thinking styles might lead to 'black and white' thinking (reducing several categories to just two) and 'personalization' (seeing oneself as more personally implicated than one is) in relation to the schema. However, recent neonate and infant research shows that very young children are extremely sensitive to visual, auditory and kinaesthetic cues in the environment. These perceptions then form the hazy mélange of 'felt meaning' experience that Layden calls 'The Cloud'. Where there have been very powerful early maladaptive experiences such as abuse, neglect or inconsistency, the child learns that the world is not a good place and that others cannot be trusted. Since they are not able to understand the motives of caregivers, they may conclude that the only explanation for their predicament must lie in their own 'badness'.

By the time the client reaches therapy as an adult, such trauma is likely to be a relatively inaccessible mélange of 'bad' visceral, felt meaning with very fragmented accompanying cognitions. Because of the visceral haziness of 'The Cloud', the child, and later the adult, has few retrieval clues to access the memories, which means that they cannot be well processed, cognitively or emotionally. Like the 'fear structure' of Foa and Kozak (1986), the experiences may lie like molten lava close to the surface of the mind. They can, however, easily erupt as overwhelming emotion at any moment. As the matching memories themselves are not easily retrievable, the experience of overwhelming emotion may be all the more baffling and scary to the client herself and to those around her.

LORNA

Lorna had strong schematic memories from childhood. In one of these memories, she was accused by her parents of having failed to discharge duties that most people would consider unfair impositions on a young child, such as being able to anticipate that her younger brother might fall in a shallow pond while she was responsible for him. She did not then have the sophisticated conceptual thinking that would have been necessary to defend herself and could only think of herself as 'unworthy of' her parents' trust. This and other similar incidents led to the development of an 'unworthiness' schema that is now activated when she is unfairly criticized at work. The discharge of feeling which results from the activation of the schema prevents her from being able to find any of her normal adult responses, so that, as in childhood, she experiences powerlessness and humiliation. She is effectively having to deal with stress from the actual current situation and, at the same time, with some restimulated stress from memories of childhood. She might be able to deal with either stress but the combination of the two is what results in the feeling of being overwhelmed.

CHRISSY

Another client, Chrissy, had been feeling sad after getting caught in the rain one day. She couldn't see why this had upset her so much but, while processing the experience, recalled being left in a wet nappy in a cold house as her parents locked themselves in their bedroom and refused to come out to her.

The integration of schemas into the cognitive model has had an important influence on the development and practice of cognitive therapy. For example, when a therapist is aiming to help the adult client develop more flexible and functionally adaptable ways of thinking, they may be dealing with pre-verbal experience, resulting in severe limitations in using a highly verbal intervention to try to impact on these schema.

WHEN IS SCHEMA WORK APPROPRIATE AND INAPPROPRIATE?

Cognitive therapy, as we have discussed before, works from the principle of parsimony – beginning with work at the symptom level, especially with automatic thoughts. For example, Beck et al. (1979) stressed that when people are very depressed, hopelessness and difficulty in concentrating can limit the client's capacity to enter into 'insight' work. Trying to 'work through' the depressive symptoms by cognitive techniques alone may not only prove inadequate but may even worsen the level of bad feelings. Such work becomes more possible as some of the symptoms of depression begin to lift. Blackburn and Davidson (1995) estimate that around 75 per cent of the intervention in standard cognitive therapy of depression is concerned with symptom-level work, typically working with behavioural responses to the passivity of depression and the countering of negative automatic thoughts experienced by the depressed person. The remaining quarter of treatment may be concerned with underlying issues and preventative strategies.

As the work proceeds and the therapist builds up a conceptualization, deeper beliefs, including core beliefs, become evident. It may of course be that in working directly on behavioural passivity and hopelessness, one is already working on underlying schema such as 'I am cursed' or 'I cannot act powerfully in my life'. As this present-oriented and symptom-level work unfolds, most clients will begin to reveal certain facts about previous experiences, including childhood experiences. The cognitive therapist is able to use the conceptualization to fit all these pieces of information into the overall picture. The therapist may, for example, invite the client to talk about childhood experiences and then ask, 'What beliefs or rules of living do you think developed from those experiences?' It sometimes surprises therapists how easily clients can answer this question; describing clear, often stark, core beliefs that they were not previously consciously aware of. Schemas are unlikely to become a major focus of therapy, however, unless the client's material actually demands that they be put on the agenda and the therapist begins to conclude that such underlying issues are likely to predispose the client to a relapse of symptoms unless tackled therapeutically.

Where the client's functioning before the current emotional problem was reasonably good, without marked personality disturbance, it may often be enough to merely unveil the core beliefs. This unveiling alerts the client to their existence and raises awareness of how they operate, particularly the way they are activated and how they send disturbed feelings 'cascading' down to the symptom level. It may not always be necessary to work on modifying the core beliefs – the client's increased awareness of the beliefs in itself will lead to changes, as the following example illustrates.

KEITH

Keith, a 40-year-old computer project worker, had been prone to depression and anxiety since adolescence. He became depressed again after his job was threatened by organizational changes at work. He had frequent negative automatic thoughts such as, 'I'm falling behind at work'; 'They think my work is under par'; 'They thought my report was rubbish'; and 'The others are way ahead of me'. The therapy was limited to a maximum of eight sessions. In the first six sessions Keith was able to learn cognitive techniques and, in particular, to vigorously challenge his negative automatic thoughts. His BDI score fell from 23 to 8 (from moderate to a non-clinical score). During these early sessions, Keith occasionally spoke about his childhood, usually rather reluctantly. His description was of an 'unremarkable' childhood and it seemed difficult to link this with his 'worrying' cognitive style. In Session 6, the client and I (FW) went over this again and tried to draw out a formulation together. Keith suddenly said: 'The thing is they didn't seem to worry about me … maybe they didn't worry enough'. I added: 'Did that leave you to do all the worrying?' In Session 7, Keith reported that this question had led to an 'Ah-ha' experience and he surprised me by bringing in a very detailed formulation he had worked on by himself, with two pages of closely written textual notes with examples of his childhood experiences. We talked the conceptualization through in Session 7 and as part of his 'blueprint' at the end of therapy (see Chapter 8), but it was not otherwise 'worked through'. Keith reported himself happy to finish therapy at the end of Session 8. His feedback included positive comments about how helpful it had been to look at some of the historical roots of his difficulties.

With the development of schema-focused therapy come concerns about its use. We have observed that therapists from other disciplines are more likely to believe that core beliefs and early experience are where the action is. They tend to want to dive into these areas early on in therapy, neglecting to fully explore maintenance cycles and day-to-day aspects of the client's problems, perhaps feeling that that they are not doing 'real therapy' without bringing up the past.

However, core belief work is not, as yet, fully evaluated, and is where the greatest likelihood of therapy-induced problems can occur. When we are exposing and examining long-term core constructs, the individual can be extremely vulnerable, and the risk is that difficult material is uncovered before the client has learned ways of coping with the consequences of uncovering such meanings.

The downward arrow method is simple, but powerful, and often leads to emotional consequences, as the client unmasks what he or she 'truly' believes, but which may have been out of awareness. Unpacking a seemingly straightforward negative thought can lead to uncovering difficult and sensitive meanings, and if this is done too early in therapy, before the person is able to cope with the consequences, then he or she may end up feeling much worse.

CLARE

Clare, who had asked for help with bouts of depression, felt terrible when she had a minor disagreement with someone at work. She had told her supervisor that she had not understood her instructions, and the supervisor was dismissive and unhelpful. Clare felt very 'stupid' and 'useless' and also frightened that her supervisor could now see what a failure Clare really was. On looking at the event in depth in her therapy session, Clare saw that a fall-out with the supervisor meant, to her, that she was 'useless' and 'a failure', and this meant that she would 'always be alone': once people find out how useless I am, they won't want to know. Uncovering this meaning led Clare to feel much worse, bringing up many childhood memories of being severely reprimanded for small mistakes, and being punished by being left alone for long periods of time. For a while, she was left interpreting her world in terms of these beliefs, collecting examples in her mind, and remembering the past in terms of failures. However, another line that could have been taken to lift Clare's mood earlier on in therapy, and to help her develop skills in taking her thoughts and beliefs as hypotheses, not facts, would be to work with her assumption 'If people are stroppy with me, this means I've got something wrong', perhaps helping her to see that her supervisor was wrong to be dismissive and unhelpful to Clare, reflecting the supervisors' problems, not Clare's. Such work would help lift Clare's mood, rather than leading her to be overwhelmed with earlier feelings. Then, uncovering her underlying beliefs would be valuable, helping her to understand and re-evaluate the meanings she was giving to day-to-day events.

James (2001) and James and Barton (2004: 434) emphasize the need for therapists to think through the possible emotional reactions and consequences of accessing core beliefs, and suggest that hypotheses about core beliefs are brought gradually and sensitively into a course of therapy, not suddenly and in confrontation. Beliefs can be mood dependent. When depressed, the person may believe themselves to be useless and worthless. However, when feeling better, these apparently 'core' beliefs vanish, the person feeling once again reasonably well. Therefore, going in at the level of core beliefs can be counterproductive if not aversive (James et al., 2004). In addition, therapists need to have sufficient skill and expertise, therapy time and supervision to do this kind of work.

In order to do core-belief work safely, James and Barton propose the following:

- Collaboratively decide with the client if, when and how to work on core beliefs;
- Start working early on in the session to allow sufficient time for appropriate work;
- Be mindful of the person's style of thinking. For example if someone has a tendency to be black and white, the perspective may shift dramatically;
- Be mindful of how low mood tends to lead to overgeneralized negative memories, so that the individual finds it difficult to remember anything that can offer a different perspective. For example, when low, Clare could remember very few examples that counteracted her belief 'I am useless at relationships' whereas there were many examples of good friendships and relationships in her life (with her sister, two friends at school, one boyfriend and her stepaunt) which she was able to see when less low;
- Work to enable the client to think more specifically and in detail about memories, and to be able to put things into context, before doing schema work. For Clare, this meant being able to see the supervisor's reaction in the context of the job situation (a stressed, open-plan office environment with little time or space for proper discussion) and what was going on for the supervisor (recently split up with her husband, problems with her oldest daughter) rather than automatically in terms of Clare;
- Blackburn et al. (2001) observe that trainee cognitive therapists quickly become skilled at eliciting negative thoughts and beliefs, but are less prompt and skilled at using methods to change such material, perhaps hoping or believing that change will occur as a result of insight alone. We need to be able to work with whatever thoughts come up in therapy, and be adept at methods of guided discovery and testing thoughts, so the client is not 'left hanging'.

The stepped-care approach is also useful in deciding when and where to start working at a 'deeper' level (Davidson, 2000). Stepped care is a means of delivering services in the most parsimonious way, by starting with the simplest interventions and only using longer, more intensive or expensive forms of therapy where there is clear evidence for their effectiveness and where they are likely to serve the client's best interests. Core-belief work is avoided for people with one episode of a problem, or someone with mild depression, or by less experienced therapists. However, it may be appropriate in the following situations:

1. When there is clear trauma emerging from early and/or previous experience;
2. With deeper 'themes' emerging strongly in the client's material;
3. When early attempts to achieve some symptom relief have definitely not worked;
4. When the client requests longer-term therapy focused on early experience.

At the two ends of the continuum between work focused mainly on 'here and now' and that focused on 'there and then' underlying issues, there is a grey area of middle ground where these decisions about the foci and length of therapy are perhaps more difficult. For the moment, we will talk about the therapeutic mode focused on underlying, schematic issues but will return to the grey area towards the end of this chapter. Supervision is valuable in making decisions about the level at which to work.

TOOLS AND TECHNIQUES FOR WORKING WITH SCHEMA

Ways of working with schema are gradually being developed, particularly through the work of Beck, Padesky, Young and Layden. As we have described earlier, schema networks may be difficult to access through language alone. Imagery techniques therefore have much to offer (Edwards, 1989, 1990; Hackmann, 1997, 2004; Layden et al., 1993; Padesky and Greenberger, 1995). Clients can be asked to report significant images occurring at moments of difficulty or to induce an image of their difficulties or situation, which can then be explored for their incipient meanings. Therapist and client may attempt to transform the meaning and experience of the imagery in ways that may prove more helpful to the client. Two-chair methods from Gestalt can help reform the images and allow change in meaning as the following illustrates:

MANESH

Manesh had struggled for years with depression related to underlying fears of being 'found out' and rejected but could not make sense of why this should be so. He articulated possible beliefs – 'People abandon me'; 'I am going to be found out' – which were activated when feeling low. When he was one-year-old, he was left with his aunt for a few weeks while his mother was in hospital, but could not make sense of why this should have affected him. Although, rationally, he could tell himself that he was not abandoned – his mother had to go to hospital and it was not his fault – he still had an underlying sense that something bad would happen if he was not 'good'. In a two-chair dialogue, Manesh talked to his young self, allowed himself to express how upset he was, and comforted the child. This was an emotional turning point in therapy.

Continua, positive data logs (Padesky, 1994; Padesky and Greenberger, 1995), and schema diaries (Young and Klosko, 1994) enable old beliefs to be evaluated and weakened, and new beliefs to be constructed. In *continua* work the client is asked to map out how he sees himself in relation to others. For example, for Sam, who holds the rigid belief 'I'm useless', the therapist would encourage him to define 'useless' more closely: what does it mean? Useless at what? What does the opposite concept, 'useful', mean? Once the concepts have been discussed, Sam defines either end of the continuum: 0 and 100 per cent 'useful' (Figure 7.3).

Figure 7.3   Continuum for the concept of 'useful'

0 per cent useful ←————————————————————————→ 100 per cent useful
Someone who has nothing   Spends all their time doing good things for other people
Lies around all day in bed   Involved in charity work, politics
No job, no friends   Brings up children
Looks after elderly parents and neighbours
Someone everyone calls on in an emergency

We then ask Sam to say where, realistically, he fits on the continuum. After he has located himself, we begin to map out how different people he knows would make out on the positive and negative criteria. We can then explore the concepts more. For example, Mother Theresa, or other people who serve others all the time, might be seen as the most 'useful', but are these people Sam would want as close friends? If people are not 'useful' in any way, does this make them unacceptable human beings, or those worthy of help? The idea, as in standard cognitive therapy, is to try to 'stretch out' these inflexible categories, so that the client can begin to realize how inaccurate and counterproductive they really are.

Positive diaries encourage clients to keep a diary of all the positive self-attributes and achievements they can detect. Very often therapy starts focusing on episodes of negative thoughts and moods; with positive diaries we are aiming to highlight the good in the person's life. Initially, Sam found it hard to find evidence for being a 'useful, worthwhile person' and we needed to illuminate all the tiny, day-to-day actions that contributed to his life. Sam then started to notice how many times he interacted in a positive way with other people – chatting to the postman, holding the door for a colleague, making someone else laugh with a terrible joke – and how many times he achieved what he set out to do: 'I got up this morning; I got dressed. I put the rubbish out. I stayed at work all day, and finished two tasks I set out to complete'. Such activities would have previously been discounted; by keeping a diary over several weeks, Sam could begin to chip away at the notion of being 'useless'. Positive diaries provide powerful evidence to disconfirm the self-prejudice induced by maladaptive schema (Greenberger and Padesky, 1995; Padesky, 1994).

Young et al. (2003) provide a comprehensive array of techniques specially adapted for schema-focused work. Schema flashcards are a valuable means of highlighting when the client's responses are being dictated by the activation of schema, with the experience of strong affect making it impossible to realistically appraise situations. When noticing 'schema activation', or times when strong feelings are activated, based more on past beliefs than present reality, the schema flashcard written on a postcard or in a notebook, invites the client to think, in

Figure 7.4   Schema issues and the therapeutic relationship

Phase I – Dealing with one's own countertransference reaction

1. **Do not retaliate**
   Schematic material can be very provoking and disheartening to the therapist.
   Remember that this is why the person needs therapy. It is just something
   that they do, not all of what they are that is the problem. Try to 'hold' the
   difficulty.
2. **Do not offer immediate 'easy' reassurance**
   Being a nice person, you will be very tempted to reassure the client: 'Of course,
   you can trust me …', '… I won't abandon you …'. If you do this, however, you run
   the danger of not seizing the moment and taking the chance to work with the
   schema while it is 'hot'. You may also be reacting like other people in the client's
   life – most usually in a schema-confirming way. Again, try to hold the difficulty and
   then open it for examination and 'working through'.

Phase II – Responding therapeutically

3. **Express empathy for the schema**
   'It's understandable that, given your circumstance, you've come to think that
   you can't trust people [i.e. in the case of a mistrust schema]. Most people who'd
   had those experiences would end up feeling that way.'
4. **Acknowledge the schema and suggest it is a problem that can be solved
   collaboratively**
   'In a way, it is good that it has come up now. It means that we can take the time
   to work out ways of stopping it from getting in the way of the things you want
   to do in your life.'

---

the cool light of day, what is going on, and distinguish feelings arising from past
beliefs from present-realities.

Other cognitive interventions include 'life review' or 'historical test of schema',
a process of drawing out a life history and trying to locate the development of
core beliefs and schemas alongside it. Experiential techniques include 'schema
dialogue', an adaptation of Beck's role-playing technique, where either therapist or client can take the role of either schema or anti-schema. Behavioural
interventions include collaboratively working on new behaviours that the
client 'can try on for size'; for example, 'acting as if' they did have more self-
esteem. Another aspect of behavioural work can include behavioural-pattern
breaking using experiments to test out different forms of behaviour.

Young and colleagues suggest that the therapeutic relationship is central in
schema-focused work and that the therapist can play a role of 'limited reparenting' where the therapist tries to offer a therapeutic relationship that counteracts the
schema. Such reparenting can be helpful but, in our view, should be approached
with caution and monitored in supervision.

RESPONDING TO SCHEMA ISSUES IN
THE THERAPEUTIC RELATIONSHIP

We would like to end this chapter by giving our view of possible responses when therapists become aware that their client has a schema-based issue. The first thing is obviously to be aware of the schema. This often comes about because the therapist experiences the countertransferential 'pull' of the schema. We have drawn up a brief résumé in Figure 7.4. Fittingly, it owes much to the work of Kahn (1991), who writes to show how humanistic therapy and psychodynamic therapy are converging in their view of the therapeutic relationship. We would like the cognitive voice to be added to this debate. We invite the reader to use the template in Figure 7.4 to imagine how she or he would react to an interpersonal marker that occurred with a client, Wes.

WES

The first sentence that Wes said in therapy was to ask his therapist (FW) what his qualifications were. This is a relatively unusual but not unreasonable request. Wes, however, raised this question four times during the next eight sessions, every other session in fact. On the last occasion, Wes said: 'Don't take this personally but I'm not sure if you are a good enough therapist to work with me'. By this time, it had emerged that Wes came from an indulgently 'laissez-faire' family on whom he was dependent but with whom he was also very angry. His visits home invariably resulted in him storming off before the scheduled end of the visit. His current therapist was his fifth, most of whom he had 'provoked' (his own word) into terminating therapy with him. The therapist was determined to stay the course (in this case 20 contracted sessions) with him and not reject him, saying; 'I know it's hard to know if I am the therapist for you but that's your question, I intend to stick around and do my work until you tell me otherwise'. The therapist rightly suspected that this would be an up and down struggle and made sure that he took the situation to supervision regularly.

CONCLUSION

The tools and techniques of cognitive therapy discussed in these three chapters are many and varied, some unique to cognitive approaches, some borrowed from other disciplines, including behaviour therapy, Gestalt therapy, emotion-based psychotherapy and meditation. We have stressed, however, that cognitive therapy, while using such techniques, is more than the sum of its parts, and must always be integrated with the cognitive conceptualization within a good therapeutic relationship. This should ensure that techniques will impact on the deepest level of cognition possible, be that on assumptions, core beliefs or schemas.

The overall aim of any technique in cognitive therapy is to target and modify the client's belief systems, a process which is guided by the client's individual conceptualization, which provides a sound understanding of what that belief system is, where it came from and how it works in practice. Thus, cognitive therapy becomes a dynamic therapy soundly based on an individual formulation, rather than a set of self-help techniques. In the words of Weishaar:

> Cognitive Therapy, viewed as a set of techniques, is not likely to be successful in treating the range of disorders confronting clinicians. Yet, Cognitive Therapy based in a theoretical framework, grounded in psychological literature, and presented within a sustaining therapeutic relationship has wide-ranging utility. (1993: 27)

If we are tempted to simply utilize techniques, we are missing the key ingredients.

On the specific question of working in a schema-focused way, it is important to acknowledge that there may well be a large 'grey area' concerning the presence of 'schemas' and/or 'personality disorders' in clients and in people – therapists included – in general. While some cognitive therapists have tried to make hard and fast divisions between 'standard' and 'schema-focused' cognitive therapy, we think it is far more likely that a number of different mixes of the two approaches would be distributed on a continuum. The significance of this view is that cognitive therapists may well find themselves working on the schema level in both medium- and short-term work as well as in longer-term work (Young et al., 2003). The fact that the cognitive therapist is now much better equipped to work flexibly is one of the most exciting developments of cognitive therapy today.

Further Reading

Beck, A. T., Freeman, A. & Davis, D. (Eds.). (2003). *Cognitive therapy of personality disorders* (Rev. ed.). New York: Guilford Press.

Fennell, M. (1998). *Overcoming low self esteem*. London: Robinson.

Greenberger, D. & Padesky, C. (1995). *Mind over mood*. New York: Guilford Press. (**Chapter 9.**)

Hackmann, A. (1997). The transformation of meaning in cognitive therapy. In M. Powell. & C. Brewin (Eds.), *The transformation of meaning in psychological therapies* (pp. 125–140). Chichester: Wiley.

James, I. A. (2001). Schema therapy: The next generation, but should it carry a health warning? *Behavioural and Cognitive Psychotherapy*, 29: 401–407.

Layden, M. A., Newman, C. F., Freeman, A. & Morse, S. B. (1993). *Cognitive therapy of borderline personality disorder*. Boston, MA: Allyn & Bacon.

Young, J. & Klosko, J. (1994). *Reinventing your life*. New York: Plume.

Young, J., Klosko, J. & Weishaar, M. E. (2003). *Schema therapy: A practitioner's guide*. New York: Guilford Press.

NOTE

1 It is surely time that psychiatric units for offenders with mental health problems should cease to be referred to as 'Personality Disorder Units.'

8 Difficulties in Cognitive Therapy

When reading or hearing about cognitive therapy, it is possible to gain the impression that cognitive approaches allow for easy case conceptualization, progressing smoothly into the use of aptly chosen techniques to which the client responds in a positive way, taking on board the model and always doing homework. The result is clear symptom reduction and a happier client. However, things do not always happen like they say in the books. Beck and colleagues aptly remind us that 'the course of therapy, like true love, is not always smooth' (1979: 295). In our experience, the textbook case of cognitive therapy, while common enough to allow for a great deal of job satisfaction, is the exception rather than the rule. By no means all therapy sessions present major obstacles to be overcome but the cognitive therapist has to be on the lookout for difficulties that may arise, sometimes perniciously. Such obstacles may be seen as upsetting the flow of therapy. They may arise from misunderstandings or the therapist having an 'off day'. Obstacles almost always – if viewed and used in the service of therapy – provide valuable material for understanding and working with the client. They can facilitate the client's conceptualization and give greater understanding of the kinds of problems the client is experiencing, as well as areas the therapist needs to work on. To quote Judith Beck: 'Problems of one kind or another arise with nearly every patient in cognitive therapy … [A] reasonable goal is therefore not to avoid problems altogether but rather to learn to uncover and specify problems, to conceptualize how they arose, and to plan how to remediate them' (1995: 300).

We, as therapists and people, can also learn a great deal from difficulties that arise during therapy, in terms of conceptualizing ourselves and highlighting our own issues that may impact on our therapeutic abilities, and learn from the ways in which our clients negotiate difficulties.

In this chapter, we describe the common difficulties facing the cognitive therapist. Obviously, the list is not exhaustive, but we hope to give a flavour of the way cognitive therapy approaches solving such difficulties. The chapter is divided into two sections covering common difficulties in carrying out cognitive therapy; and difficulties in the therapeutic relationship. To a large extent, separating difficulties in the therapeutic relationship from other problems is arbitrary. We may see all problems as arising within the context of the therapeutic relationship and therefore constituting a relationship difficulty. However, cognitive therapy, in keeping with its pragmatic philosophy, suggests moving from the simplest level to the more complex, starting with a bottom-up approach. Thus, one might assume first that a problem is caused by a simple misunderstanding rather than diving in at the level of schema or 'client resistance'. Almost always, the main principles of problem resolution follow the main principles of cognitive therapy: gain regular feedback to find out what kind of problems exist; conceptualize the problems; work collaboratively towards resolution; and work in the most parsimonious way. It is easy to overlook such principles when faced with the intricacies and complexities of therapy. Hence, we stress throughout the chapter the value of feedback and supervision to throw light on our difficulties.

WHEN IS A PROBLEM A PROBLEM?

Some problems are glaringly obvious: the client does not turn up, ends therapy prematurely, makes a complaint against us, and simply does not find the therapy at all helpful. Others are more specific or subtle such as recurrent difficulties in identifying or challenging thoughts or the client never doing homework, but always having a plausible excuse. Judith Beck (1995) summarizes the problems that may occur in cognitive therapy as fitting into several categories: diagnosis, conceptualization and treatment planning; therapeutic alliance; structure and/or pace of the sessions; socializing the client into the cognitive way of working; dealing with automatic thoughts; accomplishing therapeutic goals; and the client's processing of the session content. She goes on to provide a list of questions therapists can ask themselves whenever problems arise, such as 'Does the client believe, at least somewhat, that therapy can help?' Leahy (2001) defines cognitive behavioural 'resistance' as anything in the client's behaviour, thinking, emotional responses and interpersonal style which interferes with the person's ability to use therapy and acquire the ability to handle problems outside therapy, and interferes with what he calls the 'demand characteristics' of therapy, its emphasis on the here and now, structure, problem-solving orientation, psycho-educational approach, active nature and focus on self help and meeting goals.

Measures such as the BDI and BAI, as well as regular reviews of the client's mood, allow us to assess whether or not the client is improving or meeting therapy goals. One of the great strengths of cognitive therapy in identifying difficulties is in its use of regular feedback, throughout and at the end of both therapy as a whole and each individual session. We aim for the client to be able to give us feedback about what is going on, such as 'I don't follow what you're saying'; 'That doesn't make sense'; or 'You're not understanding/listening to me'. We may pick up problems indirectly: the client agreeing verbally but looking puzzled. However, the ideal of feedback does not always work. Clients may be hesitant to say they do not understand in case they are thought to be stupid or they may not like to question the therapist as an 'authority figure' because of fear of rejection. The therapist, one way or another, may fear negative feedback and therefore not be open to it in the sessions. The value of ongoing supervision, both with a supervisor and self-supervision, may lie in the degree to which it is able to help the therapist to see some of their blind spots that are not apparent from the client's feedback. A great deal can be learned by therapists allowing time at the end of each session to reflect on or listen to tapes of the session, and giving themselves supervision and feedback.

PROBLEMS IN IDENTIFYING
EMOTIONS AND THOUGHTS

The bedrock of cognitive therapy lies in identifying specific thoughts, relating these thoughts to emotion, behaviour and physiology, and learning to see alternative perspectives. Identifying thoughts and finding alternative meanings is a common area of difficulty. Some people report that they do not have, or are not aware of, particular thoughts, finding it difficult to separate out thoughts and feelings. It is a common experience for the emotion to precede any conscious thinking, leading to difficulties in picking out thoughts from the mass of cognitions and emotions that accompany strong affect. Clients may not tell us what is really going on, fearing that if they describe their thoughts, strange as they often are, we will think them mad.

There are three main areas of difficulty when working with thoughts (Grant et al., 2004).

THE CLIENT HAS DIFFICULTY IN BEING
AWARE OF, OR LABELLING, EMOTIONS

Feelings may be global, rather than specific, such as generally feeling 'bad' or 'crap' without a strong sense of specific triggers, or connection to particular situations. People who have been deeply traumatized, either early on in life or later on because of traumatic events, may have learned to avoid, or blunt, affect in order to avoid being overwhelmed; and for some people emotions may never have been discussed or labelled, leading to long-term difficulties in 'knowing how I feel'. Cultural and gender issues may lead to different ways of labelling emotions: making a sweeping gender stereotype, it can be more difficult for men to label emotion than for women.

One way to work with this is to use physical sensations as indicators of emotion, asking 'What was going on in your body just then?' rather than 'How were you feeling?' Keeping a careful diary of physical symptoms and possible feelings may help with being specific – for example, noticing headaches or a sinking feeling in the stomach can help label feelings of 'stress' or 'fear', or underlying anger or sadness. In addition, the concept of cognitive specificity can be helpful, showing how specific thoughts and emotions are linked – for example, someone who has a strong sense of moral right and wrong for others, expressed as 'shoulds' and 'oughts', which are regularly transgressed by others, may experience anger; those with strong moral rules for the self may experience guilt.

THE CLIENT IS NOT AWARE OF
SPECIFIC THOUGHTS, DESPITE BEING
AWARE OF FEELINGS

This may be because thoughts are being mislabelled, or not recognized for some reason. People often mix up thoughts and feelings, reporting, 'I felt like

I was going mad' whereas 'I am going mad' is in fact a thought. People may report thoughts in the form of questions, such as 'Why me?' when something bad happens to them. It is often useful to seek out their implicit answers to the question to obtain the meaning – for example, 'I'm cursed'. It is very difficult to challenge a thought such as 'Why me?', whereas the concept of the client being cursed, or deserving bad things happening to them can be explored. Some people relate their important emotions more to images than to words. Questions about imagery, asking if the client gets a picture in their mind, can sometimes help us reach thoughts that purely verbal questions cannot. It may be helpful to use metaphors such as 'Is there something that represents how you felt?' when talking about what the image represents and its meanings (Hackmann, 1997, 2004).

Finding the right questions to ask in order to elicit thoughts may involve a process of trial and error – for example, by asking 'Why were you feeling that way?', the therapist might expect the client to say, 'Because I was thinking what a lousy person I am', whereas the 'why' question may elicit responses like 'I don't know', or 'Because I was feeling bad'. Putting words into the client's mouth is sometimes tempting, but generally best avoided; however, it can be valuable to say something along the lines of 'I guess if it was me, I might be thinking ...' or 'A lot of people who feel like that think x; I wonder if that is true for you too?'

When clients are struggling to find words for thoughts, it is important to use the person's own voice, words and metaphors, asking questions such as 'What was so bad about that situation for you?'; 'What were you telling yourself at that time?'; 'If there was a little critical voice inside, what would it be saying then?' Role playing the situation and stopping at points of high emotion can elicit the key thoughts at the time.

KAY

Kay had no idea why she felt so anxious and panicky when she went out. She knew she was not going to collapse or make a fool of herself, and did not think she had any social concerns, but still experienced panic attacks. I (DS) asked her to invoke some of her panicky feelings in the session, and hyperventilate to reproduce some of the sensations. Then we walked to the hospital bookshop, and I asked her to start a conversation with the shop assistant about the books. She managed to do this without any problem. I asked Kay what was going through her mind, and she reported: 'That was OK, I didn't care what she thought of me. It didn't matter if I looked like a scared little mouse'. We then discussed some of the other thoughts that came up, and she realized she was always concerned that people would see her as 'nothing', or 'a little mouse', and judge her badly if she was to show anxiety.

THOUGHTS AND FEELINGS DO NOT SEEM TO MATCH

A client may report feeling panicky in a situation, shaking and sweating, but the thought may be 'It's OK, I'll cope', or when asked, 'What did you think would happen?', might answer, 'Nothing'. In this case, difficulties in identifying the content of negative, fearful or depressing thoughts may arise because the client may describe to us the answer to the thoughts or a positive way of thinking rather than what was really going on: she is coming in at the end point of a stream of thinking. The client may believe that the aim of therapy is to 'think positive' and will therefore be reluctant to describe negative thoughts. For example, when asking anxious clients to describe what they thought might happen in a feared situation, they may say something along the lines of 'Well, I knew nothing would happen', rather than the scared thought of 'I thought I was going to die'. We may need to actively encourage our clients to express what was really going on, mad, crazy or irrational as it may sound, and discuss any fears clients have about speaking their minds. Also, they may need to go back over the sequence in their minds, to catch the first, frightening thought: 'Oh my god, here come the symptoms, I'm going to lose it' before talking themselves out of it ('Stay calm, it's OK, you'll be alright').

DIFFICULTIES IN MODIFYING THOUGHTS AND MEANINGS

IT MAKES SENSE ... BUT ...

The 'yes ... but ...' syndrome is a common problem, where the client agrees in principle with the idea being discussed yet 'buts' it: 'I understand that I'm thinking very negatively, but I do not know how to change'. Buts are common on thought records: the client may come up with an alternative thought, but then overrule it with a 'yes ... but ...'. One answer is to treat the 'but' in the way of any other negative thought, using downward-arrow approaches to understand what underlies the word. For example, Sasha, the insurance clerk whom we described in Chapter 1, had a long-standing problem with worry, leading to many physical symptoms and inability to get on with many aspects of her life without paralyzing anxiety. She had a great deal of knowledge about ways of managing worry and stress and was able to challenge her worrying thoughts, but it made no difference to how she felt. Every discussion and intervention led to her saying 'I know all that ... but ... it doesn't make any difference, or it's too difficult'. Sasha and I (DS) looked at her beliefs about worrying, discussing the role of worry in her life, in particular her constant worrying about doing something wrong at work.

Therapist: What are the disadvantages for you of worrying so much?
Sasha: I know it is making me feel awful. It's so difficult going to work. My husband is getting fed up with me. They must be fed up with me at work asking if I've done it properly. I know all that. I know practically every time I worry about something it turns out OK and I wonder why I made such a fuss. I know I'm being stupid ...

Therapist: But ...?

Sasha: But I just can't stop worrying.

Therapist: You know it's 'stupid' but you can't stop it. It's like you know in your head but something else is telling you to worry. How about we hear from the something else ... the 'but'?

Sasha: But if I didn't worry, I might make a real mess up of my job. I have to worry about it because if I didn't then I might miss something. I'd make a mistake and not even know about it!

Therapist: And then what?

Sasha: I'd just want to die. People would think 'she's made a real mess'.

Therapist: So I guess the but is protecting you from making a mess, like an insurance policy against rejection?

Sasha: Yes, but ... I guess it is an expensive one.

Therapist: So how about looking at whether you need to be insured in the first place. Or at least find a cheaper policy.

Sasha: Yes, but ... it's kind of terrifying thinking about being under-insured.

The 'yes ... buts' had many strands for Sasha, requiring unpacking her fears about change which she found very difficult to articulate. Using downward-arrow techniques and metaphors can help to explore the underlying issues, arriving at the emotion rather than challenging thoughts on the surface level. For Sasha, once she recognized her real terror of changing, she began to substitute the word 'and' instead of 'but' whenever she thought to herself about changing. A simple cognitive shift enabled her to acknowledge and recognize her feelings, rather than allowing them to 'but' her into her old patterns of worrying.

DEALING WITH CONTENT WHEN WE NEED TO DEAL WITH PROCESS

In Sasha's example, above, looking at her positive beliefs about worry, her metacognitive beliefs, proved more fruitful than attempting to work with every thought. At times we need to focus on process rather than content issues. For example socially phobic people conduct extensive post-mortems in their minds after a social interaction, going over and over what was said, how they came across, whether there was any evidence to show how incompetent they were. Attempting to evaluate the reality of such thoughts may be useful to a degree, but there may well be more mileage in looking at the process, and the pros and cons of post mortems (e.g. I may find evidence to reassure me and feel better, but on the other hand thinking over and over makes me feel awful and I may not be a good judge of what others were thinking). For people who worry excessively, and those with obsessive-compulsive problems, there is often more value in looking at metacognitive beliefs rather than content (Wells, 2000). Positive beliefs about worry, or positive beliefs about the need to ruminate, mean that whatever answer can be found for specific thoughts, another one or a hundred will take their place. In this case, thought records can only go a certain distance, and we need to identify beliefs about worry or rumination, and use reattribution methods and behavioural experiments to test out the validity of such beliefs.

CHALLENGING FACTS NOT DISTORTIONS

Sometimes what sounds like a juicy negative thought to challenge is more like a reality, and to try to look for alternatives leaves the client feeling misunderstood, or their difficulties trivialized. For example, Moira was feeling awful as a result of thinking about her relationship with her son: she believed that she had been a bad mother. Moira and I (DS) attempted to look at alternatives to this way of thinking: What was the evidence for her being a bad mother? What was the evidence against? For Moira, the evidence against her being a bad mother was thin on the ground. Her child had been taken into care at a young age because Moira was extremely depressed. The depression had left her unable to cope with her baby; when she was finally reunited with her child, they had not bonded and were unable to form a good relationship. Therefore, it seemed nonsensical for Moira to look at ways in which she had been a good mother. Instead, we talked around the meaning of her not being a good mother; her beliefs that having a child automatically meant that she should have been a good parent; how difficult it had been, because of her circumstances, to look after her baby; how she had done the best for her child by putting him into care. Moira's belief that she was not a good mother did not change; however, she began to be slightly more accepting of her difficulties, and look instead at her feelings of loss for her child.

Stirling Moorey (1996; Moorey and Greer, 2002) describes how Beck's model developed in relation to relatively stable emotional states such as clinical depression and anxiety. The model has to be modified to fit situations where a client is adapting to strongly adverse life events. In this case, rather than initially trying to modify meanings, we spend more time listening, empathizing, and building up a collaborative and supportive relationship in which the client may well find their own resolution without explicit cognitive work, akin to person-centred and emotional processing therapy. The cognitive aspect involves identifying ways in which the way of thinking, or dealing with situations, is unhelpful as opposed to biased. For example, when working with people with terminal cancer, cognitive therapy can enable the person to look at how ruminating about how little time one has left or regretting what one will be missing by dying, gets in the way of making the best use of the time available. For others, cognitive work would be about the meaning given to the process of adaptation: another person might not allow themselves to feel sad or distressed, believing 'I have to put on a brave face and cope, whatever': in which case, we could look at the pros and cons of 'coping', and use cognitive approaches to identify and test out 'helpful non-coping' such as telling a partner how low one feels and gaining support.

'I UNDERSTAND IT IN MY HEAD: BUT I DO NOT FEEL ANY DIFFERENT'

Another frequent difficulty is in the process of the working through of therapeutic change, moving from 'head' to 'heart'. In cognitive therapy, the individual may find that therapy makes intellectual sense but does not result in feeling any different. Sometimes this can be a matter of repetition and what Ellis (1962) calls 'work and practice': if the client has felt this way for a long time it will take time and practice to change. The time taken to work through from the head level to the gut feelings can be normalized by the therapist and may even be worth anticipating at the early stages of therapy. At other times, the client's difficulties in feeling any different are an indication that one needs to move to another cognitive level.

Where trauma occurs before a child has developed linguistic abilities, the impact may be coded not in language but, rather, in other sensory modalities, such as touch, tone of voice, bodily sensations or shapes that have no meaning, called 'The Cloud' by Layden et al. (1993). We need then to switch to more emotional ways of working, using experiments, imagery, drawings, role-play or methods such as Gestalt 'two chairs' to dialogue between different voices of the self, as shown in the example of Manesh on page 154. We may also be attempting to use standard methods to work with core beliefs; again, we may need to switch to more appropriate methods such as continua or positive data logs described in Chapter 7.

DIFFICULTIES WITH BEHAVIOURAL EXPERIMENTS

The idea of conducting experiments to test out beliefs that have been held for a long time, or dropping safety behaviours, not doing things to try and cope with what can seem like overwhelming emotions is, not surprisingly, a challenging area for therapists and clients alike. In research evaluating SP/SR used during cognitive therapy training, trainees reported that experiments, although the most rewarding in terms of emotional change, were the most anxiety-provoking aspect, requiring most support from the therapist (Bennett-Levy, 2003). There are many common pitfalls that need to be taken into account when devising experiments and, when things do not go according to plan, we need to be flexible in making the outcome a useful one for the client. The best policy with experiments is to try and prevent problems arising, by careful advance planning, predicting possible difficulties in advance and making sure the outcome, whatever it is, is a no-lose one. Rouf et al. (2004) give an excellent overview of common pitfalls, including:

- Aiming too high, or too low, with experiments: if it is too easy, then no real learning can occur; if too anxiety-provoking, high affect may impair carrying out the experiment, or learning from it;
- Not taking into account therapists' or clients' reservations; not listening to doubts; checking that we are not 'bullying' our clients or asking them to do something we would not do ourselves;
- Testing the untestable: working on predictions that are too much in the future or even after death (e.g. testing whether blasphemous thoughts will lead to eternal misery, or whether panic attacks are linked with later heart disease);
- The client carries out the experiment but is using subtle or not-so-subtle safety behaviours so it is not possible to fully assess the outcome (managing to go shopping in a busy supermarket but never looking at anyone else, or chewing gum to reduce anxiety);

- The prediction comes true: a client worried about being sick when panicky threw up in the therapy session; another person collecting evidence from other people about their opinions of her was told by one that she was, as she feared, rather boring;
- There may be issues of physical safety and working within sensible limits – for example, a client who wanted to test out her beliefs about being safer than she thought suggested walking alone around dark areas at night; another middle-aged, overweight man suggested running a mile very fast to test his new-found beliefs that his chest pains did not mean heart disease.

Conducting experiments can also challenge the therapeutic relationship, where something does not go according to plan and the client believes the therapist was at fault (which may or may not be the case), or where boundary issues become relevant when conducting experiments outside the therapy setting, such as working with agoraphobic people testing fears of fainting in a shopping centre (see for example Rouf et al., 2004; Sanders and Wills, 2003). We need therefore to think, predict and be open to discuss the outcome and any difficulties that arise with experiments, and deal respectfully with boundary issues. For examples of common pitfalls, and vignettes of when all does not go according to plan, we recommend Bennett-Levy et al. (2004).

DIFFICULTIES WITH STRUCTURING SESSIONS AND AGENDAS

Wills (2005a) found that setting agendas and keeping sessions structured were the most difficult skills to master for counsellors undertaking cognitive therapy training, and is a commonly reported problem of both trainees and experienced therapists alike (Burns, 1999b). We have all had sessions that wander, meander or appear aimless, where we seem in a battle with the client to work out an agenda, the person being determined to 'tell all' and launch into the session topic before we have got a clear idea of what to cover. Difficulties arise if the therapist has not, at the beginning of therapy, fully explained the purpose of agendas by 'socializing' the person as discussed in Chapter 4, and where the client may come along to therapy expecting to be able to spend the time talking through whatever is on top without interruption.

Difficulties with agendas may occur because the client is generally unclear and disorganized, finding it hard to keep focused on one issue, which may happen with people who are very depressed. In this case, we may need to work harder to keep the session on focus, making sure we pick only one or two small session items and stick to these. Regular summaries help, reflecting 'Where are we now? We seem to have gone off course'. Having a written agenda literally out on the table for both to look at can help keep sessions on track.

People may come along to therapy saying they 'don't know' what to cover – the problems may seem overwhelming, or they avoid thinking about them during the week. It can help to ask clients, as a homework task, to spend half an hour before sessions thinking about and writing down clearly what they want to achieve during the time, or what is most important to cover. If a client predicts that therapy is more use without an agenda, we could experiment – one session being agenda-less, another with an agenda – to see what works best. Similarly therapists may be reluctant to do agendas, or regularly forget to do them, perhaps having reservations about their value or whether agendas inhibit spontaneous and potentially more valuable issues from arising. In which case, the therapist could try to work with and without agendas, as above. Difficulties with agendas and structure may arise for clients who believe 'I have to tell my therapist every detail otherwise she won't understand', or 'Unless I say everything, I may miss something important', in which case it helps to identify the rule, and encourage the client to try out saying only a few things about the problem, to see how much information is necessary to work with an issue. We may have difficulties keeping sessions structured when the client is ruminating in sessions, so we are hearing a long stream of a thinking process. Reflecting on what is going on, and identifying metacognitive beliefs about rumination, as above, can help.

We have found in practice that some people like structure, and other clients always seem to stray off, or find it hard to say exactly what they want to cover until the session has got going. The answer probably lies in being flexible, while keeping a general eye on the issue of structure, and taking any chronic problems to supervision.

DIFFICULTIES WITH HOMEWORK

Homework is an integral part of cognitive therapy, and, indeed, completion of homework is linked to the success or otherwise of therapy (Garland and Scott, 2002; Kazantzis and Lampropoulos, 2002). Homework also presents some of the most common difficulties in cognitive therapy, often simply by being forgotten or otherwise not completed, not understood, or itself causing the client problems (see Figure 8.1, which includes information from Burns, 1999b).

While it is gratifying for both client and therapist for homework to proceed smoothly, difficulties with homework can also be a vital part of therapeutic change, allowing for understanding of the problems the client is facing in 'real life' and enabling the client to work them through. The conceptualization can be very useful in dealing with difficulties with homework. Some clients' responses to homework can be anticipated early on in therapy: for example, clients who are perfectionist or obsessional may well be paralysed by the need to produce the perfect homework, or be unable to complete a thought record unless every single thought is recorded, a task which becomes so onerous as to be 'best forgotten'. Where procrastination is part of the client's picture, homework can prove both a useful behavioural experiment and a source of further data.

One obvious problem arises when the therapist does not ask the client, from one week to another, how they got on with homework, thus giving a powerful message that the work was not really necessary or valuable. Therefore, reviewing homework must be integrated into the beginning of every session. Another common

Figure 8.1   Common Difficulties with Homework

- The homework is not understood;
- The therapist has not explained it properly;
- The therapist did not work through an example in the session;
- Homework relies on an ability the client is not skilled in – e.g. expressing the self in writing, difficulties in reading or hearing therapy tapes; or experiments involving skills the client does not have;
- The client cannot see the point of doing homework;
- The homework is too frightening (e.g. behavioural experiments);
- The client has a general tendency to avoid or put off difficult things;
- Emotional reasoning: 'I don't feel like doing it so I won't do it'; 'I'll start when I feel like it'
- Specific beliefs get in the way: 'I have to do it right or perfectly'; 'If anyone sees my writing they'll think badly of me';
- The therapist forgets to ask about last week's homework so the client thinks it is not important;
- The term 'homework' brings up difficult memories;
- Depression and hopelessness get in the way of starting homework;
- The client forgets due to memory problems, perhaps related to depression;
- Social concerns: e.g. someone else may see a diary with negative consequences;
- Homework relies on other people who are not cooperative or able to help;
- The client does not have the time or energy;
- Specific thinking biases;
- Not doing homework is a way of expressing anger or negative feelings towards the therapist;
- Low frustration tolerance: it feels bad or difficult, so it's easier not to do it;
- Issues of shame about the problems, about writing;
- Difficulties with concentration;
- Needing to understand 'why' I am like I am before doing anything to change;
- Fear of change.

problem is that the client simply forgets the homework. It is therefore necessary to have some written record, for both client and therapist, of what the homework was; in addition, we have consistently found therapy tapes to be a valuable reminder for our clients. The client may fear the therapists' response if homework is not done 'correctly', awakening previous experiences of being chastized for things going wrong. It may be that the client does not know how to do the assignment, and both therapist and client were unaware of this. For example, a socially anxious client was unable to do a homework assignment of holding a short conversation with a colleague at work. Rather than being too anxious about the consequences, he simply did not know how to initiate a conversation. In this case, the task highlighted an important area for the client to work on.

We may need to explore the pros and cons of doing homework, as well as the person's motivations, perhaps linked to concerns about changing, or thoughts such as 'I can't be bothered, what's the point' which get in the way. The client's response to homework must be accepted in an understanding and collaborative way, viewing difficulties as problems to be solved jointly rather than a failure on the part of the client. The relevant therapist skill is the ability to negotiate 'no-lose' homework: whatever happens the client finds the experience valuable. For example, finding that a client is unable to keep a record of thoughts highlights a tendency to suppress any difficult thoughts that come to mind. Another person with chronic fatigue syndrome was asked to schedule in one enjoyable and restful activity for him every day, which he found impossible. His difficulty in doing this task highlighted strongly to him his need to do 'useful' things, or activities that were useful to others, to the expense of himself. Whether the homework is done or not, the results can be analysed in cognitive terms and tied to the formulation.

In practice, we all have examples of goals we would really like to attain: a tidier house; getting more exercise; spending less time watching TV; losing weight; or generally moving towards being 'better' people. However, the desire to change is not actually matched by moves towards putting the changes into practice; such changes are more likely to be sabotaged by a variety of mundane and human factors rather than by subconscious forces. Difficulties in doing homework may then be normalized, and tackled in the same way as one would tackle getting started on a variety of projects: Is the problem a lack of motivation, and if so, what does that mean? Is the problem a lack of information? Needing more help from others? Needing to get other tasks out of the way before being able to get down to homework? In this way, understanding the difficulties may lead to simple solutions, or may reveal important issues that need to be addressed.

IT'S SOMEONE ELSE'S PROBLEM

'How can some people treat me so badly?'
'Very easily' replied Albert Ellis. 'Some people are very good at it'. (Ellis, 1993)

Problems can arise when the client wants to solve his or her problem by getting someone else to behave differently: 'I want my partner to treat me better'; 'I'd be OK if my boss gave me the recognition I need at work' and so on. On occasions, it is possibly true, and the individual would be better off with a nicer partner or boss. Sometimes it can seem heartless to say that people have to take responsibility for their problems, even if someone else is causing them. Unless we are working with couples or groups, in individual therapy, we can only look at the client's contribution to interpersonal issues, related to underlying rules and beliefs, and what action the individual can or cannot take. People can inadvertently draw complimentary responses from other people (the socially phobic person behaving oddly; the angry person making everyone else uptight) and these can be fruitfully looked at in therapy.

If the client is 'going on' about how badly someone else is behaving, and how 'He makes me feel X', rather than focusing on the other person, ask 'How can you respond when he does that?', thereby bringing the discussion back to the client. We can examine feelings, related to specific thoughts ('How dare he'; 'He hates me'). We can also say, 'Let's work on some ways which will increase the possibility that your partner will treat you better. For example, we can look at you being clear about what you'd like him to do and be able to tell him without being angry or sulky. How does that sound?' However, in the worst case scenario, the partner may never come up with the metaphorical goods, so we also need to look at what would happen if the client got a negative response.

DEALING WITH STUCK POINTS

Cognitive therapy is, no doubt, a challenging therapy to work with, for both therapist and client, and is perhaps more active and demanding on therapist energies than other forms of counselling and therapy, particularly when learning the model or working with people with difficulties which are newer to us. As a result, it is not uncommon for the therapist to get overconcerned about the technical aspects of therapy to an extent that is actually paralyzing: rather than listening to what the client has to say, we may be thinking about what kind of intervention may be required, whether we are 'doing it right', and whether we should be reading more journals on the client's difficulties before being able to help the client. Although these technical aspects of therapy are important, they are to be used in the service of therapy rather than to its detriment. It is not uncommon for trainees, as well as more experienced, cognitive therapists to throw all the basics out of the window in order to practise cognitive techniques, but in the process somehow get lost. Again, when the therapist is unsure where to go next, it is tempting to try yet another technique. However, at stuck points or at points where the therapist is not sure where to go next, it is usually far more helpful to collaborate with the client to jointly think of a solution. Simply reflecting back to the client: 'It seems as if we are going round in circles and we're not clear where to go from here: what do you think?' allows for more collaboration than just trying something out in the hope that it will work.

Thinking and reflection time, for both client and therapist, is essential. Reflection is well known to be a component of adult education theory as well as a key aspect of developing therapist skills (see Bennett-Levy, 2005) and time to think, reflect and digest is necessary for both therapists and clients. Cognitive therapy can be very demanding on the energy, and not therefore conducive to having an 'off day'. However, we have often been surprised at how such apparent therapist off days, when our brains do not want to do good cognitive therapy, have resulted in useful sessions: when we have gone back to basics, listened more, collected more information, summarized and used good therapy skills, sessions have moved on from a stuck phase to useful material or insights for future work. The concept of going back to basics is also useful for trainees, when feeling that they should be more interventionist but unsure of where to go next.

The Gestalt concept of the 'fertile void' can be valuable when used in cognitive therapy. The 'fertile void' (Van Dusen, 1958) describes a place where one is seemingly stuck, where old doors have been closed but new ones have not yet opened. Rather than viewing such a place in a negative light, and rushing forward, the void can be a place to stop, take stock, and reflect before deciding where to go next. Similarly, therapy may be rushing ahead without sufficient time for the client to reflect and absorb: in which case, suggestions include making time in sessions to summarize and think, asking clients to write down summaries and their thoughts on therapy so far, or spacing out sessions.

THERAPY RESULTS IN LITTLE CHANGE

We have emphasized throughout the book the empirical nature of cognitive therapy, seeking to measure what is going on, and measure changes in the client's mood or presenting problems. Hence, as therapy proceeds, we regularly assess whether or not the therapy is 'working' or whether either a different way of working, or even a different form of therapy, is required (Beck et al., 1979). If short-term standard cognitive therapy is going to be helpful to the client, some form of change is usually evident after a few sessions. It is always encouraging if client and therapist are able to come up with at least a preliminary conceptualization of the difficulties in the first session or two, leading, if not to improvements in mood, at least to increased hope that things might get better. This is not always the case, however. Although it is important, and therapeutically effective, for the therapist to be 'upbeat' and optimistic about the therapy, it is also important not to raise false hopes, especially in people who have tried different forms of therapy to no avail. Initially only contracting for a few sessions and reviewing after this time to see if the therapy is on course enables us to be both optimistic and realistic. Should the therapy not work, other solutions such as long-term therapy, referral on to another agency or a combination of therapy and medication may well be called for.

We stress the importance of making realistic expectations about what is possible when clients continue to have severe life difficulties. We, or our client, may have expectations that therapy will enable the scores on the BDI to come to the normal, non-depressed range. However, the client may seem able to feel better in sessions, but the messages from partners, friends or family and ongoing social and environmental difficulties are likely to hold more impact and require addressing in order to facilitate long-term change.

LOW MOTIVATION TO CHANGE

While we may assume that our clients want to see us, this may not always be the case (Leahy, 2001). Therapy may arise as a result of family pressures, difficulties in a relationship or generally pressure from others; keeping a job, or avoiding a prison sentence, may be contingent on receiving therapy. Not surprisingly, the client may not engage well. Clients who are severely depressed may have little motivation to attend or engage in therapy, feeling too hopeless to believe that there is any point in trying to change. Whatever the difficulty in motivation, it clearly needs addressing at an early stage. For clients who are not there of their own free wills, finding something that they can, personally, get out of therapy may increase motivation: keeping a relationship may be one goal, but feeling better or meeting important goals in life may be more powerful incentives. For severely depressed people, moving slowly towards increasing levels of activity, using activity scheduling, may increase their general motivation; the use of anti-depressant medication may also lift these clients' mood sufficiently to enable them to engage in the process of change.

We cannot underestimate the effects of the individual's situation and environment on their motivation and ability to change. While the client may be willing, their spouse or family may like things as they are, or resent the therapist for meddling in personal affairs. Helping clients to feel better about themselves is extremely difficult when their world includes few or no supportive relationships. The consequences of feeling better – being more assertive, less anxious and so on – need to be carefully assessed in the context of the individual's world. Sometimes, working with the client's partner or family can be very helpful, exploring their attitudes to and concerns about therapy. Working in the therapeutic world, it is sometimes easy for us to forget that the stigma of mental illness and psychotherapies is still alive and well: we may need to convince the client's partner that we are not aiming to brainwash the client or stuff their head full of 'false memories'.

MISMATCHES

Not all clients are suitable for cognitive therapy, or at least some will need a highly modified form of it. Safran and Segal (1990) have devised a scale for calculating suitability and Young et al. (2003) review when short-term, standard cognitive therapy may not be appropriate. It is worth reviewing such criteria, discussed in Chapter 4, when assessing why therapy may not be helping. Just as not all clients may be suitable for cognitive therapy, the same may be true of therapists. Most of the things that go wrong in cognitive therapy have an echo in both therapist and client, reminding us of the interpersonal nature of therapy. Some therapists may feel embarrassed or reluctant to be seen as directive, which can inhibit the ability to structure the session or set homework. This can lead to a sense of vagueness or half-heartedness in the therapist that can be experienced as confusing by the client. We look further at therapy–therapist matches in Chapter 11. At this stage, we move to looking at how difficulties in the therapeutic relationship are identified and resolved in cognitive therapy.

DIFFICULTIES IN THE THERAPEUTIC RELATIONSHIP

Difficulties in the therapeutic relationship can be broadly defined as anything that threatens the core conditions of the relationship, including therapeutic empathy, listening to the client, keeping the boundaries, and keeping a structure both within sessions and across therapy. One of the most common relationship difficulties is a problem with collaboration. Rather than client and therapist working together, in an open manner, the therapist may become 'the expert' and start to offer directive advice, or do all the work in sessions; tasks may be set, not negotiated; the client may become 'over compliant' or 'non compliant', for example agreeing with the therapist on homework tasks and then not carrying them out. The client may find a collaborative relationship very difficult, related to themes of distrust, low confidence in having anything to offer, or believing that the therapist ought to be the expert. In addition, the client may simply not know how to be collaborative, or may fear change. During therapy, the client may not cooperate or may 'go through the motions' but not really engage with therapy. The client may avoid looking at issues of importance previously agreed on, or avoid feeling or expressing any emotion, making the sessions dry and sterile.

Problems may arise if the client and therapist do not share the same conceptualization of the client's problems. The therapist may have arrived at a working conceptualization of the client's difficulties, and the client may agree in principle with the model but not believe that it applies to them personally. These differences can cause relationship difficulties even before therapy commences. The therapist may have difficulty in empathizing with the client, seeing the person as a mass of problems rather than as the person she or he is or arguing with the client. Both client and therapist may end up in the role of client.

Although it is possible to define and describe difficulties in the therapeutic relationship, in practice, actual difficulties may be missed. The therapeutic relationship involves engagement at the level of emotion and of interpersonal communication that may be non-verbal, and therefore hard at times to describe. However, when difficulties are encountered, something almost intangible occurs: a vague feeling of discomfort, or behaviours that on the surface look straightforward but do not ring true, such as therapist or client being persistently late for sessions, always armed with a good excuse. A helpful marker is the shift from the sessions seeming alive, with a sense of therapist and client working together in an active way, to a dead feeling, where one or other or both are going through the motions without any movement. Only when stepping back and trying to describe and analyse what is occurring, can the difficulties be understood and conceptualized.

Various factors external to the client and therapist may cause difficulties in the therapeutic relationship (Wright and Davis, 1994). These include the type or length of therapy, the situation, such as medical, mental health or educational sessions where there is strong pressure to 'cure' people in a fixed length of time and long waiting lists, social or cultural factors, financial issues, or effects of the client's real life social circumstances. Difficulties in the therapeutic relationship may reflect a mismatch between the client's needs and the therapist's style (Wright and Davis, 1994). For example, the high level of structure, Socratic questioning, or the empirical approach in cognitive therapy may not suit some clients, being so incompatible with their beliefs and assumptions as to make developing a therapeutic relationship extremely difficult. While some clients may want us to be active and directive, others prefer a non-directive or relatively inactive therapeutic style.

The client's problems themselves may impinge on the therapeutic relationship: for example, if the client is very depressed and hopeless, the therapist needs to be more energetic and hopeful; panic or phobic clients want the therapist's help in avoiding anxiety, and may therefore resent the cognitive therapist's attempts to elicit anxiety in sessions. Therefore, both individual therapist and client characteristics and the characteristics of the therapy can cause difficulties.

Newman (1994) outlines four common areas of difficulty within the relationship in cognitive therapy, which he calls 'resistance'. These include:

1. Not doing agreed homework tasks;
2. Reacting to improvements with scepticism;
3. Showing high levels of expressed emotion to the therapist;
4. Subtly avoiding things within sessions.

WORKING WITH DIFFICULTIES IN THE THERAPEUTIC RELATIONSHIP

A number of stages are involved in working with difficulties in the therapeutic relationship: assessment and weaving the issues into the conceptualization, then collaboratively sharing and working on the issues with the client (Sanders and Wills, 1999).

ASSESSMENT: BECOMING A PARTICIPANT OBSERVER

The first step to working with difficulties in the therapeutic relationship is to identify and assess what is going on (Newman, 1994; Safran and Segal, 1990). It can be very difficult to identify problems or difficulties at the time, since we are by definition a participant in the relationship with the client. Both therapist and client are likely to 'pull' from each other responses that will maintain their beliefs. Inevitably, the therapist will get sucked into the client's way of being, leading to a 'dysfunctional cognitive-interpersonal cycle' (Safran and Muran, 2003).

Safran and Muran (2003) describe a model for both identifying 'rupture markers' when the therapeutic relationship becomes strained or impaired, and intervening, using the context of the therapeutic relationship, initially to observe as well as participate in the difficulties. Methods of mindfulness – being able to observe and experience, in an open and non-judgmental way – allow the process of stepping outside one's immediate experience and thereby not only observing the experience but also changing the nature of the experience itself (Segal et al., 2003; Teasdale, 1996). Rather than being 'hooked' in the interaction, such as may happen during conversation outside of therapy, the therapist is also aware of being a participant in the encounter. The therapist then 'unhooks' from the interaction to avoid becoming so engaged in the interaction that the client's schema are, yet again, confirmed. In psychoanalytic therapy, the process is called developing an 'observing ego', 'observing self', or 'internal supervisor' (Casement, 1985). During the 'hooked' stage, the individual feels, for example, anxious, thinks anxious thoughts and behaves anxiously. During the 'unhooked' or observing stage, the person is able to observe him or herself being anxious. In the therapy situation, once the interaction is both experienced and observed, it is possible to discuss what is happening and generate hypotheses for the conceptualization.

Assessing difficulties in the relationship also requires regular supervision focusing on process issues. This may involve listening to therapy tapes, and stopping at various points to assess what was going on for the therapist and client at this stage. Once observed, we can begin to ask ourselves what is going on and what we can do about it. Newman (1994) suggests a number of questions we can ask:

- What is the function of the client's behaviour? What does the client fear would happen if the difficulties were not there?
- How do the problems fit with the client's conceptualization?
- When and under what circumstances has the client been similarly affected in the past?
- What therapist or client beliefs are feeding the current situation – what schema maintenance behaviours are in operation?
- Does the therapist or client lack certain skills that make it difficult to collaborate with therapy or resolve the present difficulties?
- Are there environmental factors influencing the therapy?
- Does the conceptualization need revision?

COLLABORATION

Once difficulties are identified and assessed, therapist and client work together to conceptualize and deal with the difficulties. The therapist shares her or his thoughts, as appropriate, in the service of collaboratively working with the difficulties. This process must be guided by the conceptualization, and is both extremely valuable and also a stage of therapy where things can go wrong. Interventions focusing on the relationship can be threatening to clients who have had no experience of being able to discuss or resolve relationship difficulties. Therefore, grounding the interventions in the conceptualization is essential. Here-and-now examples within the session are valuable to explore difficulties, using guided discovery to identify the client's thoughts and feelings at times of alliance ruptures. The therapist can ask the client: 'When I said x, it looked as though it was uncomfortable: what went through your mind just then?'

Therapists must acknowledge their own contribution to the experience, and not blame or pathologize the client (Kahn, 1991). Rather than saying, 'I feel like you are trying to control the interaction', therapists may offer their own feelings: 'I feel like I am involved in a struggle with you at the moment. I am not sure what is going on: How does this relate to your feelings right now?' The therapist may wish to say: 'I feel like I am giving you a lecture at the moment, and am not sure why this is so', or 'I feel quite puzzled when you tell me you are sad but laugh at the same time'. The therapist's response does not aim to reassure the client, but holds the moment by implying that they can sort out the problem together (Kahn, 1991). Layden et al. (1993) operationalize working on the therapeutic relationship in terms of questions the therapist can ask her/himself before offering interventions at the level of the therapeutic relationship: 'How will my patient benefit from this intervention?' and 'How will I benefit from this intervention?' If the answer to the latter is more apparent than the answer to the former, the intervention should be postponed and reflected on, by self-reflection and supervision.

The process of learning cognitive therapy involves both mastering techniques and integrating these into the context of the relationship, juggling the art and science of therapy, a process that develops as the therapist's skills increase. For those new to the model, remembering the 'therapy' in cognitive therapy at all times is extremely important, and if in doubt about what to do or where to go next, reflect, summarize, empathize, listen or even leave a short silence rather than throwing in another technique or becoming directive in order to feel more in control. We know that on its own a good therapeutic relationship is helpful; the converse is also true, that a bad therapeutic relationship, despite a technically proficient therapy, is likely to do more harm than good. Making the relationship the refuge when not sure where to go next allows both client and therapist thinking time in a safe way.

Waddington (2002), in a review of the therapeutic relationship, sets out tasks for the therapist to enable us to look after our therapeutic relationships:

- Elicit the client's view of the relationship by asking for regular feedback;
- Aim to generate hope in the relationship, by encouraging the client to believe in the possibility of change;
- Use cognitive skills to establish a good relationship, using collaboration, guided discovery, thought records and other cognitive methods;
- Pay attention to and work with difficulties in the relationship, rather than attributing them to 'client resistance';
- Use cognitive methods on the self, to enable the therapist to deal with one's own issues which impact on therapy;
- Pay attention to generalization from the therapeutic relationship, exploring the way in which issues in the therapeutic relationship, such as ruptures or ways of dealing with conflict, mirror other relationships, and how what is learned within therapy might act to improve other relationships;
- Use supervision to focus on relationship issues.

CONCLUSION

We have, in this chapter, given a flavour of the difficulties which may arise in cognitive therapy and a flavour of the way in which a cognitive therapist might set about solving such difficulties. Some arise from the tasks and methods of cognitive therapy; other issues, to do with the interpersonal nature of the encounter, are likely to be familiar across all therapies. The philosophy behind problem resolution may be expressed as Occam's razor: *Entia non sunt multiplicanda praeter necessitatem*, or, for non Latin-speakers, 'Entities ought not to be multiplied except from necessity'. Translated into cognitive therapy terms, this means that the best solution is one that gives the most benefit for the least effort, and therefore the simplest. We have stressed the importance of a 'bottom-up' approach to dealing with difficulties, and the importance of collaboration at whatever level the difficulties occur. At times this means acknowledging our own contribution to the encounter: in the words of Albert Ellis (Dryden, 1991), being willing to be a FFHB – a 'fucked up, fallible human being' – at times of dealing with difficulties is essential (and these authors, Sanders and Wills, frequently compete with each to see who can be more of a FFHB than the other). If the therapist is able to be 'real' and admit to mistakes or uncertainties, this can be both a powerful model and a means of challenging assumptions or schemas within sessions.

Further Reading

Burns, D. (1999). *The feeling good handbook*. Harmondsworth: Penguin. (**Section 6.**)

Leahy, R. (2001). *Overcoming resistance in cognitive therapy*. New York: Guilford Press.

Leahy, R. (2003). *Roadblocks in cognitive behavioural therapy*. New York: Guilford Press.

Safran, J. D. & Muran, J. C. (2003). *Negotiating the therapeutic alliance: A relational treatment guide*. New York: Guilford Press.

9 Ending Therapy and Preventing Relapse

Cognitive therapy is, frequently, time-limited, focusing on the goals that the client brings to therapy, and the success, or otherwise, in meeting those goals. Cognitive therapy's reputation for being a short-term therapy leaves it open to the criticism that it does not get to the root of a client's problems and potentially leaves the client stranded at the end. In this chapter, we look at the issues surrounding ending therapy, and making sure that the client neither feels that their core difficulties have not been solved, nor feels left high and dry when therapy finishes. We discuss how to assess when to finish, the stages of ending, the value of offering follow-up sessions, and ways of helping people prepare for future difficulties and write a 'blueprint' for long-term coping. We also look at what happens when endings do not go according to plan; when the client abruptly terminates or disappears; when the client does not feel any better at the end of therapy; or when other unresolved issues get in the way of a satisfactory ending.

ENDINGS IN COGNITIVE THERAPY

Beck originally developed cognitive therapy for depression to be conducted over 12 to 20 sessions, and research evidence has shown that the therapy can be, and often is, very effective in this kind of time frame. This relatively short-term aspect has made the cognitive approach a popular one where time and resources are under particular constraints: for example, therapy settings within the Health Service. No doubt, also, the brief nature of cognitive therapy means that client and therapist are more likely to work parsimoniously and efficiently: 'Being under sentence of termination doth most marvellously concentrate the material' (Dryden and Feltham, 1992: 159). A short time frame would normally allow for full work at the 'bottom end', symptom and thought level, and a certain amount of work on assumptions, and possibly begin to reframe beliefs, depending on the kinds and length of problems the client brings to therapy. However, a short time frame would probably only allow a certain amount of working through at the 'top end' of the formulation, and normally major assumption and/or core-belief work is held to take considerably longer periods of therapy. For example, if a client's main goal is to get rid of panic attacks and be able to go out more and progress with their life, then short-term work can be effective, and both help the client with the presenting problem and, directly or indirectly, begin to change some beliefs or improve self-esteem. For depression, short-term work can alleviate the current episode, and equip the person with methods for dealing with future episodes. If the client has long-term, enduring difficulties in many areas of life, although good work can be done in short-term therapy, it is probably necessary to work also at the level of beliefs, thereby necessitating longer therapy.

Whether short- or long-term therapy is needed can to some extent be estimated during the assessment phase of the work and taken into account when setting goals. Ending therapy is therefore a phase of therapy that, in fact, starts right at the beginning when negotiating a contract with the client (Wills, 1997). During goal setting, the topic of ending is noted, for example by asking the client to think about questions such as 'How will your life be different once therapy is finished?' and 'How will we know when we've finished?' Commonly, the therapist gives the client an exact number of sessions that are available: something in the region of 6 to 20 for anxiety, 12 to 20 for depression, and so on. Whether the therapy is likely to last one month or one or two years, it is important to be explicit about the dates when the therapy will be reviewed, as well as being explicit about the possible time scale of therapy and therefore about the ending. Both client and therapist need frequent reminders of where the therapy has got to, which includes looking back at the progress made and forward to future sessions. Sometimes it is helpful to remind the client how many sessions are left at every session; sometimes incorporating reviews every few sessions serves as a reminder without appearing too much like a number cruncher. Some clients have difficulties ending things and working through these difficulties may help them, perhaps for the first time, to have the experience of a satisfactory ending to an important relationship. Whatever the number of sessions, frequent reviews every six sessions or so enable both client and therapist to check that they are on course. Sometimes it may even be appropriate to end somewhat ahead of schedule.

Another important characteristic of cognitive therapy is that it aims to help clients to become their own therapists, by teaching them ways of helping themselves across a number of situations or problems. Although, when working as any form of therapist, our clients are the centre of our professional lives, the therapy may not be so central to the client's life, and learning goes on apart from and after the sessions. As stated by Judith Beck: 'A therapist who views himself as responsible for helping the patient with every problem risks engendering or reinforcing dependence and deprives the patient of the opportunity to test and strengthen her skills' (1995: 269). One of the key advantages of the cognitive approach is its ability to transfer the benefits of work during therapy to the client's life after therapy. Such generalization and transfer of learning can be major factors in preventing relapse. The message throughout therapy is that the real work is a function of what goes on between sessions as well as within sessions, expressed as a concentration on homework and practising therapeutic gains across different situations. The cognitive approach seems to have a key advantage in helping to militate against the 'wash out' of gains over time (Hollon, 2003). Therefore, ending therapy is concerned with what the client has learned and how he or she will cope with various different situations or difficulties in the future.

Leading on from this 'learning' function of cognitive therapy are the ways in which ending therapy might be extremely difficult for some people, for example those whose hopelessness prevents them from being able to generalize from sessions or those with issues of dependence who believe themselves incapable of disengaging from the therapist and coping alone. Thus, the stage of ending, as for other stages of therapy, requires both identification of and working through such issues. Therapists too may have issues about ending with some clients, for instance where pressures from workplace constraints mean that we can only offer a fixed number of sessions, thereby ending therapy with some clients earlier than we would like; where we feel we have not done a 'good enough job'; where there are unresolved therapeutic relationship issues; or where endings bring up other issues in ourselves.

THE PROCESS OF ENDING

Termination is more than an act signifying the end of therapy; it is an integral part of the process of therapy and, if properly understood and managed, may be an important factor in the instigation of change. (Yalom, 1975: 365)

Ending therapy can represent a real or symbolic loss, and how it is handled can make a difference to the outcome. Endings can be planned and deliberate, known about at the beginning and reached as planned but, not uncommonly, therapy ends prematurely if the client terminates early and unexpectedly, or the therapist changes jobs or geographical area; illness or unexpected life events can also interrupt therapy. Despite the importance of endings in therapy, and clinical experience of unclear or 'messy' endings, they seem surprisingly under-discussed in the cognitive therapy literature, with the exception of Safran and Segal (1990), Safran and Muran (2003) and Judith Beck (1995). Beck and colleagues pertinently remind us of the importance of handling endings well: 'Because cognitive therapy is time-limited, the problems associated with termination are usually not as complex as those associated with longer forms of treatment. However, much of the benefit of cognitive therapy can be lost through in-appropriate or inept closure' (1979: 317).

One way of understanding the end of cognitive therapy is to conceptualize it as a process or stage that needs to be given an appropriate amount of time and attention, rather than a sudden cessation of activity, with four main tasks (Horton, 2006):

1. Seeking resolution of issues around ending;
2. Exploring ways of consolidating learning and change;
3. Identifying obstacles to maintaining changes;
4. Evaluating the outcomes of therapy and the effectiveness of therapeutic process and relationship.

Having a good formulation of the client's beliefs and assumptions is an invaluable aid in predicting and working with potential difficulties in ending therapy.

On approaching ending, therapists can ask themselves: 'What does this client's conceptualization tell me about how the client is likely to see ending?' The client's response to ending can be identified and worked with in a collaborative way, and be seen as the opportunity for one last piece of, perhaps crucial, therapeutic learning. For example, beliefs concerned with dependency on others or that the client is unable to cope alone are likely to be activated during the ending of therapy, particularly if client and therapist have formed a good therapeutic relationship. For other clients, where therapy has been less helpful, beliefs such as 'No one can help me' may be activated and strengthened. If such issues have already emerged, as we hope they would have done in good therapy, then they will already have been incorporated into the conceptualization and thus will have shown themselves in attempts to predict the course of therapy. For some clients, these predictions can be very valuable as they allow the therapist to offer the client the chance to make a deliberately good end to the therapy. This, having been an elusive experience for them in other types of relationships, can therefore prove to be a very valuable learning experience and an excellent way to finish therapy.

Ending therapy involves assessing the client's readiness for the end of therapy, addressing and resolving remaining issues, bringing about appropriate closure of the relationship, and consolidating what has been gained and learned during therapy so that the client can carry on using these gains after therapy has ended. The extent to which each of these stages is emphasized depends on the individual client and the therapy situation.

ASSESSING WHEN TO END COGNITIVE THERAPY

The usual criteria for when to stop therapy are when the allocated number of sessions has been completed and, ideally, the client feels better about the presenting problems, is acting differently in life, or at least working in that direction, and is able to predict and prevent future difficulties. The client's goals for therapy and the extent to which they have been met need to be the main guiding factors, and the simplest, and most collaborative, way of assessing when to end therapy is to ask the client. It is important, however, that the goals, set by both client and therapist, are realistic. Therapy is not likely to resolve all problems, remove all symptoms or result in a 'complete cure', and people may well still experience the symptoms that led them to seek help in the first place. It is also not realistic for any of us to expect never to feel anxious, low, upset or angry again. Therefore one of the goals of therapy may have been to be more accepting of emotions and distress. This may be particularly important for people who do not easily express or experience feelings, who may be feeling significantly more emotionally fluid since starting therapy, perhaps noticing and expressing emotions in a way that was previously uncharacteristic.

One way of beginning the end of therapy is to increase the time between sessions. Even when good progress has been made, clients quite often wish to have a period of consolidation before ending. The therapist and client may meet weekly during the initial stages of therapy, but may then spread out the sessions to every two or three weeks. In addition, clients are encouraged to see the therapist for follow-up sessions approximately three, six and twelve months after ending. Spacing sessions in this way enables the client to have more time between sessions in which to practise and consolidate gains made during therapy, and also allows any potential difficulties to arise before therapy has ended.

There may be times when ending is less clear. The client may have doubts about ending therapy or may want to end therapy 'early', when important issues are left dangling. Some people may want to stop, understandably, at the point of feeling better, perhaps wanting to avoid looking at underlying issues or assumptions in case further work makes them feel worse for a while. The client may 'give up' on therapy before giving it a good try. In this case, therapist and client can work out the pros and cons of both ending therapy and continuing (Beck, 1995) in order, collaboratively, to arrive at a decision. Towards the end of therapy the therapist can act as 'devil's advocate' for the client: the client can put forward the arguments in favour of ending therapy and how to cope in future, and the therapist can attempt to challenge these, to help the client clarify possible issues in ending therapy.

DEALING WITH UNRESOLVED ISSUES AND ENDING THE THERAPEUTIC RELATIONSHIP

During the final stages of cognitive therapy, the client may identify issues that have not been resolved during previous sessions, requiring collaboration in working out how best to deal with these issues. It may be possible to negotiate a number of additional sessions; it may be more appropriate to look for other sources of help such as relationship therapy. Some clients may bring important issues to the last session, with the flavour of a 'parting shot', leaving the therapist puzzled, frustrated or annoyed, which may mean that therapy ends with an 'unfinished' feeling. It may be that these issues are too difficult or threatening for the client to work with them or they may have been brought up as a way of continuing the therapeutic relationship. It is important to try to discuss what has happened and offer some understanding in terms of the client's conceptualization.

The end of the therapy relationship may evoke a variety of feelings including loss and grief, and Safran and Segal (1990) note that ending therapy can activate specific interpersonal schema, such as those of abandonment and dependence. Addressing and discussing these feelings is an important part of the stage of ending therapy, enabling the client's reactions to be understood as part of the overall conceptualization. The client can be encouraged to look at any similarities between ending therapy and other endings, and invited to think about how they usually handle saying goodbye, and whether they wish to try out a different, more satisfactory way of ending the relationship, as the following example illustrates.

JOANNA

Joanna found ending any relationship extremely difficult, the feelings evoked in her being almost unbearable. She tended to always leave without saying goodbye, promising to get in touch before a friend left and then not contacting her, leaving relationships at the first sign that things may be going wrong. Her beliefs included: 'People always abandon me eventually'; 'There's no point in saying goodbye. They'll go anyway'. Her way of coping with endings avoided the pain of confronting her loss, but led to great dissatisfaction and a feeling of something missing. Towards the end of the allocated time, Joanna, predictably, started to cancel or to miss appointments. Given the pressures in the NHS to discharge people who do not attend a certain number of appointments, I (DS) was tempted to give up on Joanna, thus confirming her beliefs, but persisted instead in contacting her after a missed appointment to offer her another. When she eventually came back we were able to explore her feelings around ending her sessions, and identify ways in which she could try out a different approach to ending with me. We both worked out a way to say a more satisfactory 'goodbye' that she was able to test out in therapy.

Ending the relationship can also be a positive experience for people who have learned something about themselves and the nature of relationships through the relationship with the therapist. It may have been healing in some way or a chance for the client to work out ways of being assertive. The relationship may have been an opportunity to be honest about difficulties, and being able to discuss these with another person without being judged can enable the client to examine ways in which she or he can be honest in other relationships. During the ending phase, some clients may find it valuable to reflect on the nature of the therapeutic relationship and what has been learned about other relationships.

It is also important to discuss why change happened, and how the client attributes responsibility for change. A client who says 'If it wasn't for you ...' or 'You've made me so much better' may give the therapist a warm, self-satisfied glow. However, this should be used not to boost the therapist's self-esteem but as an opportunity to attribute progress to the client. One response to such praise might be to ask the client the proportion of the work in therapy done by the client versus therapist, or the amount of time the client has been tackling the problems (24 hours a day, 7 days a week) versus the amount of time the therapist has put in (10 hours). Dismissing their own contribution to therapy may relate to the client's beliefs around dependency or powerlessness, therefore the ending can be used to enable the person to develop alternative beliefs. Another response to ending therapy may be for the client to feel angry about the need to seek 'professional help' in the first place. Although such a response to coming for help is often looked at during the early stages of therapy, sometimes the client may have found the process of therapy to have made sense in a way that leads them to question 'Why couldn't I do it for myself?' Such responses, as for other responses to ending therapy, need careful attention.

The ending of therapy is a stage for the therapist as well as the client. If the therapist has found the client particularly difficult to work with, or therapy has not been particularly helpful, they may feel a sense of disappointment at not being able to help or relief at finishing with the client. Alternatively, sometimes it is difficult for us to end therapy at the point at which the client is improving or becoming more emotionally accessible and therefore more rewarding to work with, or where a client's developmental stage is mirroring one's own, as shown in the next example.

PAUL

Paul presented with depression, difficulties at work and questioned what he was doing with his life. During his first session, he was angry at 'having' to see me (DS), did not think there was any point in just talking about things, and simply wanted a prescription for Prozac. At the end of the first session, he reported that despite his misgivings he had found talking helpful, and was a bit more hopeful that he could sort things out. He turned out to be an easy and rewarding client to work with: he took to the cognitive model with ease, devouring the recommended self-help books, and began to make long-overdue changes to his life. He was able to make use of the depression, looking back and seeing it as a valuable indicator that he needed to take stock. I felt sad at ending therapy with him, partly because he represented an 'easy' case among a sea of more complex clients, and partly because, on reflection, I realized that some of the issues he was successfully tackling, with the flavour of a 'mid-life crisis', were those that I, too, felt were close to my own heart.

The therapist's feelings, both positive and negative, are often best dealt with during supervision, giving an opportunity to end the therapy successfully for the therapist as well as for the client. Sometimes, issues in ending are systemic: both authors have to struggle to avoid endings being driven by the needs of the clients on our waiting lists.

PREPARING FOR THE FUTURE: LONG-TERM COPING

As therapist and client begin to reach the end of therapy, they begin to review the progress that has been made and what implications the gains or lack of gains have for the ending of therapy. Cognitive therapy, as we have discussed, stresses its active and self-help nature. To a large extent, the therapy moves from more activity on the part of the therapist at the early stages, to more activity on the part of the client later on. Handing over the reins of therapy is completed at the

Figure 9.1   Therapy Flashcard

Reminder of what I have Learned:

There are times when I'm anxious, but try and swim along with it: nothing awful is going to happen.

I've been anxious many times and it's felt like something bad is going to happen, but it never has.

I know nothing bad is going to happen because during therapy I faced my worst fear: going into a public place and feeling really anxious – and still, nothing bad happened. Nobody noticed, nobody is judging me.

Even if I feel anxious and sick, I'm not going to be sick.

Even if I did feel very ill, it would not be a complete disaster: other people would help.

Don't get out of the habit of doing things – keep going despite how I feel. Make friends even if it is a bit frightening.

I KNOW I CAN DO THINGS
DON'T DWELL ON HOW I FEEL ALL THE TIME
DON'T DWELL ON THE SLIGHTEST MISTAKE I'VE MADE
IMAGINE PUTTING ALL THE WORRIES IN MY HEAD IN A RUBBISH BIN
IF I DON'T FEEL LIKE DOING SOMETHING, DO IT ANYWAY, AS AN EXPERIMENT

---

end stages. Ideally, the client will have practised new ways of seeing things, of thinking or of acting in different situations, enabling therapy gains to be generalized to a wide range of situations and life issues. Clients often need concrete reminders of progress. The pen-and-paper nature of this type of therapy enables the clients to collect written information in a therapy file or notebook, along with tapes of sessions, handouts and books. Flashcards give clients instant reminders of key points during the therapy. A therapy flashcard is shown in Figure 9.1.

Another model used in practice is a Positive Cycle, such as that shown in Figure 9.2. The early stages of therapy focused on Elaine's negative spiral, the factors maintaining her low mood and negative feelings about herself. Later on in therapy, we drew up a positive spiral, incorporating things she needed to do in order to carry on feeling well and work on improving her self esteem and accepting herself. She stuck the positive cycle on her fridge, as a reminder of the direction she wanted to stay facing.

The method of 'point counterpoint', similar to rational role play (Cromarty and Marks, 1995) can test whether someone is able to fully challenge old thoughts and assumptions. The therapist takes the voice of the old assumption or belief ('I'm rubbish if I make mistakes'; 'I've got to worry all the time to prevent bad things happening'; 'Silly cow'; 'I'm useless'; 'Don't go out just in case') and the client argues back with a new perspective, giving a counterpoint to each

Figure 9.2 Negative and Positive Cycles

A: Negative Cycle

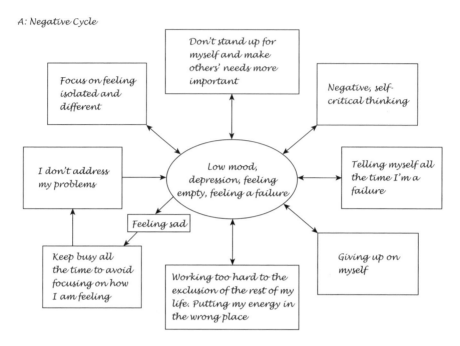

B: Positive Cycle

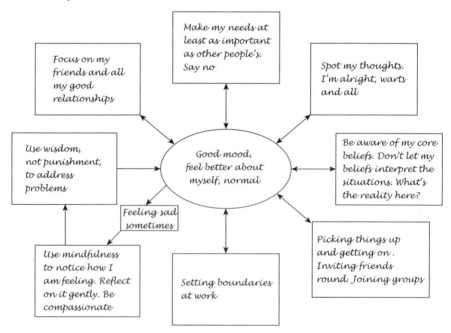

negative point the therapist voices. This needs to be done with compassion and a certain amount of humour, so we are not labelling the person, merely giving a voice to what he or she used to say about the self or the world. By hearing the negative view, and coming up with a different perspective, the client is able to practise what needs to be said when the old voices come back (Mooney and Padesky, 2000).

Although cognitive therapy aims to help the client to learn approaches that can be applied across many different situations, successful therapy does not, unfortunately, always guarantee an easy, problem-free life. Both therapist and client may, however, be reluctant to bring up the thorny issue of what happens if things go wrong – the therapist wanting to engender hope, and the client preferring not to think about future problems. But given that progress is rarely in a straight line, and that most people have some form of setback at some stage, knowing what to do is crucial.

One useful strategy is to help clients to find ways so that they do not turn a setback into a disaster, 'building a floor' under their feet that will limit how far they can fall. Setback does not necessarily mean relapse; relapse does not necessarily mean that the client is back to square one. Theoretical models of the process of change are valuable in highlighting the organic nature of change, and how we move through stages. Prochaska (2000) describes six stages:

1. Precontemplation, when we are not aware of the problem;
2. Contemplation, when we become aware and think about it;
3. Preparation, working out what to do and when to do it;
4. Action, doing something about it;
5. Maintenance, keeping up progress;
6. Relapse, when the change begins to slip.

Should clients start to experience problems, rather than viewing them as being back to square one, it can be helpful to look at ways they can get back on to the cycle, identifying the need for change and what to do in order to change. Other theoretical models include the Lewin-Kolb learning cycle (Bennett-Levy et al., 2004), which highlights the importance of reflection time as well as preparation and action in making changes.

BLUEPRINTS

During the process of ending therapy, the client can be asked to work on a 'blueprint', or first aid book, of how beneficial change will be maintained and how future problems may be handled. This process is described by Judith Beck:

> The therapist encourages the patient to read through and organise all her therapy notes so she can easily refer to them in future. For homework, she may write a synopsis of the important points and skills she has learned in therapy and review this list with the therapist … [T]he therapist prepares the client for setbacks

early in treatment. Nearing termination, the therapist encourages the patient to compose a coping card specifying what to do if a setback occurs after therapy has ended. (1995: 278)

Working on a blueprint involves at least two sessions for the client to think about the questions and work through them with the therapist. An example of a completed blueprint is given in Figure 9.3.

The stages of working on a blueprint involve inviting the client to think about what kind of difficulties may be encountered in future. What kind of problems led up to the client requesting help? Is it likely that these problems will recur? If so, what can be done? What are the early signs of problems? Who else may be able to help? The client can be encouraged to carry on working on the issues identified during therapy after therapy has ended. An important goal is for

Figure 9.3 Cognitive Therapy Blueprint

What have I learned?	Modifying my thoughts can change my feelings. I don't necessarily need tablets. I can challenge my thoughts – they are just thoughts, not facts.
	Don't slump into depression – do something. Recognize the early signs and do something about them. Allow myself to receive support from my family.
How can I build on this? What's my Plan of Action?	I can define how I want to be: more light hearted. I can learn to worry less. I can actively plan more enjoyable activities: go to the cinema; go for walks at weekends. Get my work–home life in balance. Don't allow myself to stay in bed and ruminate.
What will make it difficult for me to put this Plan of Action into practice?	Taking work home. Not going to work feeling fresh. Getting into a cycle of 'no time', 'no motivation'. Not spotting the early signs.
How will I deal with these difficulties?	Keep on reviewing the costs and benefits of positive and negative actions and thoughts. Ask J. to remind me of what I need to do and to help spot the early signs.
What might lead to a setback? For example, stresses, life problems, relationships and so on.	Problems at work. Ill health.
If I do have a setback, what will I do about it?	Seek help early from family and friends, GP, therapist. Read the self-help books and reminders of therapy. Read this blueprint! Re-start activity scheduling and writing down thoughts.

clients to become their own therapists, or be able to use informal support networks rather than automatically relying on professional help. An example of a 'self-therapy' session is given by Judith Beck (1995), where the client can set aside time to conduct a session with herself, incorporating the usual structure of agenda, reviews, and so on.

OFFERING FOLLOW-UP SESSIONS

Many therapists will routinely offer clients one or more follow-up sessions after therapy has ended in order to review progress and work on difficulties. Offering follow-up sessions may be valuable, particularly for those clients with long-term difficulties or personality disorders. Therapist and client need to decide whether to arrange regular reviews, regardless of how the client is feeling, or more open access, that is, the client being able to contact the therapist for emergency sessions. However, continuing contact with the therapist may be a means for the client or therapist to avoid saying goodbye and having to deal with the resulting feelings of loss, or avoiding issues of dependency. We need, therefore, to be aware of the hazards as well as potential benefits of offering follow-up sessions.

SUDDEN ENDINGS

The progression of therapy through the beginning, middle to the end stages often involves satisfactory completion of each of those stages. However, we have all had the experience of clients who suddenly terminate therapy, leaving a sense of incompletion for the therapist and uncertainty about 'where we went wrong'. Such feelings indicate that there is some kind of ideal way for therapy to end, contravened by the client who just disappears, implying that the client has ended before the therapist thinks they 'should'. In a truly collaborative relationship, the client's wishes regarding termination are those on which decisions are made: thus, if the client wants to end, the therapist respects this decision and is able to deal with his or her own issues accordingly. The client's wishes to end therapy can be openly discussed, the pros and cons of ending weighed up, and the therapist can encourage the client to give honest feedback. Should the therapist want to carry on where the client wishes to end, it is possible that client and therapist are working from different conceptualizations: the therapist may believe that schema-driven issues are at the root of the problems and need to be worked on before ending, while the client might be happy to feel a bit better and get back to 'coping'.

The client's conceptualization can be used as a way of approaching sudden endings: for example, the client who has learned not to trust people, developing the belief that 'No one can really help you anyway', is likely to translate whatever happens in therapy in terms of the belief; thus, one difficult or unproductive session may lead to schema confirmation and the end of therapy. The desire to end therapy can, ideally, be both understood and handled using the case conceptualization.

The 'sudden death' kind of ending requires careful handling. When clients simply disappear we need to think about our responsibilities to follow up these people. Again, returning to the client's conceptualization, 'walking in their shoes' and carefully discussing and reviewing previous sessions may help us to understand what is going on. Sudden ending may be a way for the client to cope with the ending, or may be a way of communicating with the therapist, as in the earlier example of Joanna. The client may be acting out interpersonal strategies, part of which may be to suddenly disappear only to suddenly reappear later on. Whether or not we take the active step of contacting the client may depend on the client's particular issues. For example, following the disappearance of a client who believed 'Nobody really cares about me', the decision to pursue him was well justified by his successful re-entry into therapy. People who default from therapy, ending abruptly and not responding to letters or phone calls, can haunt us for some time: what has happened to the client? Is he or she alright? Did I do something wrong? Could I have done better? Such issues are best taken to supervision, and are in our experience a potential source of valuable clinical learning.

RELAPSE PREVENTION AND RELAPSE SIGNATURES

Cognitive therapy has focused on relapse prevention for many psychological problems, and the evidence suggests that relapse following cognitive therapy is lower than following other forms of therapy or pharmacotherapy (Butler, 2001; Hollon, 2003; Nathan and Gorman, 2002; Strunk and DeRubeis, 2001). As discussed earlier, the ending stage of therapy involves looking at what might happen should the client feel he or she is going back to square one, or seemingly insurmountable difficulties begin to arise. However, relapse can and does occur, possibly associated with the re-emergence of core issues following successful work with the client's presenting problems such as depression. One way of conceptualizing relapse prevention for these clients is to enable them to view difficulties as equivalent to chronic conditions such as diabetes, which, when looked after properly, have less impact on the individual's life than when ignored. A car analogy may be helpful: the yellow light indicates that the oil is seriously low, but it is more helpful to check and top up the oil on a regular basis than to only use the warning sign. Similarly, if the client is prone to react in a certain way when particular beliefs and assumptions are triggered, and therefore remain vulnerable to relapse, regular maintenance is crucial. Such maintenance may be in the form of regular booster sessions, regular self-reviews by the client, and learning to identify the early warning signals and respond quickly rather than waiting until a serious problem develops.

One of the keys in preventing serious relapse may be to identify early signs, and intervene by putting action plans and blueprints into practice, before problems escalate. Studies of people with repeated episodes of depression show that the process of becoming depressed can become increasingly autonomous: one slight hint or reminder of what depression feels like, the beginnings of low mood or rumination, and the person will switch mode and escalate into depression

(Segal et al., 2002). As part of mindfulness-based cognitive therapy, identifying these early markers, or 'relapse signatures' while the mood is still stable, can enable the person to take action to stop switching mode by choosing one of the skills he or she has been practising (Segal et al., 2002). Such relapse signatures for depression may include:

- Becoming more irritable;
- Withdrawing and not wanting to see people;
- Changes in sleep and eating patterns, tiredness;
- A reduction in exercise;
- Not dealing with work and things that may come up;
- Putting off deadlines.

Segal et al. (2002) stress that each person's signature is unique, and being aware of these signs, without becoming hyper-vigilant for them, is important. However, they also stress that while it is easy when feeling well to list these warning signs and see the importance of taking notice of them, when depressed, the person may not see the point of heeding them at all, or doing anything about the problem: 'I'm back to square one'. Therefore, it is also important to work out what other people could do to help detect the early signs of relapse. Segal and colleagues suggest three questions that need clear, written answers, to facilitate relapse prevention:

- What in the past has prevented me from noticing and attending to these feelings (e.g. pushing them away, denial, distraction, alcohol, arguments, blaming others)?
- How can I include other family members in my early warning system for detecting relapse?
- If depression strikes what can I do to look after myself to get me through this low period?

CONCLUSION

The end of cognitive therapy is a stage that starts right at the beginning and ends with the process of follow-up sessions. Ideally, the ending of the meetings between therapist and client is not an end to therapy, since the aim is for the client to become his or her own therapist, and be able to generalize learning to other situations or problems. The learning associated with ending therapy works both ways: ending with each of our clients gives us the opportunity to reflect on the work that we did, to reflect on the conceptualization of the particular client we developed and evolved, and, most importantly, to reflect on how we might consolidate or change our practice as a result of the journey with each individual. Blueprinting and relapse prevention are helpful notions for both client and therapist.

Further Reading

Horton, I. (2006). Structuring work with clients. In I. Horton & C. Feltham (Eds.), *Handbook of counselling and psychotherapy* (2nd ed.) (pp. 118–126). London: Sage Publications.

Murdin, L. (1999). *How much is enough? Endings in psychotherapy and counselling*. London: Routledge.

Part three

The Wider Context of Cognitive Therapy

10 Applications of Cognitive Therapy

Christine Padesky (1998) has said, possibly with tongue in cheek, that learning cognitive therapy was easy for her because there was at the time of her training, in the late 1970s, only one 'application' that had to be learned – that of Beck et al's (1979) seminal work on the cognitive therapy of depression. An aspirant cognitive therapist who took this remark too seriously might experience a sense of dysphoria when considering the range of applications that may now have to be learned. In the 2004 European CBT conference in Manchester, there were a bewildering array of symposia on 39 different areas of application. It appears that there is no problem known to human kind that cognitive therapists will not turn their hand to fixing. Cognitive models and therapy interventions have been developed in many areas, as shown in Table 10.1, and such work has been invaluable in helping people with problems such as panic, depression, obsessive-compulsive disorder, hypochondriasis, eating disorders or sleep disorders among many others.

Therefore, when learning cognitive therapy, we have to learn not only the general principles but also its applications to particular problems. Each application is based on similar overall principles, but in line with the concept of 'cognitive specificity', has significant variations on the exact way such principles are applied to various types of problems. A further complication is that people more often than not come for help with a number of different problems, co-morbidity of different psychological difficulties being the norm rather than the exception. Whatever mélange of issues our clients arrive with, we need to tease out the strands and apply the methods according to the specific problem.

In this chapter we explain some key features of the concept of 'applications of cognitive therapy'. We show such principles in action for the two most common reasons people seek psychological help: anxiety and depression. Some other general principles will then be used to illustrate how to work with common psychological processes, drawing on examples from the ever-widening web of cognitive therapy applications. We look at some of the settings in which cognitive therapy might be applied, including group work, couples and the growing area of self-help, bibliotherapy and using on-line resources and discuss the pros and cons of using therapy protocols. At the end of the chapter we list a number of texts on application to different problems. One of the messages we wish to give the reader, particularly those new to the approach, is that we do not all have to be experts on all these therapy variations. A good cognitive therapist will know how to go about finding out how to work with particular clients and be able to implement these variations

Table 10.1   Applications of Cognitive Behavioural Therapies

CT/CBT has been developed for people with the following types of problems:	CT/CBT is applied in the following types of settings:
Anxiety problems:	Mental health
	In patient
• Panic	Primary care
• Agoraphobia	Medical settings
• Social phobias	Elderly
• Simple and complex phobias	Child and adolescent
• Health anxiety	Youth work
• General anxiety	Forensic
• Worry	Education
	Social work
Post-traumatic stress disorder	Probation
	Human resources
Obsessive-compulsive disorder:	Employee assistance programmes
	Life coaching
• Obsessive rituals	
• Obsessive thoughts	Individual therapy
	Groups
Depression – moderate	Couples
Long-term, chronic depression	Bibliotherapy
Treatment-resistant and recurrent depression	Self-help groups
Post-natal depression	On-line resources
Suicidality	Telephone
Deliberate self-harm	Email
Survivors of childhood sexual abuse	
Health anxiety	
Somatization	
Unexplained medical symptoms	
Adjustment to chronic health problems	
Chronic pain	
Chronic fatigue syndrome	
Skin disorders	
Trichotillomania	
Medical problems – e.g. rumatoid arthritis	
Sleep problems	
Eating disorders	
Relationship problems	
Sexual problems	
Psychotic disorders	
Manic depression	
Hearing voices	
Delusions	
Hallucinations	
Complex personality problems	
'Personality disorders'	
Drug and alcohol problems	
Dual diagnosis	

Table 10.1   (Continued)

CT/CBT has been developed for people with the following types of problems:	CT/CBT is applied in the following types of settings:
Anger, hostility, violence Stress	
Learning disability ADHD Autism and Asperger's syndrome Stuttering Dyslexia	

fairly quickly. Both the authors have worked in various settings and, therefore, have had to become familiar with many human conditions. In our experience, however, clients can usually tolerate the therapist beginning from a position of not always completely understanding all aspects of their difficulties provided that the therapist expresses the desire to find out more about them and confidence in being able to do so. It is, in fact, our experience that the stance of 'Let's find out about this together' is actually often a good starting point with clients and begins the process of collaboration. We start, therefore, with some general principles of application.

THE CONCEPT OF APPLICATION

One of the defining features of cognitive therapy is the way that it is built on empirically researched models of psychological problems such as anxiety and depression (Salkovskis, 2002). Clark (1996) describes how the starting point for the development of a cognitive model is often a clinical observation or insight. For example, Beck's early work was based on his observation of specific negative thoughts in the depressed patients he was at that time seeing for psychoanalysis. Clinical and non-clinical research is then used to build up an understanding of the cognitive, emotional and behavioural 'architecture' of the problem. Treatment interventions are then devised to impact on the psychological mechanisms that cause and maintain these problems. As these interventions are tried and tested, they are built into whole models of intervention that are in turn tested for effectiveness. Therapists in the field are only encouraged to use these interventions when a good level of confidence in the treatment model has been achieved.

Many emotional disorders have separate and unique cognitive profiles and, therefore, have conceptualizations that are 'general' to many clients with those disorders. As we have stressed in Chapter 2, however, these general conceptualization and therapeutic approaches are 'individualized' to the unique client in question, allowing for a specific and individual formulation and therapy plan for each person we see. Each different problem has both similarities and differences. We illustrate these similarities and differences by using examples from anxiety and depression.

COGNITIVE MODELS OF ANXIETY AND DEPRESSION

The basic cognitive models of depression and anxiety are shown in Figure 10.1.

Seeing the two generic conceptualizations for anxiety and depression alongside each other helps us to see that the two models have many basic similarities. They trace out, for example, a similar pattern of influence between the thoughts, feelings and behaviours associated with depression and anxiety respectively. We can also see that there is different content in the levels of cognition, and significantly different types of problematic behaviours that would need to be targeted in order for the maintenance cycle to be disrupted, broken down and modified.

Figure 10.1 Generic Conceptualizations for Depression and Anxiety

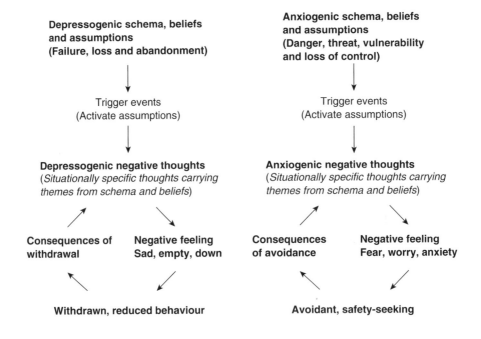

COGNITIVE CONTENT AND PROCESSES IN DEPRESSION

The content of a client's cognitions when depressed refers to thoughts that are likely to generate depressed feelings and withdrawing patterns of behaviour. At the deepest level of cognition – schema and core beliefs – the content seems to be most characterized by themes of loss and defeat (Beck, 1967,.1976; Beck et al., 1979). The theme of loss often has a very wide meaning for the depressed person. It may concern the loss of something specific like a partner, health or a job or career.

The sense of loss can, however, reach beyond objective loss to a sense of loss of faith in oneself or even the loss of having any sure sense of self at all. Given the strong links between depression and loss, it is perhaps surprising that the cognitive therapy literature has had comparatively little to say about grief and bereavement. Beck et al. (1979) describe the 'cognitive triad' where a negative sense about the self combines with a negative sense about the world and a lack of faith in the future that we might term 'hopelessness'. Hopelessness is seen as particularly powerful in determining the strength of depression. Most people can tolerate negative feelings about themselves and their lives in the short term, provided that they can see some 'light at the end of the tunnel'. The negative feelings become intolerable, however, if there is no sense of any possible release from suffering in the future. Beck et al. (1993) see hopelessness as a particularly lethal aspect of depression and strongly link hopelessness with increased danger of self-harm and suicide, and recommend that hopelessness is specifically assessed and targeted in therapy.

Cognitive theory can be strongly linked to evolutionary theory (Beck, 1991; Beck and Emery, 1985; Gilbert, 1992, 2000a). In brief, an evolutionary perspective in the cognitive therapy of depression would suggest that, after defeat, there is survival value in withdrawing resources from previous invested objects and then having a period of 'hibernation'. For example, common sense often supports the idea that it is not necessarily wise to rush into finding a new partner after the failure or loss of a relationship. Conventional wisdom – not always wrong in these matters – suggests that there is a danger of acquiring an ill-chosen new partner 'on the rebound'. Equally, if a business is failing, at some point it will become time to 'cut one's losses' and withdraw from the enterprise. In general, we allow for people in such situations to be 'a bit down' and withdrawn, at least for a while. The problem may come not so much with the initial negative reaction, but with the fact that the person in effect stays asleep when the spring arrives (Beck, 1996).

Gilbert (1992, 2000a) has suggested that evolutionary mechanisms often have an on–off mechanism. They are switched on for a while to cope with relatively short-term emergencies but once the immediate emergency has passed, they then need to be switched off. The problem with depression is that the deeper or more long lasting it becomes, the harder it can be to switch it off in this way. Gilbert (1992, 2000a) provides more support for the evolutionary idea by suggesting that 'shame', linked to low self esteem (Fennell, 1998), is also often part of the picture in depression. Again 'shame' may have ancient roots as an adaptive behaviour to cover the requirement for submission at times of defeat. Submission may be motivated by the desire to prevent further attacks by becoming the smallest threat possible. Linking psychological problems with evolutionary advantage fits well with Beck's strong desire to destigmatize many of the so called 'psychiatric' conditions, motivated by the desire to take what clients had to say about the condition seriously and not undermine it by labelling it as driven by 'unconscious factors' or 'conditioning' (Beck, 1976).

As well as factors connected to cognitive content, there are also distinctive cognitive processes that reinforce the operation of the vicious cycle in depression.

One of the best known is that of rumination. Rumination is a deliberative thinking style that keeps going over and over negative events. Sometimes the person believes that if he or she keeps going over and over things, he or she will somehow eventually find 'the answer'. Ruminative patterns are reinforced by the fact that the depressed person withdraws from many aspects of their previously normal routine, for example by going out less and seeing much less of other people. In the absence of other activity, the client's daytime hours may therefore become filled with ruminative thought. At night, sleep, often already disrupted, may become further disrupted by rumination, staying awake and going over and over life issues. In addition to rumination, there are other well-known cognitive effects of depression: difficulty in concentration, negative attentional bias and a negative, globalized memory (Brewin, 1998; Williams, 1992), which some describe as 'depressing and fuzzy'.

COGNITIVE CONTENT AND PROCESSES IN ANXIETY

The salient cognitive content of anxiety concerns the appraisal of threat and danger and the preoccupation with reaching safety. The experience of anxiety is often linked to the balance of different ways of thinking:

- Overestimating the likelihood of occurrence of an event;
- Overestimating the cost of an event;
- Underestimating how the person may cope with the situation;
- Underestimating rescue factors – how others may help, for example.

These four can be put into an equation (Salkovskis, 1996):

$$\text{Anxiety} = \frac{\text{Perceived likelihood that threat will happen} \times \text{Perceived cost/awfulness}}{\text{Perceived ability to cope} + \text{Perceived rescue factors}}$$

The more likely and the more awful the threat is perceived as being, the greater the anxiety. This anxiety may, however, be lessened by the appraisal of one's coping abilities and/or the possibility of 'rescue'. The more the person appraises such mediating benefits as likely, the lesser the degree of anxiety will be. For example, for a person with health anxiety, the actual health risk may be seen as highly unlikely, such as becoming HIV positive or getting a brain tumour, but the cost of illness is seen as so terrible and extreme, combined with the sense that there would be no help available from any direction, that the anxiety becomes uncontrollable. For those with phobias such as a fear of driving, although the person may have a good sense of rescue factors should an accident occur, the likelihood is overestimated. One client estimated the chances of being involved in a motorway crash were 80 per cent, whereas the statistical probability is less than 1:100,000.

Underlying beliefs in anxiety often show a preoccupation with oneself as vulnerable and with being unable to call upon help from a world seen as indifferent and dangerous. One anxious client picked up on the survival metaphor often attached to anxiety by describing his fears about some of his work colleagues as 'predators, circling round the sheepfold looking for stray lambs to devour'. Sometimes these negative conceptions may relate to schemas and core beliefs picked up in early experiences during which the client's caretakers dwelt on the dangers of life. Some clients, such as the man who gave the predator analogy, however, remember their caretakers as being rather lacking in vigilance for danger and seem to have drawn the conclusion that they, therefore, must develop extra vigilance to compensate for this 'carelessness'.

Beck and Emery (1985) point out that there is often a crucial difference between perceptions of time dimensions in anxiety and depression. The sense of loss in depression has often already happened. The 'loss' in anxiety lies in the future and could therefore still be avoided. Assumptions and rules of living that stress the benefits of vigilance, safety seeking, control and avoidance are therefore common. Anxious people are often mentally and/or physically preparing for any possible eventuality, however unlikely. It often seems to the client that threats are in imminent danger of happening, most classically in panic attacks. The client's anxious negative automatic thoughts often reflect this sense of imminent danger. The power of imagery is particularly strong in anxiety so that thinking that a danger might happen can lead to powerful images that are often experienced almost as if that danger *is* happening now. In social anxiety, for example, it has been shown that clients are sure that people are scrutinizing them critically. The client's attention is so monopolized by these negative images that the evidence of the images of what other people are doing is more compelling than the evidence of what those people are *actually* doing (Wells, 1997).

It has become clearer that the core cognitive processes in anxiety lie in the focus of attention and in the way that anxiety sufferers pay attention to supposedly potentially dangerous situations. Metacognitions that stress the positive functions of anxiety and worry – for example, 'If I worry a lot about my course work, I will be likely to get a higher grade' – have been shown to play a key role in the maintenance cycle of many types of anxiety (Papageorgiou and Wells, 2003; Wells, 1997; Wells and Matthews, 1994).

BEHAVIOURAL RESPONSES IN DEPRESSION AND ANXIETY

The different types of cognitive content and processes in anxiety and depression will naturally be linked to different types of problematic behaviours. The major behavioural features of depression are those of social withdrawal, isolation and physical atrophy. Behavioural interventions are therefore focused on 'activation' (Fennell, 1989). In anxiety, problematic behaviours will be more likely to be of the avoidant and safety-seeking type. Interventions are almost always based, therefore, on helping anxious clients to 'face up to' situations they have been avoiding and to drop the safety-seeking behaviours that may prevent them from disconfirming their fearful beliefs about the outcomes of such situations. Avoidance also, however, occurs in a different form in depression. Guidano and Liotti (1983) make a very telling and slightly ironic point about depressed clients: these deactivated people may show the capacity to become amazingly 'active' when it comes to not doing things. The time-frame perspective is again helpful in understanding the lack of activity: it seems that the depressed person becomes strongly adapted to past loss, but, at the moment of brief contemplation of future action, has an automatic closing down reaction, probably motivated by the desire to avoid further defeat and loss (Emery, 1999).

RELATING CONCEPTUAL MODELS TO THERAPY INTERVENTIONS IN DEPRESSION AND ANXIETY

As we have described in Chapter 2, while there are some variations in the way that conceptualization models are formatted, all of them share a fundamental form that differentiates between, first, the current maintenance cycle of the problem and, second, the underlying mechanisms of the problem. This section will describe ways of working with each of the maintenance cycles for depression and anxiety, and then with a common approach to their underlying cycles.

DEPRESSION

Emery has suggested that relatively brief cognitive therapy of depression:

> ... is foremost an educational approach to treatment. It involves teaching clients two things: 1) concepts that can help them better understand and cope with depression, and 2) specific skills that enable them to confront and master the symptoms of depression and the dysfunctional beliefs that predispose them to this disorder ... The heart of the programme is teaching two main skills: the ability to act differently and think differently ... This programme uses two tools to bring about this correction: the action schedule and the thought record. (1999: 5)

The activity schedule or Weekly Activity Diary as described on page 129 is a good place to start in the therapy of depression, in that the method not only immediately targets behavioural activation but also engages with the client's thinking processes. There are two main ways in which the activity schedule can be used. First, clients can be asked to give a description of their week, such as filling in, for homework, how they spend their time each day. For some people who are very low, the therapist may need to go over the past few days with the client during the session and fill out the form there and then. When the client brings their outline of the week, it is likely to contain rich data for exploration in the next session. Ratings of achievement and enjoyment (see Chapter 5) can be added, to enable client and therapist to get a picture of the client's week – with low and high points – and a sense of whether anything is enjoyable or satisfactory. The next phase is to use the schedule to *plan* for days ahead, perhaps adding some more enjoyable items into the week to overcome the common problem in depression of loss of pleasure. When first using this technique, I (FW) made the mistake of asking clients to plan the week ahead. It now, however, seems generally better to get the client to plan flexibly and for just a day or two ahead, which seems to be a less daunting and more doable task to clients. Emery (1999) makes a nice suggestion that clients who have planned some days ahead can be encouraged to write or say a few intentional sentences about what they will do that day: 'Today I will get up by 9 am and be dressed and ready to go out by 10 am. I will visit my friend for coffee, and take my library books back'; 'Tomorrow I will go to the job centre and make an appointment. I will then walk around the park'. These statements can reinforce the client's intention to act. They may also carry metameaning, sometimes representing a shift from a 'why bother' frame of mind to a 'can do' frame of mind. This cognitive shift indicates that, despite looking like a profoundly behavioural intervention, activity diaries also hold the potential for cognitive change and behavioural experiments (Bennett-Levy et al., 2004; Emery, 1999).

MIKE

Mike was a young client who had become understandably depressed following a serious illness. During his slow recovery, he frequently felt a sense of self-disgust because 'I never do anything'. The therapist suggested that they retrospectively fill out a schedule for the last two days. This revealed the fact that Mike had been to work on both days, cleaned the house, met a friend for a drink, read two chapters of a novel and watched a favourite film on TV. The therapist had to admit that Mike had greatly exceeded his own activity level in those two days!

Thought records completed by Mike continually revealed the same perfectionist demands that he 'should' fill the day with achievement and judge himself harshly when he didn't do so. His father had belonged to an extreme Protestant sect that had beliefs that seemed to reflect the old motto, 'The Devil makes work for idle hands'. In this way, the seemingly straightforward behavioural task of monitoring activities serves to identify other issues maintaining the depression, and leads on to cognitively focused work, identifying and changing negative thinking and underlying assumptions.

With a greater understanding of cognitive processes in depression, including those processes linked to relapse for people who experience repeated episodes of depression, come newer ideas for therapy such as mindfulness-based cognitive therapy (Segal et al., 2002). Mindfulness training is based on the idea that depressive relapse is strongly linked to a change in the person's relationship to their thoughts, and by enabling the person to take a different relationship to his thinking, relapse can be avoided. The Mindfulness-based Cognitive Therapy (MBCT) maintenance programme for the prevention of depressive relapse consists of eight weekly group sessions, each lasting 2 hours, consisting of psychoeducational elements, cognitive therapy and mindfulness meditation:

1. Automatic Pilot
2. Dealing with barriers
3. Mindfulness of the breath
4. Staying present
5. Allowing/Letting be
6. Thoughts are not facts
7. How can I best take care of myself?
8. Using what has been learnt to deal with future moods.

  Segal et al. subjected MBCT to a clinical trial with 145 people who had suffered from depression on three sites in Canada, Wales and England. A group of people getting MBCT was compared with a group getting 'treatment as usual'. The MBCT group had significantly lower relapse rates. MBCT seemed particularly effective with the most vulnerable people – those who had had three or more previous episodes. Although it is early days, MBCT does appear to be an exciting and valuable development, and the ideas can be incorporated into individual therapy (Fennell, 2004).

YASMIN

Yasmin was an overseas student suffering from dysthymic depression. She was particularly troubled by negative rumination over whether she had chosen the right course and career path. This can obviously be a legitimate concern, yet it was a cycle she had been through many times before, indicating that the key problem was a pattern of ruminating in search of certainty in an inherently uncertain situation.

  Thought-record-based exploration of her thoughts floundered on the fact that the relevant evidence would not emerge for many years, after pursuing a career for some time. After this realization, Yasmin was, however, able to experiment in taking a more mindful approach to these ruminations with some success.

ANXIETY

Interventions for anxiety focus on the client's thinking about future, supposedly dangerous, events and on an overactivated behaviour style strongly orientated towards avoidance and safety seeking. This raises an epistemological difficulty to begin with in that events that have happened can be more realistically evaluated and appraised – there are likely to be witnesses and evidence in relation to them. Events in the future, however, are harder to assess and obtain evidence for. We have already seen, however, the four components of the anxiety formula, appraising the likelihood, cost and sense of rescue, and how a change in any one of them can result in a lessening of anxiety. The therapist can therefore be particularly alert to any of these factors arising in the thoughts and beliefs of the client, reviewing them in thought records and testing them using behavioural experiments.

There will, however, be issues that will be intrinsically harder to deal with by thought challenging or experiments. These issues may include fears about becoming ill, for example, developing a second episode of breast cancer *is* more likely for a woman who has already experienced it once and this end result is so extremely bad that, for many people, putting any attention on the thought of it would be likely to lead to anxiety. People's worries may concern realistic events: dying, for example, is something we are all certain to do at some stage; the world is in some areas a dangerous place, and environmental disasters, terrorism and terrible unexpected accidents can and do occur. When working with clients where worry is a central feature, such as generalized anxiety disorder (GAD), many therapists describe the sense of trying to dispute the indisputable, stuck in a blind alley of remote possibilities. The worry is fully understandable and in a sense indisputable so that it may be better to think of ways of either 'achieving closure of the worry' or taking attention from it.

The problem with worry is not so much in the content of the worries as in the interminability of the worry process. After a while, the worry process feeds on itself. Cognitive responses to anxiety, GAD and worry have been immensely strengthened in recent years by the addition of strategies that work more on undermining anxiety processes than working to undermine or change the content of anxious thoughts and beliefs. Such strategies include worry management (Butler and Hope, 1995), attentional training (Mansell, 2000; Wells, 2000) and mindfulness strategies (Kabat-Zinn, 2004, 2005), described in Chapter 5. The process of worrying may well be buttressed by meta-cognitive beliefs about the effects of worrying – these include 'positive' worry beliefs such as 'Worrying helps me to stay on top of things', as well as 'negative' worry beliefs, such as 'Worrying like this will drive me mad'. Such beliefs mean that the process of worry is never effectively closed down. Wells (1997) offers a helpful inventory for identifying these beliefs and guidelines on how to challenge them.

Worry-management strategies such as Butler and Hope's worry decision tree that we describe on page 118 offers a set of pragmatic steps that lead to a way out of the worry. The method invites clear definition of the problem and offers a path that leads to either acting to counteract the worries (doing something) or seeing that one can accept them and let them be (accept and distract). Precisely identifying what the worries are, in so many words, is important because global, amorphous beliefs possess greater ability to 'stick around', whereas precise thoughts carry the seeds of action and thereby their own resolution. For example, being 'scared all the time' is paralyzing, whereas 'worrying about how we will pay the mortgage' suggests the utility of a plan to 'make the mortgage payments'. Another way to manage worry is to accept it. Hayes et al. (2004) have highlighted the role of acceptance of problems as a first stage in the change process. It can be helpful to, as it were, let the worry into the house, give it a cup of tea and wave it farewell after a chat. Such acceptance resonates well with mindfulness, a method and approach which will no doubt prove to be as valuable in anxiety as depression.

Avoidance is common in anxiety. Traditionally, avoidance is tackled by the principle of 'facing the fear' by using exposure – the process of graduated approach to feared objects, by using a hierarchy of situations, starting with the easiest and proceeding to the more difficult. This procedure is probably best known through the step-by-step desensitization such as used in phobias or agoraphobia: going to the front door, going down the path, walking to the gate, walking to the post box, walking to the shop, and so on. Such exposure work, while valuable, has now evolved into behavioural experiments aimed at testing out beliefs, thereby facilitating not only behavioural but cognitive change. The example below shows how the idea of a hierarchy can be used in a very different type of situation – recovering from trauma.

CATHY

Cathy had been involved in a very nasty motorway pile up. Although she was not hurt and initially seemed to have got over the accident well, about a month after her recovery she started showing strong trauma symptoms with flashbacks, anxiety and avoidance. She was unable to get into a car. She lived in a new housing estate, which had been built on the assumption that car travel using the nearby motorway was the modern mode of living. An initial hierarchy succeeded in getting Cathy into a car quite quickly but then it emerged that she got very strong trauma symptoms when she came near a motorway. She had to stop, get out of the car and then return home. The therapist introduced the idea of another graduated programme. Together they devised a programme with 15 steps. The first step was to drive near to and look at a motorway. The second step was to drive on a bridge over the motorway. The third step was stop on that bridge and look at the motorway. Subsequent steps involved driving short distances on the motorway between exits that were close to each other. These steps gradually built up to longer driving trips along the motorway, culminating in a final step of getting to the town, about 70 miles away, to which Cathy had been driving on the day of her accident. It took her about three months with lots of ups and downs to complete this programme. It ended with a lovely therapeutic moment when she telephoned me (FW) from the town to say that she had, literally and metaphorically, 'made it'.

Although graduated exposure programmes, like the one above, have been strongly associated with behavioural aims – getting Cathy driving again – a cognitive approach would seek also to capitalize on the cognitive potential of what can be seen as a series of behavioural experiments. The cognitive gain implied in the small but telling phrase 'made it' shows how successfully engaging with activities like a graduated programme can have a significant impact on self-concept. As part of running this graduated step programme, Cathy was encouraged to work on her negative automatic thoughts as she tried to complete various steps. These negative thoughts ranged from reasonable and possibly true fearful thoughts such as, 'Other cars will beep their horns at me because I am going so slow' to catastrophic predictions like 'I'll never get off this motorway alive'. Cathy found it helpful to work through these types of thoughts after the event but had only limited success in being able to challenge them at the time of driving on the motorway. She was, however, able to find something that seems in retrospect to have combined elements of both distraction and mindfulness. It is sometimes hard to fully articulate what these kinds of strategies actually do consist of but perhaps that is not so important if the client is able to do them anyway. Cathy referred to her new type of attention while driving as 'Putting on my road-first mind' and added to her therapist, 'Whatever gets you through, eh?'.

WORKING WITH BELIEFS IN DEPRESSION AND ANXIETY

Although we have, in this book, made a distinction between 'standard cognitive therapy' and 'schema-focused cognitive therapy', in our experience the distinction between the two different ways of working may not be completely clear. Many clients we see bring along at least elements of issues influenced by underlying beliefs. The therapy with Cathy and Mike within the format of 'standard cognitive therapy' had such moments, and we give these as examples of the way in which underlying beliefs influence the way standard cognitive therapy might be conducted.

MIKE

We mentioned earlier the tensions created by Mike's father's religious strictness. Mike had always been closer to his mother and was therefore devastated when she died when he was 18 years old. He had just started university and experienced severe loneliness and unhappiness there, compounded by the fact that his father remarried within a year of his mother's death. Mike had never really talked through his feelings about his mother's death, believing that he had to be 'brave' and conquer these sad feelings. As he reviewed his depressed feelings in thought records, he increasingly noted the similarity of these feelings with those that he had felt at the time of his mother's death. It seemed helpful to give him space to talk about this. The issue raised itself again, however, as therapy drew towards its concluding sessions. I (FW) had thought that Mike had not particularly 'bonded' with him but noted signs of increasing distress as ending therapy was discussed. Further exploration of this revealed that Mike did have schematic feelings about abandonment (Young et al., 2003). He had therefore 'held back' in the relationship, as was his wont in other relationships, but still felt a sense of loss as termination of therapy approached. Mike related these feelings and behavioural patterns to the death of his mother. This new material allowed a particularly meaningful focus for ending therapy so that some of these feelings could be worked through in a way that was sensitive and also allowed Mike to negotiate for his needs, for example, by defining his preferred level of follow-up contact.

CATHY

About halfway through the graduated programme with Cathy, she rang the therapist to say that her sister had told her that she must tell him something she had recently revealed to her. Cathy wouldn't say what this was on the telephone but said that she would explain when she next saw the therapist. In the subsequent session, half an hour passed by without Cathy referring to the call. When the therapist asked about it, however, she said that she had been sexually abused as a child. Within the spectrum of abuse, these experiences were at the less severe end. The abuser, who was an uncle, did not proceed far with his advances. The experiences had happened twice and her parents had confronted the abuser and he stopped thereafter. Nonetheless, Cathy said that the memories of this had come into her mind after her motorway accident. It turned out that she had had a number of other such traumatic experiences, for example, one with a 'prowler'. For various complex reasons, Cathy seemed to have developed a style of dealing with worries by saying that she didn't have them – 'I am laid back. Nothing gets to me'. And yet she also had issues consistent with a 'vulnerability schema'. She and the therapist eventually worked out that only traumatic worries could break through this screen of being 'laid back'. As well as working on the motorway-driving programme, therefore, Cathy's therapy also included some revisiting of her traumatic memories via imagery (Hackman, 1998; Layden et al., 1993) and reconstructive narrative work (Edwards, 1990; Young et al., 2003).

COMMON PROCESSES IN COGNITIVE THERAPY: A DIFFERENT VIEW OF APPLICATION

Cognitive therapy and cognitive models have evolved for specific problems or 'disorders', implying, as described earlier, that in order to help people with these problems, we have to know about specific applications. However, as highlighted throughout the book, many common processes operate across the psychological problems, and a knowledge of these processes, how to spot them and how to intervene, gives cognitive therapists a wide repertoire of helpful skills across a number of problems. While processes are common, how they are expressed in terms of particular problems depends on the person's current concern and focus. For example, the main concern in eating disorders is to do with shape and weight; in worry and general anxiety, the person is concerned about the impact of their worrying thoughts and their safety within the world; and in obsessive-compulsive disorder, the concerns are around responsibility and contamination. Harvey et al. (2004) give a very readable summary of a transdiagnostic approach, and this is reassuring in the face of a bewildering sea of applications. Rather than having to learn a multitude of different methods and approaches, an understanding of a handful of common processes such as attention, memory, patterns of thinking and reasoning, avoidance and safety behaviours, and how to work with these, gives us a huge repertoire, tool box and mode of understanding for the range of difficulties our clients bring. Being able to then see how these processes work for our client leads to individual formulations and plans for therapy. In the following section we describe one common process, that of self-focused attention, and how this is formulated and worked with in social anxiety.

SELF-FOCUSED ATTENTION

Attending to internal cues rather than the external world, and paying attention to information consistent with one's beliefs rather than objective reality, is seen in many problems. The person in the midst of a panic attack is focused only on the internal sensations of a racing heart and sweating; and when depressed, negative thoughts and memories are attended to while other, more comforting or positive aspects of the environment or life, are not seen. By paying attention to internal mood states and to information consistent with beliefs, the person is not able to see other information which may be useful to aid disconfirmation of negative beliefs and reinforce learning new beliefs. The person stuck in self-focused attention is also more likely to make internal attributions to events, such as blaming the self for external problems such as setbacks at work or arguments, which may in any case be out of the person's control.

Working with attention can enable the person to pay more attention to external information and thereby break the cycle of attending to, and interpreting, only internal stimuli. Methods such as attention training and mindfulness enable people to focus more widely, without judgment. Cognitive methods such as positive data logs, experiments to collect a range of information from the environment or people, and thought records also aim to help broaden attention and attend to previously ignored information. Thus, where attention is seen as a core, maintaining process, a range of methods can be valuable.

SELF-FOCUSSING INTERVENTIONS IN SOCIAL ANXIETY

Adrian Wells, David Clark and others have developed a robust model of the way clients with social anxiety function in social situations (Clark and Wells, 1995) and the central role taken by 'self-focused attention' or 'self-consciousness'.

This kind of self-consciousness may be thought of as an 'interacting cognitive subsystem' (Teadsale, 1996) or 'mode' (Beck, 1996) in that it involves a series of complex triggering mechanisms between thoughts, emotions, physical sensations and behaviours. All these phenomena give continuous feedback to the sense of self-consciousness and thus keep it firmly in place.

ELLIE

Ellie was a person who generally thought of herself as quite confident. However, she had a history of suffering from intense periods of anxiety and worry and had been taking SSRI medication on and off for years. She had recently been appointed to a science teaching job where her duties included giving demonstrations of scientific procedures to students. Ellie found these demonstrations generally very difficult, especially when mature students were present. She and the therapist drew up the conceptualization (based on Clark and Wells, 1995) presented in Figure 10.2.

Figure 10.2   A Conceptualization for Social Anxiety ('Ellie')

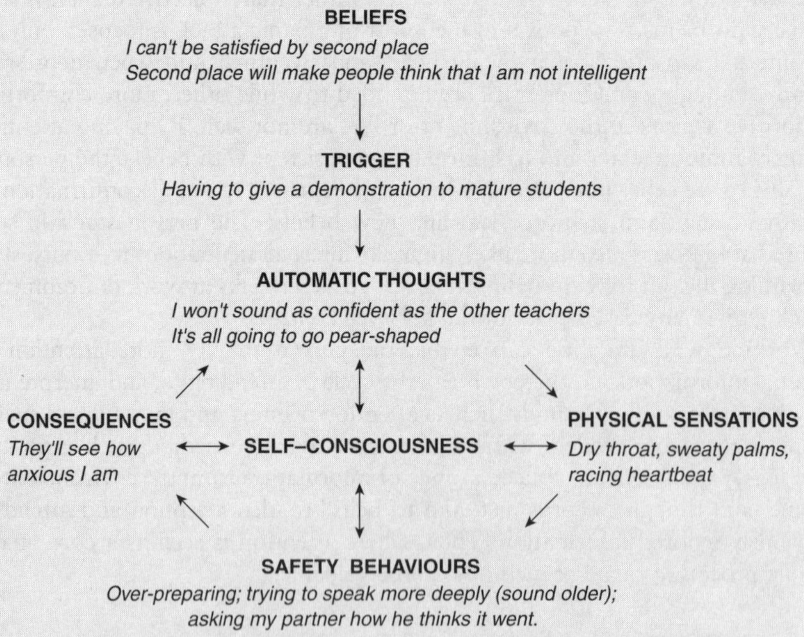

BELIEFS
I can't be satisfied by second place
Second place will make people think that I am not intelligent

TRIGGER
Having to give a demonstration to mature students

AUTOMATIC THOUGHTS
I won't sound as confident as the other teachers
It's all going to go pear-shaped

CONSEQUENCES ←→ **SELF–CONSCIOUSNESS** ←→ **PHYSICAL SENSATIONS**
They'll see how anxious I am *Dry throat, sweaty palms, racing heartbeat*

SAFETY BEHAVIOURS
Over-preparing; trying to speak more deeply (sound older); asking my partner how he thinks it went.

Knowledge of the cognitive model of social anxiety not only allows such a conceptualization to be drawn up but it also helps to quickly establish a common language for the problem and the therapy:

Therapist: So, when all this [the presentation] is going on, then, do you feel quite self conscious?

Ellie: Yeah, that's it, exactly. Mmm. Not half!

Therapist: And it's hard to act naturally then.

Ellie: Yes, I feel so tense. I feel like it is already going all pear shaped and it kind of gets worse and worse ... goes from bad to worse. I'd like to just run out but I can't. I have to tough it out.

Therapist: So the cognitive model I was telling you about suggests that it is in fact the feeling of self-consciousness that drives the whole thing ... so perhaps if we can lessen that, we would lessen the whole anxiety reaction?

Ellie: Well, yeah ... but it is something that I have had for a long time. I'm not sure how easy it will be to change that.

An important result of self-focused attention is that it drains attention from observing external events. This lack of external attention may be one reason why socially anxious clients are so convinced that people in their environment are critically examining them. When they are in the mode of self-consciousness, these perceptions are dominated by the internal fearful images and these people do not pay enough attention to what is actually going on in the environment. Behavioural experiments are then often directed to getting clients to observe their environment more directly. There are of course always likely to be at least some fashionista-type people who may be critically examining one from top to toe. In general, however, the presence of such persons is mostly balanced by others who may quite like the look of one and by many more who may be relatively, if not supremely, indifferent. Ellie learned to make more neutral appraisals of how people were reacting to her demonstrations and also that she could be more direct at asking for feedback. The greatest moment of emotional change, however, seemed to come when she experimented with dropping safety behaviours, especially seeking reassurance from her partner.

During demonstrations, Ellie thought: *'The students think I'm hopeless at this'* and *'They'll all fail their exams'* or *'They'll think that I am not intelligent'*. This latter thought seemed to be the 'hot' one and related back to quite a competitive childhood and education. Ellie realized that she was extremely focused on herself and her own performance during her demonstrations, and was unable to provide any convincing evidence that her thoughts were true. The biggest change for her, though, came when she realized that she consulted her partner for reassurance. This could only be a *safety behaviour* because the partner was not present at her demonstrations and his reassuring evidence did not carry much weight. Ellie found that by dropping this behaviour she instantly felt much better and quite quickly began to be able to reassure herself much more. Other experiments involved paying attention externally to see how her students were, in fact, reacting.

BEYOND THE ONE TO ONE:
COGNITIVE THERAPY IN GROUPS,
COUPLES AND SELF-HELP

Cognitive therapy initially developed as an individual form of therapy, and one-to-one work remains the traditional model. However, access to therapy in this format is extremely resource-limited, and for public services in most parts of the country there are long waiting lists – demand always exceeds supply. In addition, there are situations where therapy is practised in pairs or units, such as couple therapy or family therapy. Overall, the pressure is on to improve access without reducing effectiveness (Lovell and Richards, 2000).

Group work is an obvious and well-used method of delivering therapy, and cognitive therapy works well in this setting. As well as learning and applying specific and effective methods, there are general factors across group work (Dryden, 1998; Yalom and Leszcz, 2005) which can, for some people, make it preferable to individual therapy: instillation of hope, meeting people with similar problems and finding that one is not alone with difficulties, sharing others' experiences, and translating an individual painful problem into a common, shared understanding. Group therapy has been shown to be effective. For example, for many people with anxiety problems, group work can be as effective as individual therapy (Morrison, 2001; White, 2000; White et al., 1992; White and Freeman, 2000). Jim White's work involves setting up large 'stress control' groups – structured, didactic groups of up to 50 people – with very much an educational flavour. Participants are encouraged to 'become their own therapists' and are actively discouraged from talking about their own problems in the group. While necessary for large group work, avoiding problem discussion helps focus on anxiety-reduction methods and solutions rather than difficulties. The two- and three-year follow-up studies on these groups are extremely encouraging (White, 1998a; 1998b), with up to three quarters of participants maintaining improvements at two years. Large day-long workshops on anxiety management have shown very good results (Brown et al., 2000), and that they are as effective as the small-group format. As well as applications for anxiety, group work can be effective for people with depression, low self-esteem, schizophrenia, sleep disorders, chronic fatigue syndrome, medical problems, pain, anger difficulties and many other problems, and can be used in settings such as in-patient, primary care or education. For further details of group cognitive therapy, we recommend Free (1999), White (2000), White and Freeman (2000) and Scott and Stradling (1998).

There is good evidence to show that self-help methods can be very helpful (see White, 2000). Self-help materials can be very useful to clients on long waiting lists, instilling hope and beginning clients on the process of helping themselves, and may cut down the number of sessions. There are now many self-help books available, some of which are listed in our Appendix at the end of the book. In addition, the internet and computer technology provide a rich resource which is beginning to show effective results, such as the Overcoming Depression programme developed by Chris Williams and others in Glasgow (Williams and Whitfield, 2001) and Marks et al.'s (2004) fear fighter programme.

Results from group therapy and self-help are very encouraging. But, can they replace individual work or is it a case of 'dumbing down' therapy? The evidence to date is that while many clients can find groups helpful, these may not be appropriate for everyone. Individual work is more helpful for clients who are depressed, those with complex difficulties and those with obsessive-compulsive disorders (Morrison, 2001), although it may be that group work has a place for these people while they wait for individual therapy. Groups probably have higher drop-out rates than individual work, and face the challenge of being relevant to mixed groups with a variety of individual problems. Depending on the setting, it can be difficult to recruit sufficient numbers to groups without some customers having to wait a long time until groups are ready to start. With self-help methods such as bibliotherapy and computer-assisted packages, there may be issues around maintaining motivation, or the therapeutic effects of other people's interest in overcoming the difficulties. It may be that a combination of both self-help with some therapist contact, as and when needed, will address problems of diluting effectiveness while increasing access to resources. The jury is to some extent out, but with the massive development of internet resources, and significant potential to reach many people, it is a case of watching with interest.

USING PROTOCOLS IN COGNITIVE THERAPY

As the applications have widened, so too have the number of 'protocols' or specific guidelines for working with different problem areas. The earliest protocol within cognitive therapy was Beck's manual for depression (Beck et al., 1979), where the specific approaches and methods were detailed so that all therapists could use identical methods. Against a background of analytic therapy, where the techniques and methods were harder to put into operation, Beck started the quest to know what works and why, so the methods could have general applicability. The development of applications of cognitive therapy and research into their effectiveness have followed this tradition of a degree of manualization and standardization of the stages and methods of therapy. It is necessary to produce therapist protocols for research trials so that therapists in the trial can make sure they are offering the same procedures as each other. Without this uniformity, the trial is not a fair test of the therapy model. After successful trials, protocols can be published so that other therapists can work to guidelines that have been shown to be successful for specific problems. For example, Leahy and Holland (2000) describe up-to-date protocols and structured therapy plans for the main anxiety problems and depression; Steketee (1999a, 1999b) offers similar protocols for obsessive-compulsive disorder. Padesky and Greenberger (1995) describe protocols for using the manual 'Mind over Mood' with people with a variety of problems including anxiety, depression, anger and personality issues. The core features of cognitive therapy are common to many of the problems, but differences lie in the way the problems are formulated and in the specific interventions used.

In many ways, the idea of a standard approach for standard problems is reassuring: therapists can know they are using tried and tested methods and people receiving the therapy know they are getting what is deemed best, and most effective, practice for their particular difficulties. However, the area of protocols is by no means clear, and their effectiveness and value in therapy remains controversial.

The main controversy is around standard therapy versus using individual formulations, worked out with specific clients. At the very heart of cognitive therapy is the development of individual client conceptualizations which guide our understanding of the client and the direction of therapy; against this, we have the development of specific protocols for specific problems which are shown to be effective. How do we, as therapists, balance these two apparently contradictory ways of working?

PROTOCOLS VERSUS INDIVIDUAL CONCEPTUALIZATION

Some therapists and counsellors, particularly those from disciplines other than cognitive or behavioural, will start to feel rather alarmed by the ideas of protocols and manuals for conducting therapy, given that their philosophy and training are geared towards treating each client as an individual with individual problems. The idea of a protocol implies that there is a correct way to work with clients and that this way is separable from the client's individuality.

The protocol debate centres around the finding that there are certain active ingredients which have been shown to be effective for clients with anxiety problems such as phobias and OCD, and without which the therapy may be less effective (Emmelkamp et al., 1994; Schulte, 1997; Schulte et al., 1992). Giving therapists free reign to design their own therapy for the individual may mean that such active ingredients are left out. For example, people with specific phobias are by definition scared of the thing that they are phobic about and do not want to be exposed to their fears. They may predict: 'I couldn't do it' or 'I'll be overwhelmed with anxiety'. As therapists it is difficult to go against our compassion and encourage clients to do something which they fear will make them worse, but challenging these fears, both for ourselves and our clients, may be necessary to helping them overcome specific fears and phobias.

NICOLA

Nicola was 34 years old when I (DS) first saw her and had been phobic of spiders for most of her life. The phobia was having an increasing impact on her life, meaning that going to strange places was difficult, she had to check out any rooms she went in and felt uncomfortable being at home on her own in case a spider appeared and she would not be able to deal with it. Nicola was also troubled with periods of low mood during which her phobia would get much worse. She had been for counselling and help many times, often focused on her mood, building self esteem, understanding how her fears may be important to her relationships, looking at the origins – work which she found had given her valuable insights but had not tackled the phobia.

Nicola simply refused to do any exposure work with spiders. We spent several sessions in preparation, formulating her difficulties and fears, attempting to decatastrophize her predictions about herself and spiders. However, she would not do the exposure work and remained very phobic. She asked her GP to refer her several times, each time really wanting to make a fresh start and really try, but each time I had collected spiders for the exposure work and lovingly kept them alive and happy for their important work in therapy, Nicola would cancel or not turn up and the unemployed spiders would be returned to their webs. Nicola reported that therapy had been helpful for many things, but no progress was made on her phobia without the exposure work. Therefore if we take as a successful outcome symptom reduction, the therapy could not work without the active ingredient of contact with spiders.

Research on protocol-based therapy has mostly been conducted within research trials, often the more behavioural end of cognitive behavioural therapy (Wilson, 1997), which by definition include a fairly homogeneous population and using symptom reduction as a positive outcome. Clients with complex and multifaceted difficulties more common in clinical practice would not be included in such research. Nicola may have felt better, been more proactive in her life and developed greater self esteem, but not following the therapy protocol would mean that she would be in the 'treatment failure' group. So, the protocol versus individual therapy debate needs to take into account what the meaning of good outcome is.

The conceptualization approach to cognitive therapy is based on the idea that, although ideas can be helpfully gleaned from general models and protocols, in the end the treatment of the individual client will be best formulated according to an individual assessment of that client. This is built into the rationale of cognitive therapy theory which emphasizes the fact that people will react to events, including the experience of having cognitive therapy, according to their idiosyncratic cognitive frameworks. Given that clients often present with complicated issues, it can feel good for a therapist to go into the session with a framework for both understanding and working with the client. This framework can act both as a map to locate where we are and as a rudder to guide us forward. If, for example, a person who is disabled by panic attacks can experience a marked reduction in attacks from a manualized, six-session, protocol-based therapy, then it would make far more sense for the therapy to proceed along standard lines than to spend many sessions building up a detailed formulation. The framework or protocol, however, should never lead us to impose ideas or activities on the client. It should help us to negotiate an individual approach to the client based on general principles. The art and skill in cognitive therapy may well lie in being able to develop models and therapy plans which are unique to the individual in all their idiosyncrasies, and yet follow methods and approaches that have been found to be helpful for specific problems. This combination of the general and particular is the science and art of therapy.

CONCLUSION

The development of cognitive therapy appears to be a show that will run and run. This chapter has shown how cognitive therapy developed around specific applications of its concepts and interventions to specific problem areas. While the chapter has of necessity had to adopt a limited focus on what might be regarded as the 'classical applications' of cognitive therapy, the model itself has spread to ever wider areas. Even within the relatively narrow confines of these classical applications, however, it can be seen that innovation is the name of the game, with major new developments coming on stream every three to four years and this is all very exciting in many ways. However, the dizzy rate of change and the increasing amount of desirable knowledge for working in the various provinces of cognitive therapy raises the question of whether at some point, greater specialization within it will be called for. The further point from that concerns whether there will still be a place for the generalists, such as the writers. We obviously like to think that there will be but will examine this issue in a more dispassionate way in the next chapter.

Further Reading

These books summarize applications for different problems.

Beck, A. T., Reinecke, M. A. & Clark, D. A. (2003). *Cognitive therapy across the lifespan: Theory, research and practice.* Cambridge: Cambridge University Press.

Clark, D. M. & Fairburn, C. G. (Eds.). (1997). *The science and practice of cognitive behaviour therapy.* Oxford: Oxford University Press.

Freeman, A., Pretzer, J., Flemming, B. & Simon, K. M. (2004). *Clinical applications of cognitive therapy* (2nd ed.). Boston, MA: Kluwer Academic Publishers.

Friedberg, R. D. & McClure, J. M. (2002). *Clinical practice of cognitive therapy with children and adolescents.* New York: Guilford Press.

Grant, A., Mills, J., Mulhern, R. & Short, N. (2004). *Cognitive behavioural therapy in mental health care*. London: Sage Publications.

Morrison, A. P. (2003). *Cognitive therapy for psychosis: A formulation based approach*. London: Brunner-Routledge.

Salkovskis, P. M. (Ed.). (1996). *Frontiers of cognitive therapy*. New York: Guilford Press.

Tarrier, N., Wells, A. & Haddock, G. (Eds.). (1998). *Treating complex cases*. Chichester: Wiley.

11 Practising Cognitive Therapy in a Diverse Professional Field

One very striking fact about practising any kind of psychological therapy in the therapeutic climate of today is that one is likely to find oneself within a diverse, multidisciplinary field. There have always been many approaches to psychotherapy, and this diversity grew into a veritable 'multiverse' during which some authors estimated that there were over 400 brand therapies in existence (Norcross and Goldfried, 1992). Nobody really knows for sure if this kind of growth has continued. It seems likely that there may even have been some consolidation at least of larger groups of therapists into existing school affiliations, influenced by the need to respond to the requirements of evidence-based practice (Wills, 2005a). As well as other types of therapy, there are also different settings and agencies, such as clinics, institutes, health centres or voluntary bodies, each with its own particular organizational context within which therapy occurs. There are also different formats of therapy including self-help materials on CD-Rom and the internet, as well as individual, couple, group, family, organizational and other formats. We think that it is important for cognitive therapists to see themselves as doing their work within this complex multiverse environment and therefore wish to conclude this book with some thoughts on what it is like to work in these fields. We discuss three levels in which cognitive therapy may be used: as an eclectic addition to another model of practice; as the main model; and integratively with other approaches. We look at some of the issues arising while practising cognitive therapy and ways in which potential cognitive therapists can find out if the approach is for them. We start with a consideration of cognitive therapy in relation to other psychotherapies.

COGNITIVE THERAPY AND OTHER PSYCHOTHERAPIES

The analogy of the Berlin Wall has been used to describe the relationship between the different therapeutic schools in former times. The Wall, it can now be remembered, was a real divide between different political, economic and social systems and allowed only very limited commerce and communication between them. Similar effects have been observed within therapeutic schools. Jacobs (in Goldfried, 2000), for example, notes that training in psychoanalytic therapy results in an 'intense socialisation into the role of analyst' (p. 285) and that this socialization could serve to alienate other therapists.

Just as the Wall has now come down, so too have the barriers between therapies and there is now intense and growing communication between them. Forums, such as the Society for Exploration of Psychotherapy Integration (SEPI), allow therapists from different approaches to debate their similarities and differences. The scope for different types of eclecticism and integration can be explored in these forums. It seems that the more mature and 'seasoned' a therapist is, the more he or she is likely to appreciate these forums and to use them as vehicles for continuing professional development.

A factor that has added either piquancy or a degree of fright, according to your fancy, to these debates is a rise in the degree of competition in the market for therapy. Again, there has always been a degree of competition between therapies and therapists but this has been thrown into greater relief as health systems throughout the world have been trying to ensure that at least the therapy services funded by them are effective, both therapeutically and cost-wise. Therapists are sometimes caught with mixed loyalties in situations arising from these debates. You might, for example, be advancing a case based on evidence for the effectiveness of your approach that might highlight that other colleagues' approaches do not have such supportive evidence. We may, implicitly at least, be arguing that our approach should be preferred to theirs. Livelihoods could be at stake here. The situation might lead to a sequence of events that rebound back on us later. Will we be hung separately or hung together? To paraphrase Brecht, 'First they came for the Freudians ...'

In a way, we embrace all these developments. First, it is, as we hope we have shown throughout this book, true that therapists can learn immense lessons from each other and that sometimes we all need the view from a different perspective to help us find our 'blind spots'. Second, creative diversity is essential for ongoing development. Roth and Fonagy (1996) make the excellent point that if cognitive therapy had needed to begin life by proving its effectiveness, it may never have got off the ground. It took a period of necessary 'working up' before it could be tested in that way. In that period, cognitive therapy was more of an article of faith for the few than an empirically supported therapy. Third, we do believe, however, that therapists must attempt to put their ideas and practices to the test and eschew the sometimes arcane and evasive formulations of the past which suggested that therapeutic work could not really be evaluated. If the present systems of evaluation are deemed to be inadequate, then we must support moves to make them better. Furthermore, we should follow these evaluative practices as closely as we can within our own practice. It may not be enough in future to rely on the research efforts of others. The future is probably dependent on the development and spread of *routine* evaluation (Rowland and Goss, 2000).

USING COGNITIVE THERAPY IN OUR PROFESSIONAL WORK

In the first edition of this text, we suggested that there were three levels of application of cognitive therapy:

Firstly, using cognitive skills and concepts in a highly eclectic way;
Secondly, seeking a full training in cognitive therapy, aiming to implement a largely cognitive approach;
And thirdly, seeking integration of cognitive skills and concepts with other theoretical approaches.

We use these three levels as a template to examine in more detail some of the issues just raised.

LEVEL ONE – TECHNICAL ECLECTIC USE OF COGNITIVE SKILLS AND CONCEPTS

The developing therapist's first serious brush with cognitive ideas may well be via Albert Ellis's ABC method or Aaron Beck's concept of automatic thoughts. Trainees may attend introductory days and workshops, read texts, or generally 'dabble' with the ideas. Once therapists have grasped the concept of the negative automatic thought or of its rational-emotive-behaviour therapy equivalents such as 'awfulizing' or 'catastrophizing', it seems to be a common experience that they start to hear them very frequently – not only from clients but also from people in general, including from inside their own heads. Recognizing negative thoughts is further enhanced by the recognition of characteristic cognitive themes such as those of loss and sadness in depression and of danger in anxiety, and the recognition of characteristic cognitive distortions, as outlined in Chapter 1. These additional levels of analysis allow the therapist not only to be able to recognize negative automatic thoughts themselves but also to begin to help the client to recognize such thoughts and the accompanying themes and distortions. This may be the start of opening out a way to change some of the negative thoughts.

Another crucial concept is that of the domain of the thoughts, highlighted by both Beck and Ellis: the three sets of cognitions involving views of the self, of others and the world. Beck presents a slight variation with his concept of the cognitive triad in depression. The role of self-concept and its crucial effect on psychological health, disturbance and change has been noted in many theories of therapy such as those of Rogers and Winnicott. Self-concept may well be one of the crucial 'common factors' that tend to even out the effectiveness of different therapies (Raimy, 1975; Guidano, 1991). The therapist will therefore become very aware of negative thinking in relation to self-concept and will have some tools to work on that with the client.

In working with negative automatic thoughts in an eclectic way, it is important not to be over-simplistic about the meaning of the client's thoughts. An important aspect of how all people refer to their psychological processes is that it seems to be a natural human tendency to use shorthand language to describe our psychological functioning, especially when we are emotionally aroused. For example, we might say: 'Everyone at work criticizes me all the time. They make me feel worthless'. In fact, the experience we are trying to convey may actually be more like: 'At work, there are 20 people, two of them are critical of me. It's only two, but they are significant players. One is continuously critical and the other only sometimes. The others are okay … but then they don't defend me … although some of them are quite sympathetic afterwards. Sometimes the criticisms just bounce off me but sometimes, like today, it really upsets me and I end up feeling down, angry and frustrated'. We can look back now and see that the former is a shorthand form of the latter. We need shorthand forms because it would take forever to explain anything if we strove too hard for accuracy and, also, we need the people listening to understand the full impact of our upsetting experience. Problems can arise, however when we, emotionally aroused, begin to fully believe our shorthand versions of reality.

Both Ellis (1962) and Beck (1976) have referred to these two streams of thinking which seem to run alongside each other – in Ellis' parlance, 'the sane sentence and the insane sentence', and, in Beck's, 'parallel trains of thought'. Tapping into these internal dialogues is the first stage of developing cognitively oriented work. If, however, the therapist does not appreciate that there are *two* trains of thought, he or she is likely to get into some very unsubtle and overly persuasive arguments, with the client, thus fulfilling the stereotype of the bad (that is, dogmatically didactic) cognitive therapist.

As we have indicated at various points in the book, a more complete version of working with negative thoughts now not only requires awareness of the content of negative thoughts but also of the processes that sustain them. For example, sometimes, especially with ruminative or obsessive negative thoughts the client is only too aware that the content of the thought lacks validity but may still not be able to get their mind off it. The client skill required is the ability to be able to change the way the thought is held in attention. This can be done with the tactics of distraction and/or mindfulness and/or attention training described earlier. Shifting attention from negative thoughts is probably even harder to do than working with negative thought content but is, nonetheless, an incredibly useful skill to have available for both clients and therapists.

At the level of using cognitive methods in an eclectic way, interventions may be carried out on an occasional basis as a response to particular passages in the client's narrative. There is, as yet, no attempt to pull these sequences into an overall structured intervention or case conceptualization. There have been efforts to incorporate cognitive behavioural approaches into both social work (Sheldon, 1995) and community justice work with offenders (McGuire, 1995; McGuire and Hatcher, 2001). In the community justice field, systematic programmes have developed for both group and 'one to one' work. At this level, however, an individual probation officer or social worker might become aware that a client with whom they are working for another purpose is also depressed or anxious and might feel it could help them to use a thought record or an activity schedule and that this kind of intervention is not incompatible with the other targets they are working toward.

The downside of working at this level is that one cannot assume that using these techniques carries the same effectiveness as that demonstrated by fuller versions of the model. In research trials, a fairly prescriptive protocol is used to guide the therapy, coupled with some kind of training and/or supervision of the therapists. Cognitive therapy is not a 'magic bullet' and it is widely believed that training and supervision are vital in establishing effective practice for cognitive therapy (Padesky, 1996; Townend et al., 2002). In addition, it is important to understand the rationale for using particular techniques and the danger of eclecticism is that the wider the range of skills that eclecticism spans, the harder it is to accumulate such knowledge.

Our feeling is that success at this level is highly likely to lead the therapist to consider undertaking a fuller, conceptualization-based training. Developing such conceptualizations is the hallmark of a more concerted attempt to apply the whole model of cognitive therapy and it is to this that we now turn.

LEVEL TWO – USE OF THE COGNITIVE MODEL AS THE MAIN APPROACH

For therapists who decide to take up the cognitive model in a major way, one of the main advantages is that it can give a feeling of expertise in recognizing a specific issue for which one has a tried and tested intervention: 'If you've ever wondered "What can I do with this client next?", then cognitive therapy could be the one for you', as one of our students has put it. This puts the model in stark contrast to others, particularly the 'growth'-oriented therapies such as person-centred and Gestalt therapy, and therapies focused on longer-term personality change, such as psychodynamic psychotherapy. We are not arguing that cognitive therapy is best confined to arenas like the NHS but that its emphasis within independent practice would probably be geared towards working in more specific contexts than working with personal growth (Jones, personal communication, 1996).

In order to begin to operate the full model in practice one would need to practise using the different types of structure laid out in the earlier chapters of this book. One really should learn the model inside out before experimenting with and changing it. We use a 'should' here with a slight sense of moral absolute. The evidence, both research and clinical, is that, in its full form, cognitive therapy is valuable and effective, and 'if it ain't broke, don't fix it'. To dilute the model may well be to reduce its value. However, such adherence to structure is sometimes difficult for experienced therapists and those brought up in less structured traditions (Wills, 2005a).

Although cognitive therapy is known as a structured therapy and we see that as one of its strengths, there are quite a few dimensions to the notion of therapy structure and we believe that it may be helpful to unpick some of these strands that often tend to be twisted into the same thread.

First of all, structure can refer to templates in the therapist's head that help him or her to make sense of the client's material and to formulate some kind of sequence of steps to guide the process of therapy. This kind of structure may not be easy for the outsider to discern. It has often been remarked by those who observe Aaron Beck working on videotape that it takes them several viewings before they are able to identify the 'deep structure' of his work (Weishaar, 1993). Second, this internal structure may be matched to certain observable steps that the therapist takes; for example, ways of starting and ending sessions, certain therapeutic activities that would invariably precede others temporally. Sometimes they may not. Third, the overt and covert aspects of structure are obviously brought together in the concept of the 'therapy protocol', which, if it has been well written, should offer both a clear sequence of steps to follow based on a deeper structure designed to impact on both surface symptoms and underlying mechanisms. Using cognitive therapy 'properly' sometimes assumes that therapists wholeheartedly and consistently follow the protocols and structure, which may not always be either the case, or appropriate.

Sometimes the feeling of being in a 'programme' itself can breed a sense of resistance. Probation trainees have articulated a sense that some of their cognitive behavioural programmes are sometimes seen as representing a kind of 'thought reform' based on the official Home Office line, rather than being able to engage with the offenders' actual thinking styles in a collaborative way. As some offenders have put it, 'If this is so good for me, why do I have to be made to do it?' and 'Why don't you put your checklist down and listen to me?' (Wills, 2005b). This indeed seems to be the real crux of the matter with using protocols and manuals, especially perhaps outside the context of research trials: to what extent can we 'depart from the script'? Some people seem to argue that deviations from the script are dangerous and likely to result in decreased effectiveness. Our clinical experience, however, tells us 'departing from the script' is probably the norm and the real question must lie in the as yet unresearched and unanswered question about the differential relationship between greater and lesser degrees of structure adherence and treatment efficacy.

When the government of the DDR suggested that East Germans were unworthy of their socialist government, Brecht ironically suggested electing a new people. If therapists are unworthy of these wonderful protocols, maybe we should elect new therapists! There are a number of reasons for the seemingly pervasive tendency to depart from the script and acknowledged difficulty that therapists seem to have adhering to protocols (Beutler and Malik, 2002). Having tried to work with protocols ourselves, we can see that there might be some practical problems in this area.

First, you have to read the protocols and details of how to work with particular clinical problems and keep the tasks of a particular session fresh in your mind. Learning approaches to particular clinical issues can and should be part of continual professional development, and knowing what to do becomes easier with experience. A written summary of the areas to work on can be kept with individual client notes, and ideally, shared with the client. A practising therapist, however, is likely to know that the same stimulus material can be very differently interpreted and used by different clients. Quite often, there will be both a therapist protocol and a client protocol. A self-help book that has made all the difference for one client can find another client going into depression or rage because a single line in it carries a particular negative meaning for him. This fact is of course thoroughly in line with the cognitive theory and Epictetus' dictum that it is not by events alone that people are disturbed but by the view that they take of those events.

Second, most protocols are based on the premise of a single problem area whereas we know that for most client populations, co-morbidity is the norm rather than the exception. Co-morbidity may well require the therapist to take some deviation from a script based on only one problem area. Even where there is only one defined problem, other problems may emerge and there will be subtle variations within the inevitably somewhat general area that a protocol can cover. For example, a protocol for depression varies where bipolar, dysthymic or cyclothymic features are part of the picture.

Third, and perhaps most crucially for the cognitive therapist, clients are individuals with individual learning histories and conceptualizations. As we emphasized in Chapter 2, these beliefs, rules and cognitions will mean that they will take to similar interventions differently. It is also only right to point out that for some areas there are competing protocols, requiring some process of choice to be made.

Finally, taking all these factors together, how long might it take for the already busy clinician to learn a set of protocols needed for his everyday practice? Beutler and Malik (2002) suggest that it takes about two years' practice to master a protocol and as, in their view, most clinicians have to cover about 20 areas, it would take over 40 years to reach general protocol based competence. They wonder how pleased these octogenarian practitioners will be to arrive at general competence at that age! We cannot resist adding just one last absurd nail into this coffin by observing that our experience of writing this second edition of a book that is only seven years old has shown us only too clearly how much the fields of both theory and practice have moved on. There will clearly be a problem in ensuring that protocols are continually updated and that practitioners would need continual retraining to meet these new, updated strictures.

Though we have expanded at some length on the difficulties of using protocols, we would not wish to throw the baby out with the bath water and so we aspire to a balanced level of usage. Therapeutic decision making, itself assisted by conceptualization, would guide the balanced use of protocols:

> The challenge of protocol-driven practice is to ensure that clinicians combine clinical experience and sensitivity together with their knowledge of the research base, recognising the value and limitation of both. Against this background, clinicians should be making judgements about whether or not a particular presentation is normative, and if it is not, whether factors can be identified that militate against the recommended treatment, as Kazdin (1991) has commented, no manual (or indeed protocol) of psychological therapy can ever reflect the complexity of treatment and scope of the exchanges between therapist and patient. In our view the critical step in this process is the derivation of a formulation of the patient's problems ... (Roth and Fonagy, 1996: 51)

Schema-focused therapy and working with personality issues is at the other end of the scale from the protocol-based version of cognitive therapy and is based on freer use of structure. It is strongly endorsed that students, however, should begin by learning to use standard, structured cognitive therapy before beginning to attempt schema-focused cognitive therapy (James et al., 2004).

In some ways schema-focused cognitive therapy is more 'sexy' than the standard version and its emphasis on early experience and the therapeutic alliance in schema-focused work may make it seem more profound. Therapists from other traditions often want to skip the basics and dive in at the deep end, unfortunately offering scope for the dreaded 'amateur psychoanalyst'. The reason why it is important to master the standard model first is that it is the more parsimonious version – it is specifically short term. If we were to go 'schema hunting' with all our clients then we may eventually be drawn into an unstructured and much less effective and parsimonious way of working. Indeed, Beck has observed that analysis of some session records show that more experienced therapists may do less effective cognitive therapy than do the less experienced: process analysis of sessions seemed to suggest that the more experienced therapists sometimes appeared to give themselves more licence to wander from the formal structure of the therapy (Weishaar, 1993).

Therapists may well seek to combine cognitive ways of working with other ways of working before they have specialist training in cognitive therapy. At the pre-specialist cognitive therapy training stage, combinations would be in the more eclectic mode, that is, they would not be guided by any over-arching theoretical integration or by any case conceptualization. At the post-cognitive therapy specialist stage, combinations may be made in a more explicitly theoretical integrative way (Norcross and Goldfried, 1992), guided by a clear model of case conceptualization. It may be that, over time, there will be a strong pressure towards some cognitive therapists specializing in narrow disorder-based fields, for depression, OCD and so on. On the other hand, there will also continue to be strong demand for community-based cognitive therapy, based on more equal access across the country.

LEVEL THREE – USING STRUCTURED COGNITIVE INTERVENTIONS INTEGRATIVELY WITH OTHER APPROACHES

Beck has consistently argued that cognitive therapy is not a technique-driven approach. Many techniques, including those of diverse therapies, can be used legitimately within cognitive therapy provided that they are congruent with a genuinely cognitive case conceptualization. He further argues that because the change generated by all therapies is essentially cognitive, cognitive therapy could prove to be *the* integrative therapy (Alford and Beck, 1997; Beck, 1996). Beck (1996, 2004) has even expressed the hope that cognitive therapy will melt away as a separate therapy as many of its methods will come to be regarded as standard for psychotherapy. In a keynote address at the European Association of Behavioural and Cognitive Therapies Annual Congress, in September 2004 in Manchester, Aaron T. Beck was asked what he saw to be the future of cognitive therapy. He replied, rather surprisingly, that in a few years he hoped cognitive therapy as such would no longer exist, but that there would be one therapy, incorporating all the best and most effective components of the psychotherapies.

He sees these components as evidence based, focused, targeting meanings, collaborative and person centred.

Throughout counselling and psychotherapy, there is a general development of integrative and eclectic approaches (Goldfried, 2000). Slowly, cognitive approaches are being integrated and seen as 'the norm'. Such integration in many ways mirrors the development of person-centred work. Person-centred ways of working initially evolved as a separate psychotherapy. However, their elements have now been absorbed into cognitive therapy, where the core conditions of the therapeutic relationship are seen as 'the norm', and necessary to the model and its effectiveness. In future, instead of a person seeking help having to negotiate the minefield of therapies, and decide which form might be most suited to that person, there might be a breed of more 'generic' psychotherapists, working with people to formulate their difficulties and intervene according to the formulation.

The subject of integration is a potentially huge one and, for the purpose of this book, we wish to make only a limited foray into this area by looking at two strongly developing directions in cognitive therapy. The first is the use of experientially oriented techniques, predominantly from the humanistic therapies, alongside cognitive work. The second is the renaissance of interest in the therapeutic alliance, a concept that owes so much to the psychodynamic therapies.

Integration of Experience

We have already referred to the realization that there was a gap in the way that the earlier models of cognitive therapy dealt with emotion. It has now become absolutely clear that cognitive therapy can only have a very limited effect if it does not tap into key emotional experiences. The search is therefore now on to incorporate experiential techniques into cognitive therapy, in particular the notion of staying with emotion and the use of imagery.

In Rogerian therapy, there has always been recognition of the need to stay with and respect emotional experience. To some extent, this was acknowledged in the initial formulations of cognitive therapy, mainly in order to foster emotional change or symptom relief. We earlier noted one surprising gap in cognitive therapy, however, as the lack of emphasis on grieving processes. This is especially so as the theme of loss is so clearly identified in the cognitive therapy of depression yet merits no reference in the index of the landmark 1979 book on the subject (Beck et al., 1979). The impression is heightened by Beck's session on the well-known 'Richard' videotape, where Richard briefly mentions that his grandmother is dying. Admittedly, Richard himself does not think that it has a significant link to his current depression and yet many therapists watching that moment consider that it might have been useful to stay with it just a little longer. More reflective work on grief might be a useful way to find what may be learned and added into cognitive therapy. Stirling Moorey (1996) shows that cognitive therapy can be used to support clients struggling with adjustment reactions to adverse life circumstances, such as illness or grief reactions. His work strongly supports a more reflective, exploratory and 'staying with' style of therapy. Where adjustment to objectively negative circumstances is aimed for, the focus of cognitive therapy may well need to be more on facilitating emotional processing than on challenging negative thoughts.

Allied to the concern in cognitive therapy to find new ways of advancing the emotional immediacy of our work, there is also a new interest in working with imagery, already referred to in Chapter 7. Edwards (1989, 1990) has explored the use of Gestalt concepts and methods in this respect. Having obtained an image from the client, the therapist aims to reach the meanings that might be represented in the image. From a cognitive perspective, this offers the possibility that imagery work could be implemented along the same therapeutic track as the more usual verbal, cognitive interventions (Smucker and Dancu, 1999). Hackmann (1997, 2004) has continued this extremely creative and integrative approach to using imagery in cognitive therapy. Edwards noted the similarities between imagery work in cognitive therapy and Gestalt, illustrating his work with examples from Perls. The Gestalt therapist would help the client to understand that many features of the dream or image are projections of the client's own experiences and would typically ask the client to be that projection. As is often the case when comparing the cognitive approach with others, we are comparing an appreciation of a mental representation of a psychological feature in cognitive work with the acting out or experiencing of that feature in the other approach. The Gestalt approach in this instance would be more likely to promote emotional engagement with the client, whereas the cognitive approach might be more likely to promote 'decentring' or 'distancing' (Safran and Segal, 1990). One can imagine that there could be instances in which either of these therapeutic approaches would be more likely to be change promoting for particular clients or even for the same client at different points in the process. Finally, some kind of combination of the approaches might prove helpful to some clients, such as is used in Dialectical Behaviour Therapy for borderline clients (Linehan, 1993a, 1993b).

Integration of The Therapeutic Relationship

As cognitive therapy has developed and advanced, the therapeutic alliance has moved centre stage (Sanders and Wills, 1999, 2003). It is in this area that the integration of cognitive therapy and other therapeutic disciplines becomes prominent. One example is in the way in which cognitive therapy is beginning to recognize and use the concepts of transference and countertransference, as discussed in Chapters 3 and 7. The ideas of 'transference' and 'countertransference' were for so long such a taboo in cognitive-behavioural work that one still detects a sense of unease when cognitive therapists admit that it has crept back into their vocabulary. In their review of the interpersonal process and therapeutic relationship in cognitive therapy, Safran and Segal (1990) draw heavily on both the experiential therapies and the more recent versions of psychodynamic therapy.

It is interesting that so far there has been rather more interest in counter transference in cognitive therapy than in transference – of which, Beck et al. (1979) merely note that it should be dealt with as is any other negative automatic thought. The reasons for this underdeveloped interest in transference as compared to countertransference are likely to lie in the fact that cognitive therapy has always tried to take clients' perceptions seriously and respectfully. There may be fears that this respect might be undermined by attributing unconscious motives more explanatory power than the client's own conscious motives. Also cognitive therapists have been more likely to own their own less-than-perfect fallibility with clients in recent years and indeed have found their own tools for client analysis very useful in working on their own 'negative stuff' about therapy and clients. Such 'negative stuff' would include classic *mustabatory* (Ellis, 1962) NATs like, 'I must be able to help all my clients', and 'This client should show more gratitude for my sincere efforts to help him' (Padesky, 1996). Persons (1989) devotes a whole chapter to cognitive therapy for the cognitive therapist, including a telling list of therapist negative thoughts and their antidotes.

At present, such integration is still a very young endeavour. Therapists who have already undergone a substantial training in one of the cognitive therapies and have embedded this training into their practice can begin to think how they can undertake such integration themselves. Two main ways seem to arise in our own practice at this time. First, some kind of gap in one's work with a particular client may become evident in supervision. For example, when working with clients who have great difficulty gaining access to truly visceral emotions, such access can be greatly facilitated by the use of techniques from Gestalt therapy.

> One client, Maggie, seemed to be paralyzed by early memories of abusive parenting. Gaining access to visceral early memories via imagery and a modified version of the 'empty chair' technique allowed her to begin rapid processing of those memories.

Second, one may identify, in supervision or otherwise, a persistent block about a particular client or group of clients within oneself.

> Jim reacted badly to any mention of goals and limits in therapy. Supervision helped me (FW) to see that, not only did he have a sensitivity to any prospect of ending therapy because to him it signalled a rejection, but that I was also reacting to a barely conscious fear of my own that I did not have the time and energy to help him.

Such integration is likely to be best fostered by collaborative work with colleagues with training in other disciplines. I (FW) have been lucky enough to have regular contact, through supervision and other channels, with fellow therapists with training in other therapies. Such arrangements require a committed effort to respect and learn from other disciplines. Mutual cooperation may have the additional benefit of fostering greater unity and integrity in the professions of counselling and psychotherapy in the potentially testing years ahead.

MATCHING THE MODEL TO
THE THERAPIST

At all levels of training, trainee therapists may consider the question of what therapy approach to pursue. The trainee will often begin by matching a particular concept or technique to the perception of his own style. We make the rationalistic assumption that we choose theoretical orientations according to our basic temperament. This assumption may be an over-simplified notion and there often appears to be more than a hint of the opposite in the equation. For example, I (FW) believe that there is a strong resonance within my 'softish' personality towards the Rogerian approach. Indeed, this was where my initial therapy orientation was located. However, as soon as I began to hear about the cognitive approach in the early 1980s, it pulled strongly on a more focused part of me, working as a compensating mechanism which helped me to avoid becoming too sloppily Rogerian. I like to think that Carl would have understood this. Diana trained originally in person-centred counselling, but was immediately drawn to the structure and clarity of the cognitive approach, fitting with an organized and at times overtly bossy personality. However, the core training along with mindfulness practice provides the quieter, reflective balance to stop 'Bossy Spice' gaining the upper hand. Other person-centred therapists may have a little streak of authoritarianism in them. Several have been insightful and courageous enough to own up to this – as one put it to me: 'I use person-centredness to put the brakes on Big Brother in me' (in the Orwellian rather than the reality TV sense). It may be that 'what works for whom' is as much about the therapist doing the right kind of therapy for him or her, as it is about the client having the right kind of therapy for his or her problems.

FINDING OUT IF THE APPROACH
IS FOR YOU

One difficulty for trainee therapists of all kinds is to know how to begin to practise new skills and techniques when they feel they have little expertise in them. Should one dip a toe in the shallow end, plunge into the deep end, or start somewhere in the middle? There is very little research on the natural history of therapists, and how they develop their style over the years. Two of the stories that I (FW), as a trainer, hear quite frequently are, first, 'I tried it with x and it didn't work. Therefore, I'm not going to try it again', and, second, 'I tried it with y and it worked! [NB: there is always an exclamation mark here!] ... Therefore, it's the best thing since sliced bread'.

There is still much for us all to learn, both as individuals and as a profession, about choice of orientation. One approach might be to try different aspects of different approaches and see which of them stick in one's repertoire. The downside of such a strategy, however, is that in order to try to give therapeutic skills a sufficient trial, one may have to persist with them for some time. Persistence is especially required if the skills lie on the therapeutic end of the therapy continuum. In short, it may be hard to get really good at anything if one is continually trying different skills, and it is hard to learn anything thoroughly if we are continually experimenting with bits and pieces of methods and theories. At some stage, it may be necessary to give a concentrated range of skills a period of commitment. This commitment may to some extent preclude – at least for a while – developing others.

Most therapists are now being encouraged to learn and practise therapy models in a wholehearted as opposed to eclectic way. The British Association for Counselling and the Counselling Psychology Division of the British Psychological Society have stressed the importance of a core theoretical model in their pronouncements on training. They have also increasingly allowed for the legitimacy of integrated or eclectic core models but, for example, the course recognition procedures do seem to ask more of them. While clarity about one's model is obviously admirable, it could also be argued that any training over-focused on only one approach would be somewhat myopic or narrow-minded and would not give the trainee easy access to key debates in the field of therapy. It is inevitable, therefore, that most training courses will at least touch on theoretical concepts other than those of its core model and that trainees may decide to follow up on them either during the time of the course or later, thus strengthening the idea of informed choice of model. There has also been a trend in some regulatory and licensing bodies to require practitioners to be proficient in at least two models of practice. The two-model approach should at least eliminate the problem presented in a cartoon by Goldfried (2000) in which therapist and client confront each other thinking, 'I hope she's got the problem I treat' and 'I hope he treats the problem I have' respectively!

CONCLUSION

At whatever level therapists decide to try the cognitive approach, it is important that they are supported by good-quality supervision and training (Padesky, 1996; Townend et al., 2002). There are now a number of training courses in cognitive therapy and cognitive-behavioural therapy. The British Association of Behavioural and Cognitive Psychotherapy (BABCP) is a good source of information on courses, training events and sources of supervision and we provide other resources in the Appendix at the end of the book. To some extent, when contemplating taking on a model of therapy, the therapist has to decide if he or she wants to 'join the club' in terms of training, conferences and supervision. We would like to end our introduction to the art and science of cognitive therapy by suggesting that, if you do decide to join the cognitive family, you are likely to find yourself welcomed by a group of people who are developing fast but are not so serious that they can't be persuaded to mix some fun in with the earnest pursuit of therapy.

Appendix: Cognitive Therapy Resources

There are a huge number of books and other resources on cognitive therapy and CBT. Included in this Appendix are some of the ones we have found useful. It is now very easy to find information on the internet and we also list a few of the websites we know about and use, but each one will direct you to many other resources. A search for 'Cognitive Therapy' produces 109,000 hits on Google and 756 books on Amazon, so happy surfing and reading!

CLASSIC TEXTS WITH HISTORY AND ORIGINS OF COGNITIVE THERAPY

Beck, A. T. (1976/1989). *Cognitive therapy and the emotional disorders*. New York: Penguin.

Beck, A. T. & Emery, G. with Greenberg, R. L. (1985). *Anxiety disorders and phobias. A cognitive perspective*. New York: Basic Books.

Beck, A. T., Rush, A. J., Shaw, B. F. & Emery, G. (1979). *Cognitive therapy of depression*. New York: Guilford Press.

GENERAL

Beck, J. S. (1995). *Cognitive therapy: Basics and beyond*. New York: Guilford Press.

Bennett-Levy, J., Butler, G., Fennell, M., Hackmann, A., Mueller, M. & Westbrook, D. (2004). *The Oxford guide to behavioural experiments in cognitive therapy*. Oxford: Oxford University Press.

Hawton, K., Salkovskis, P., Kirk, J. & Clark, D. (1989). *Cognitive behaviour therapy for psychiatric problems*. Oxford: Oxford University Press.

Leahy, R. L. (2003). *Cognitive therapy techniques: A practitioners guide*. New York: Guilford Press.

Padesky, C. A. & Greenberger, D. (1995). *Clinicians guide to mind over mood*. New York: Guilford Press.

Persons, J. B. (1989). *Cognitive therapy in practice: A case formulation approach*. New York: W.W. Norton.

Sanders, D. & Wills, F. (2003). *Counselling for anxiety problems*. London: Sage Publications.

Wells, A. (1997). *Cognitive therapy of anxiety disorders*. New York: Wiley.

APPLICATIONS

Beck, A. T., Reinecke, M. A. & Clark, D. A. (2003). *Cognitive therapy across the lifespan: Theory, research and practice.* Cambridge: Cambridge University Press.

Bruch, M. & Bond, F. W. (1998). *Beyond diagnosis: Case formulation approaches in CBT.* Chichester: Wiley.

Clark, D. M. & Fairburn, C. G. (Eds.). (1997). *The science and practice of cognitive behaviour therapy.* Oxford: Oxford University Press.

Grant, A., Mills, J., Mulhern, R. & Short, N. (2004). *Cognitive behavioural therapy in mental health care.* London: Sage Publications.

Salkovskis, P. M. (Ed.). (1996). *Frontiers of cognitive therapy.* New York: Guilford Press.

SELF HELP BOOKS

Burns, D. D. (1999). *The feeling good handbook* (Rev. ed.). New York: Penguin.

Burns, D. D. (1999). *Feeling good: The new mood therapy* (Rev. ed.). New York: Avon Books.

Butler, G. & Hope, T. (1995). *Manage your mind: The mental fitness guide.* Oxford: Oxford University Press.

Fairburn, C. G. (1995). *Overcoming binge eating.* New York: Guilford Press.

Farrington, A. & Dalton, L. (2004). *Getting through depression with CBT. A young person's guide.* Oxford: Blue Stallion Publications (www.oxdev.co.uk).

Greenberger, D. & Padesky, C. (1995). *Mind over mood.* New York: Guilford Press.

Gurney-Smith, B. (2004). *Getting through anxiety with CBT. A young person's guide.* Oxford: Blue Stallion Publications (www.oxdev.co.uk).

Holdaway, C. & Connolly, N. (2004). *Getting through it with CBT. A young person's guide to cognitive behavioural therapy.* Oxford: Blue Stallion Publications (www.oxdev.co.uk).

Young, J. E. & Klosko, J. (1994). *Reinventing your life: How to break free from negative life patterns.* New York: Penguin Putnam Inc.

Also, the Constable and Robinson 'Overcoming' series:

Butler, G. (1999). *Overcoming social anxiety and shyness.* London: Constable and Robinson.

Davies, W. (2000). *Overcoming anger and irritability.* London: Constable and Robinson.

Fennell, M. (1999). *Overcoming low self-esteem.* London: Constable and Robinson.

Gilbert, P. (2000). *Overcoming depression.* London: Constable and Robinson.

Herbert, C. & Wetmore, A. (1999). *Overcoming traumatic stress.* London: Constable and Robinson.

Kennerley, H. (1997). *Overcoming anxiety.* London: Constable and Robinson.

Kennerley, H. (2000). *Overcoming childhood trauma.* London: Constable and Robinson.

Silove, D. (1997). *Overcoming panic*. London: Constable and Robinson.
Veale, D. & Willson, R. (2005). *Overcoming obsessive-compulsive disorder*. London: Constable and Robinson.

Booklets are available from Oxford Cognitive Therapy Centre on a variety of problems including depression, low self esteem, phobias, health anxiety and obsessive compulsive disorder: www.octc.co.uk

WEBSITES

British Association for Behavioural and Cognitive Psychotherapy
www.babcp.com
Training, accreditation, conferences, therapists. Valuable links including NICE guidelines and computer-assisted packages.

Oxford Cognitive Therapy Centre
www.octc.co.uk
Training, workshops, supervision, therapists, etc.

The Oxford Development Centre
www.oxdev.co.uk
Workshops, bookshop, training and therapy.

The Beck Institute for Cognitive Therapy and Research
www.beckinstitute.org
Information about training, bookshop, resources, etc.

International Association for Cognitive Psychotherapy
www.cognitivetherapyassociation.org

European Association for Behavioural and Cognitive Psychotherapies
www.eabct.com/
An umbrella organization for CBT in Europe.

www.schematherapy.com
Jeffrey Young's website with resources on schema therapy.

The Australian Association for Cognitive and Behaviour Therapy (AACBT)
www.psy.uwa.edu.au/aacbt/

www.padesky.com
Christine Padesky's website for workshops, training and resources.

CBT Arena
www.cbtarena.com/
Resources for professionals and academics and links for professional organizations.

The National Association for Cognitive-Behavioural Therapists
www.nacbt.org
Books and articles.

JOURNALS

Behavioural and Cognitive Psychotherapy
Published by Cambridge University Press for the British Association for Behavioural and Cognitive Psychotherapies.

Behaviour Research and Therapy
Published by Elsevier.

Journal of Cognitive Psychotherapy
Official publication for the International Association of Cognitive Psychotherapy, published by Springer.

Cognitive Therapy and Research
Published by Springer.

Cognitive and Behavioral Practice
Published by AABT (Association for Advancement of Behavior Therapy).

Cognitive Behaviour Therapy
Formerly *Scandinavian Journal of Behaviour Therapy*. Published by Routledge.

VIDEOTAPES AND CDs

The theory and practice of cognitive therapy
A series of tapes and CDs showing cognitive therapy in action. Available from www.padesky.com or School of Social Studies, University of Wales Newport, PO Box 180, Newport, South Wales, NP 20 5XR.

References

Alford, B. A. & Beck, A. T. (1997). *The integrative power of cognitive therapy.* New York: Guilford Press.

American Psychiatric Association (A. P. A.) (2000). *Diagnostic and statistical manual of mental disorders* (4th ed., text revision). Washington, DC: American Psychiatric Association.

BABCP (2000). *Minimum training standards for the practice of CBT.* London: BABCP.

Baer, R. A. (2003). Mindfulness training as a clinical intervention: A conceptual and empirical review. *Clinical Psychology: Science and Practice*, 10(2), 125–143.

Barlow, D. H. (2001). *Clinical handbook of psychological disorders: A step-by-step treatment manual.* New York: Guilford Press.

Bartlett, F. C. (1932). *Remembering.* New York: Columbia University Press.

Batchelor, A. & Horvath, A. (1999). The therapeutic relationship. In M. Hubble, M. Duncan & S. Miller (Eds.), *The heart and soul of change: What works in therapy* (pp. 133–178). Washington, DC: American Psychological Association.

Beck, A. T. (1967). *Depression: Clinical, experimental and theoretical aspects.* New York: Harper and Row.

Beck, A. T. (1970a). The role of fantasies in psychotherapy and psychopathology. *Journal of Nervous and Mental Disease*, 150, 3–17.

Beck, A. T. (1970b). Cognitive therapy: Nature of relation to behavior therapy. *Behaviour and Therapy*, 1, 184–200.

Beck, A. T. (1976). *Cognitive therapy and the emotional disorders.* New York: International Universities Press.

Beck, A. T. (1991). Cognitive therapy as the integrative therapy. *Journal of Psychotherapy Integration*, 1, 191–8.

Beck, A. T. (1996). Beyond belief: A theory of modes, personality and psychopathology. In P. M. Salkovskis (Ed.), *The frontiers of cognitive therapy* (pp. 1–25). New York: Guilford Press.

Beck, A. T. (2004). *Origin, evolution and current state of cognitive therapy: The inside story.* Key Note Address, Congress of the European Association of Behavioural and Cognitive Therapies, Manchester.

Beck, A. T., Weissman, A., Lester, D. & Trexler, L. (1974a). The measurement of pessimism: The hopelessness scale. *Journal of Consulting and Clinical Psychology*, 42(16), 861–865.

Beck, A. T., Schuyler, D. & Herman, I. (1974b). Development of suicide intent scales. In A. T. Beck, H. C. P. Resnik & D. J. Lettieri (Eds.), *The prediction of suicide* (pp. 45–56). Bowie, MD: Charles Press.

Beck, A. T., Rush, A. J., Shaw, B. F. & Emery, G. (1979). *Cognitive therapy of depression.* New York: Guilford Press.

Beck, A. T. & Emery, G. with Greenberg, R. L. (1985). *Anxiety disorders and phobias: A cognitive perspective.* New York: Basic Books.

Beck, A. T. & Steer, R. A. (1987). *Manual for the revised Beck Depression Inventory*. San Antonio, TX: Psychological Corporation.

Beck, A. T., Epstein, N., Brown, G. & Steer, R. A. (1988). An inventory for measuring clinical anxiety: Psychometric properties. *Journal of Consulting and Clinical Psychology*, *56*(6), 893–897.

Beck, A. T., Freeman, A. & Associates. (1990). *Cognitive therapy of personality disorders*. New York: Guilford Press.

Beck, A. T., Steer, R. A., Brown, G. K. & Weissman, A. (1991). Factor analysis of the Dysfunctional Attitude Scale in a clinical population. *Psychological Assessment*, *3*(1), 478–483.

Beck, A. T., Steer, R. A., Beck, J. S. & Newman, C. F. (1993). Hopelessness, depression, suicidal ideation, and clinical diagnosis of depression. *Suicide and Life Threatening Behaviour*, *23*(2), 139–145.

Beck, A. T., Steer, R. A., Ball, R. & Ranieri, W. (1996). Comparison of Beck Depression Inventories – I and II in psychiatric outpatients. *Journal of Personality Assessment*, *67*(3), 588–597.

Beck, A. T., Freeman, A. & Davis, D. (Eds.). (2003a). *Cognitive therapy of personality disorders* (rev. ed.). New York: Guilford Press.

Beck, A. T., Reinecke, M. A. & Clark, D. A. (2003b). *Cognitive therapy across the lifespan: Theory, research and practice*. Cambridge: Cambridge University Press.

Beck, J. (1995). *Cognitive therapy: Basics and beyond*. New York: Guilford Press.

Bennett-Levy, J. (2001). The value of self-practice of cognitive therapy techniques and self-reflection in the training of cognitive therapists. *Behavioural and Cognitive Psychotherapy*, *29*, 203–220.

Bennett-Levy, J. (2002). Navel gazing or valuable training strategy? Self-practice of therapy techniques, self-reflection, and the development of therapist expertise. In J. Henry (Ed.), *First European positive psychology conference proceedings*. Leicester: British Psychological Society.

Bennett-Levy, J. (2003). Mechanisms of change in cognitive therapy: The case of automatic thought records and behavioural experiments. *Behavioural and Cognitive Psychotherapy*, *31*, 261–277.

Bennett-Levy, J. (2005). Therapist skills: A cognitive model of their acquisition and refinement. *Behavioural and Cognitive Psychotherapy*, in press.

Bennett-Levy, J., Lee, N., Travers, K., Pohlman, S. & Hamernik, E. (2003). Cognitive therapy from the inside: enhancing therapist skills through practising what we preach. *Behavioural and Cognitive Psychotherapy*, *31*, 143–158.

Bennett-Levy, J., Butler, G., Fennell, M., Hackmann, A., Mueller, M. & Westbrook, D. (2004). *The Oxford guide to behavioural experiments in cognitive therapy*. Oxford: Oxford University Press.

Beutler, L. E. & Malik, M. L. (2002). *Re-thinking the DSM: A psychological perspective*. Washington, DC: American Psychological Association.

Bieling, P. J. & Kuyken, W. (2003). Is cognitive case formulation science or science fiction? *Clinical Psychology – Science and Practice*, *10*(1), 52–69.

Blackburn, I. M. & Davidson, K. (1995). *Cognitive therapy for depression and anxiety* (2nd ed.). Oxford: Blackwell Scientific Publications.

Blackburn, I. M., James, I. A., Milne, D. L., Baker, C., Standart, S., Garland, A. & Reichelt, F. K. (2001). The Revised Cognitive Therapy Scale (CTS-R): Psychometric properties. *Behavioural and Cognitive Psychotherapy*, *29*, 431–446.

Blenkiron, P. (2005). Stories and analogies in cognitive behavioural therapy: A review. *Behavioural and Cognitive Psychotherapy, 33*(1), 45–60.

Bowlby, J. (1969). *Attachment and loss* (vol. 1: Attachment). London: Hogarth Press and the Institute of Psychoanalysis.

Brewin, C. (1998). Intrusive memories, depression and PTSD. *The Psychologist, 11*(6), 281–283.

Brewin, C. R., Dalgleish, T. & Joseph, S. (1996). A dual representation theory of post-traumatic stress disorder. *Psychological Review, 103*, 670–686.

Brown, J. S. L., Cochrane, R. & Hancox, T. (2000). Large-scale health promotion stress workshops for the general public: A controlled evaluation. *Behavioural and Cognitive Psychotherapy, 28*(2), 139–151.

Bruch, M. & Bond, F. W. (1998). *Beyond diagnosis: Case formulation approaches in CBT*. Chichester: Wiley.

Burgess, M. & Chalder, T. (2005). *Overcoming Chronic Fatigue Syndrome*. London: Constable-Robinson.

Burns, D. D. (1999a). *The feeling good handbook* (Rev. ed.) New York: Penguin.

Burns, D. D. (1999b). *Feeling good: The new mood therapy* (Rev. ed.). New York: Avon Books.

Burns, D. D. & Auerbach, A. (1996). Therapeutic empathy in cognitive-behavioral therapy: Does it really make a difference? In P. M. Salkovskis (Ed.), *Frontiers of cognitive therapy* (pp. 135–164). New York: Guilford.

Butler, A. C. (2001). What do the data say? *Journal of Cognitive Psychotherapy, 15*(4), 287–288.

Butler, G. (1998). Clinical formulation. In A. S. Bellack & M. Hersen (Eds.), *Comprehensive clinical psychology* (pp. 1–24). Oxford: Pergamon.

Butler, G. & Hope, T. (1995). *Manage your mind: The mental fitness guide*. Oxford: Oxford University Press.

Carson, T. P. (1986). Assessment of depression. In A. R. Ciminero, K. S. Calhoun & H. E. Adams (Eds.), *Handbook of Behavioural Assessment* (2nd ed.) (pp. 404–445). New York: John Wiley and Sons.

Cartledge, P. (2001). *The Greeks*. London: BBC Worldwide.

Casement, P. (1985). *On learning from the patient*. London: Tavistock.

Chadwick, P., Williams, C. & Mackenzie, J. (2003). Impact of case formulation in cognitive behaviour therapy for psychosis. *Behaviour Research and Therapy, 41*, 671–680.

Chambless, D. L., Caputo, G. C., Bright, P. & Gallagher, R. (1984). Assessment of fear in agoraphobics: The Body Sensations Questionnaire and the Agoraphobic Cognitions Questionnaire. *Journal of Consulting and Clinical Psychology, 52*, 1090–1097.

Charlesworth, G. & Greenfield, S. (2004). Keeping conceptualisations simple: Examples with family carers of people with dementia. *Behavioural and Cognitive Psychotherapy, 32*(4), 401–410.

Clark, D. A. & Beck, A. T. (2002). *Clark–Beck Obsessive Compulsive Inventory Manual*. San Antonio, TX: Psychological Corporation.

Clark, D. M. (1986). A cognitive approach to panic. *Behaviour Research and Therapy, 24*, 461–470.

Clark, D. M. (1989). Anxiety states: Panic and general anxiety. In K. Hawton, P. M. Salkovskis, J. Kirk & D. M. Clark (Eds.), *Cognitive behaviour therapy for psychiatric problems* (pp. 52–96). Oxford: Oxford Medical Publications.

Clark, D. M. (1996). Panic disorder: From theory to therapy. In P. M. Salkovskis (Ed.), *The frontiers of cognitive therapy* (pp. 318–344). New York: Guilford Press.

Clark, D. M. & Wells, A. (1995). A cognitive model of social phobia. In R. Heimberg, M. Liebowitz, D. A. Hope & F. R. Schneier (Eds.), *Social phobia: Diagnosis, assessment and treatment* (pp. 69–93). New York: Guilford Press.

Clark, D. M. & Fairburn, C. G. (Eds.) (1997). *The science and practice of cognitive behaviour therapy.* Oxford: Oxford University Press.

Cromarty, P. & Marks, I. (1995). Does rational role-play enhance the outcome of exposure therapy in dysmorphophobia? A case study. *British Journal of Psychiatry*, 167(3), 399–402.

Davidson, G. C. (2000). Stepped care: Doing more with less? *Journal of Consulting and Clinical Psychology*, 68, 580–585.

Davies, W. (1998). *A cognitive approach to offending.* Leicester: Association for Psychological Therapy.

De Girolamo, G. & Reich, J. H. (1993). *Personality disorders.* Geneva: World Health Organisation.

Department of Health (2001). *Treatment choice in psychological therapies and counselling: Evidence based clinical practice guidelines.* London: Department of Health.

Dryden, W. (1991). *A dialogue with Albert Ellis: Against dogmas.* Buckingham: Open University Press.

Dryden, W. (1998). *Developing self acceptance. A brief, educational, small group approach.* Chichester: Wiley.

Dryden, W. & Feltham, C. (1992). *Brief counselling.* Buckingham: Open University Press.

Dryden, W. & Trower, P. (1988). *Developments in cognitive psychotherapy.* London: Sage Publications.

Dryden, W. & Feltham, C. (1994). *Developing the practice of counselling.* London: Sage Publications.

Dugas, M. J. (2002). Generalized anxiety disorder. In M. Hersen (Ed.), *Clinical behavior therapy: Adults and children* (pp. 125–143). New York: John Wiley & Sons.

European Association of Behavioural and Cognitive Therapies (EABCT). (2001). *Minimum training standards.* London: EABCT.

Edwards, D. J. A. (1989). Cognitive restructuring through guided imagery: Lessons from gestalt therapy. In A. Freeman, K. S. Simon, H. Arkowitz & L. Beutler (Eds.), *Comprehensive handbook of cognitive therapy* (pp. 283–297). New York: Plenum.

Edwards, D. J. A. (1990). Cognitive therapy and the restructuring of early memories through guided imagery. *Journal of Cognitive Psychotherapy*, 4, 33–51.

Eells, T. D. (1997). *Handbook of psychotherapy case formulation.* New York: Guilford Press.

Eells, T. D. & Lombart, K. G. (2003). Case formulation and treatment concepts among novice, experienced, and expert cognitive-behavioural and psychodynamic therapists. *Psychotherapy Research*, 13(2), 187–204.

Egan, G. (2002). *The skilled helper* (7th ed.). Monterey, CA: Brooks Cole.

Ellis, A. (1962). *Reason and emotion in psychotherapy.* New York: Lyle Stuart.

Ellis, A. (1993). Talk presented at Sheffield workshop.

Emery, G. (1999). *Overcoming depression.* Oakland, CA: New Harbinger.

Emmelkamp, P. M. G., Bouman, T. K. & Blaauw, E. (1994). Individualised versus standardised therapy: A comparative evaluation with obsessive compulsive patients. *Clinical Psychology and Psychotherapy*, 1, 95–100.

Epstein, S. (1994). Integration of the cognitive and the psychodynamic unconscious. *American Psychologist*, 49, 709–724.

Epstein, S. (1998). *Constructive thinking: The key to emotional intelligence.* Westport, CT: Praeger Publishing.

Epstein, S. (2002). Cognitive-experiential self-theory of personality. In T. Millon & M. J. Lerner (Eds.), *Comprehensive handbook of psychology* (Vol. 5) (pp. 159–184). Hoboken, NJ: Wiley.

Erikson, E. (1997). *The life cycle completed.* New York: W.W. Norton.

Fennell, M. J. V. (1989). Depression. In K. Hawton, P. M. Salkovskis, J. Kirk & D. M. Clark (Eds.), *Cognitive behaviour therapy for psychiatric problems* (pp. 169–234). Oxford: Oxford Medical Publications.

Fennell, M. J. V. (1998). Low self esteem. In N. Tarrier, A. Wells & G. Haddock (Eds.), *Treating complex cases* (pp. 217–240). Chichester: Wiley.

Fennell, M. J. V. (1999). *Overcoming low self esteem.* London: Constable Robinson.

Fennell, M. J. V. (2004). Depression, low self esteem and mindfulness. *Behaviour Research and Therapy*, 42, 1053–1067.

Fiedler, E. R., Oltheimer, T. F. & Turkheim, E. (2004). Traits associated with personality disorders and adjustment to military life. *Military Medicine*, 169(3), 207–211.

Flecknoe, P. & Sanders, D. (2004). Interpersonal difficulties. In J. Bennett-Levy, G. Butler, M. Fennell et al. (Eds.), *The Oxford guide to behavioural experiments in cognitive therapy* (pp. 393–412). Oxford: Oxford University Press.

Foa, E. & Kozak, M. J. (1986). Emotional processing of fear: Exposure to corrective information. *Psychological Bulletin*, 99, 20–35.

Free, N. K., Green, B. L., Grace, M. D., Chernus, L. A. & Whitman, R. M. (1985). Empathy and outcome in brief, focal dynamic therapy. *American Journal of Psychiatry*, 142, 917–921.

Free, N. L. (1999). *Cognitive therapy in groups: Guidelines and resources for practitioners.* London: Wiley.

Garland, A. & Scott, J. (2002). Using homework in therapy for depression. *Journal of Clinical Psychology*, 58, 489–98.

Gath, D. & Mynors-Wallis, L. (1997). Problem solving treatment in primary care. In D. M. Clark & C. G. Fairburn (Eds.), *Science and practice of cognitive behaviour therapy* (pp. 415–31). Oxford: Oxford University Press.

Gendlin, E. (1981). *Focusing.* New York: Everest House.

Gilbert, P. (1992). *Depression: The evolution of powerlessness.* Hove: Lawrence Erlbaum.

Gilbert, P. (2000a). Varieties of submissive behaviour as a form of social defence: Their evolution and role in depression. In L. Sloman & P. Gilbert (Eds.), *Subordination and defeat: An evolutionary approach to mood disorders and their therapy.* Mahwah, NJ: Lawrence Erlbaum.

Gilbert, P. (2000b). *Overcoming depression* (2nd ed.). London: Constable-Robinson.

Gilbert, P. (2000c). *Counselling for depression* (2nd ed.). London: Sage Publications.

Gilbert, P. (2001). Evolutionary approaches to psychopathology: the role of natural defences. *Australian and New Zealand Journal of Psychiatry*, 35, 17–27.

Goldfried, M. R. (Ed.). (2000). *How therapists change: Personal and professional reflections.* Washington, DC: American Psychological Association.

Grant, A., Mills, J., Mulhern, R. & Short, N. (2004). *Cognitive behavioural therapy in mental health care.* London: Sage Publications.

Greenberg, L. S. (2002). *Emotion focused psychotherapy: Coaching clients to work through their feelings.* Washington, DC: American Psychological Association.

Greenberg, L. S., Rice, L. N. & Elliott, R. (Eds.). (1997). *Facilitating emotional change: The moment by moment process.* New York: Guilford Press.

Greenberg, L. S. & Paivio, S. C. (1997). *Working with emotions: Changing core schemes.* New York: Guilford Press.

Greenberg, L. S. & Safran, J. D. (1987). *Emotion in psychotherapy: Affect, cognition and the process of change.* New York: Guilford Press.

Greenberger, D. & Padesky, C. (1995). *Mind over mood.* New York: Guilford Press.

Guidano, V. F. (1991). *The self in process: A developmental approach to psychotherapy and therapy.* New York: Guilford Press.

Guidano, V. F. & Liotti, G. (1983). *Cognitive processes and emotional disorders: A structural approach to psychotherapy.* New York: Guilford Press.

Gunderson, J. S. & Gabbard, G. D. (2000). *Psychotherapy of personality disorders.* Washington, DC: American Psychiatric Publishing.

Hackmann, A. (1997). The transformation of meaning in cognitive therapy. In M. Power & C. R. Brewin (Eds.), *Transformation of meaning in psychological therapies* (pp. 125–140). Chichester: Wiley.

Hackmann, A. (1998). Cognitive therapy with panic and agoraphobia: Working with complex cases. In N. Tarrier, A. Wells & G. Haddock (Eds.), *Treating complex cases* (pp. 27–45). Chichester: Wiley.

Hackmann, A. (2004). Mental imagery and memory in psychopathology. *Memory, 12*(4).

Harvey, A., Watkins, E., Mansell, W. & Shafran, R. (2004). *Cognitive-behavioural processes across psychological disorders.* Oxford: Oxford University Press.

Hawton, K., Salkovskis, P., Kirk, J. & Clark, D. (1989). *Cognitive behaviour therapy for psychiatric problems.* Oxford: Oxford University Press.

Hayes, S. C., Strosahl, K. D. & Wilson, K. D. (2004). *Acceptance and commitment therapy: An experiential approach to behaviour change.* New York: Guilford Press.

Hays, P. A. (1995). Multicultural applications of cognitive-behaviour therapy. *Professional Psychology: Research and Practice, 26*(3), 309–15.

Hobson, R. F. (1985). *Forms of feeling: The heart of psychotherapy.* London: Tavistock.

Holdaway, C. & Conolly, N. (2004). *Getting through it with CBT.* Oxford: Blue Stallion Publications.

Hollon, S. D. (2003). Does cognitive therapy have an enduring effect? *Cognitive Therapy and Research, 27*(1), 71–75.

Honey, P. & Mumford, A. (1992). *The manual of learning styles.* Maidenhead: Peter Honey.

Horton, I. (2006). Structuring work with clients. In C. Feltham & I. Horton (Eds.), *Handbook of counselling and psychotherapy* (2nd ed.) (pp. 118–126). London: Sage Publications.

Hubble, M., Duncan, B. & Miller, S. (1999). *The heart and soul of change: What works in therapy.* Washington, DC: American Psychological Association.

James, I. A. (2001). Schema therapy: The next generation, but should it carry a health warning? *Behavioural and Cognitive Psychotherapy, 29*, 401–407.

James, I. A. & Barton, S. (2004). Changing core beliefs with the continuum technique. *Behavioural and Cognitive Psychotherapy, 32*, 431–442.

James, I. A., Blackburn, I. M. & Reichelt, F. K. (2000). Manual of the revised cognitive therapy scale. Newcastle Upon Tyne: Newcastle Cognitive & Behavioural Therapies Centre.

James, I. A., Southam, L. & Blackburn, I. M. (2004). Schema revisited. *Clinical Psychology and Psychotherapy, 11*(4), 369–377.

Kabat-Zinn, J. (2003). Mindfulness-based interventions in context: Past, present, and future. *Clinical Psychology: Science and Practice, 10*(2), 144–156.

Kabat-Zinn, J. (2004). *Full catastrophe living.* London: Piatkus.

Kabat-Zinn, J. (2005). *Coming to our senses. Healing ourselves and the world through mindfulness.* London: Piatkus.

Kabat-Zinn, J. & Brantley, J. (2003). *Calming your anxious mind. How mindfulness and compassion can free you from anxiety, fear and panic.* Oakland, CA: New Harbinger Publications.

Kahn, M. (1991). *Between therapist and client: The new relationship.* New York: W. H. Freeman and Co.

Kazantzis, N. & Lampropoulos, G. K. (2002). Reflecting on homework in psycho-therapy: What can we conclude from research and experience? *Journal of Clinical Psychology, 58*(5), 577–585.

Keijsers, G. P., Schaap, C. P. & Hoogduin, C. A. (2000). The impact of interpersonal patient and therapist behaviour on outcome in cognitive behavioural therapy: a review of empirical studies. *Behaviour Modification, 24*(2), 264–297.

Kelly, G. (1955). *The psychology of personal constructs.* New York: W.W. Norton.

Kennerley, H. (1997). *Overcoming anxiety: A self help guide using cognitive behavioural techniques.* London: Constable-Robinson.

Kessler, R., McGonagle, K., Zhao, S., Nelson, C. B., Hughes, M., Eshelman, S., Wittchen, H. U. & Kendler, K. S. (1994). Lifetime and 12-month prevalence of DSM-III-R psychiatric disorders in the United States. *Archives of General Psychiatry, 51*, 8–19.

Kirk, J. (1989). Cognitive behavioural assessment. In K. Hawton, P. M. Salkovskis, J. Kirk & D. M. Clark (Eds.), *Cognitive behaviour therapy for psychiatric problems* (pp. 13–51). Oxford: Oxford Medical Publications.

Kolb, D. A. (1984). *Experiential learning: Experience as the source of learning and development.* Englewood Cliffs, NJ: Prentice Hall.

Kuyken, W. (in press). Research and evidence base in case formulation. In N. Tarrier (Ed.), *Case formulation in cognitive behavioural therapy: The treatment of challenging and complex cases.* London: Brunner-Routledge.

Kuyken, W., Fothergill, C. D., Musa, M. & Chadwick, P. (in press). The reliability and quality of case formulation. *Behaviour Research and Therapy.*

Laireiter, A. R. & Willutzki, U. (2003). Self-reflection and self-practice in training of cognitive behaviour therapy: An overview. *Clinical Psychology and Psychotherapy, 10*, 19–30.

Layden, M. A., Newman, C. F., Freeman, A. & Morse, S. B. (1993). *Cognitive therapy of borderline personality disorder.* Boston, MA: Allyn and Bacon.

Lazarus, A. A. (1990), Can psychotherapists transcend the shackles of their own training and superstitions? *Journal of Clinical Psychology, 40*(3), 351–358.

Lazarus, A. A. & Lazarus, C. N. (1991). *Multimodal life history inventory.* Champaign, IL: Research Press.

Leahy, R. L. (2001). *Overcoming resistance in cognitive therapy.* New York: Guilford Press.

Leahy, R. L. (2003a). *Cognitive therapy techniques: A practitioners guide.* New York: Guilford Press.

Leahy, R. L. (Ed.). (2003b). *Roadblocks in cognitive-behavioral therapy: Transforming challenges into opportunities for change.* New York: Guilford Press.

Leahy, R. L. (2004). *Contemporary cognitive therapy. Theory, research and practice.* New York: Guilford Press.

Leahy, R. L. & Holland, S. J. (2000). *Treatment plans and interventions for depression and anxiety disorders.* New York: Guilford Press.

Lewin, K. (1951). *Field theory and social science.* New York: Harper & Row.

Linehan, M. M. (1993a). *Cognitive-behavioural treatment of borderline personality disorder.* New York: Guilford Press.

Linehan, M. M. (1993b). *Skills training manual for treating borderline personality disorder.* New York: Guilford Press.

Liotti, G. (1991). Patterns of attachments and the assessment of interpersonal schemata: Understanding and changing difficult patient–therapist relationships in cognitive psychotherapy. *Journal of Cognitive Psychotherapy: An International Quarterly, 5*(2), 105–14.

Lomas, P. (1987). *The limits of interpretation.* Harmondsworth: Penguin Books.

Lovell, K. & Richards, D. (2000). Multiple access points and levels of entry (MAPLE): Ensuring choice, accessibility and equity for CBT services. *Behavioural and Cognitive Psychotherapy, 28,* 379–391.

Luborsky, L., Diguer, L., Seligman, D. A., Rosenthal, R., Krause, E. D., Johnson, S., Halperin, G., Bishop, M., Brennan, J. S. & Schweitzer, E. (1999). The researcher's own therapy allegiances: A 'wild card' in comparisons of treatment efficacy. *Clinical Psychology: Science and Practice, 6,* 95–106.

Macran, S. & Shapiro, D. (1998). The role of personal therapy for therapists: A review. *British Journal of Medical Psychology, 71,* 13–25.

Mahoney, M. J. (2003). *Constructive psychotherapy: A practical guide.* New York: Guilford Press.

Mansell, W. (2000). Conscious appraisal and modification of automatic processes in anxiety. *Behavioural and Cognitive Psychotherapy, 28*(2), 99–120.

Marks, I. M., Kenwright, M., McDonough, M., Whittaker, M. & Mataix-Cols, D. (2004). Saving clinicians' time by delegating routine aspects of therapy to a computer: A randomised controlled trial in phobia/panic disorder. *Psychological Medicine, 34,* 1–10.

Marzillier, J. (2004). The myth of evidence based psychotherapy. *The Psychologist, 17*(7), 392–395.

McGinn, L. K. & Young, J. E. (1996). Schema-focused therapy. In P. M. Salkovskis (Ed.), *Frontiers of cognitive therapy* (pp. 182–207). New York: Guilford Press.

McGuire, J. (1995). *What works: Reducing re-offending. Guidelines from research and practice.* Chincher: Wiley.

McGuire, J. (2000). *Cognitive-behavioural methods: An introduction to theory and practice.* London: Home Office.

McGuire, J. & Hatcher, R. (2001). Offence-focused problem-solving: Preliminary evaluation of a cognitive skills program. *Criminal Justice and Behaviour, 28,* 564–587.

McMahon, G. (2006). Assessment and case formulation. In C. Feltham & I. Horton (Eds.), *Handbook of counselling and psychotherapy* (2nd ed.) (pp. 109–118). London: Sage Publications.

McWilliams, N. (1999). *Psychoanalytic case formulation.* New York: Guilford Press.

Mooney, K. & Padesky, C. (2000). Applying client creativity to recurrent problems: Constructing possibilities and tolerating doubt. *Journal of Cognitive Psychotherapy, 14,* 149–161.

Moorey, S. (1996). When bad things happen to rational people: Cognitive therapy in adverse life circumstances. In P. M. Salkovskis (Ed.), *Frontiers of cognitive therapy* (pp. 450–469). New York: Guilford Press.

Moorey, S. & Greer, S. (2002). *Cognitive behavioural therapy for people with cancer.* Oxford: Oxford University Press.

Morrison, A. P. (2003). *Cognitive therapy for psychosis: A formulation based approach.* Philadelphia, PA: Brunner-Routledge.

Morrison, N. (2000). Schema-focused cognitive therapy for complex long-standing problems: A single case study. *Behavioural and Cognitive Psychotherapy, 28,* 269–283.

Morrison, N. (2001). Group cognitive therapy: Treatment of choice or sub-optimal option? *Behavioural and Cognitive Psychotherapy, 29*(3), 311–332.

Mumma, G. H. & Smith, J. L. (2001). Cognitive-behavioral-interpersonal scenarios: Interformulator reliability and convergent validity. *Journal of Psychopathology and Behavioral Assessment, 23*(4), 203–221.

Murdin, L. (1999). *How much is enough? Endings in psychotherapy and counselling.* London: Routledge.

Nathan, P. E. & Gorman, J. M. (2002). *A guide to treatments that work.* London: Oxford University Press.

Neenan, M. & Dryden, W. (2002). *Life coaching. A cognitive behavioural approach.* Hove: Brunner-Routledge.

Neighbour, R. (2004). *The inner apprentice: An awareness-centred approach to vocational training for general practice.* Oxford: Radcliffe Medical Press.

Nelmes, M. (2001). *Therapy protocols versus individual conceptualisation: The views of CBT therapists.* Unpublished MA thesis, University of Wales, Newport.

Newman, C. F. (1994). Understanding client resistance: Methods for enhancing motivation to change. *Cognitive and Behavioral Practice, 1,* 47–69.

Nolen-Hoeksema, S. N. (1991). Responses to depression and their effects on duration of depressive episodes. *Journal of Abnormal Psychology, 100,* 569–582.

Norcross, J. C. (2002a). *Purposes, processes and products of the task force on empirically supported therapy relationships.* Article for the Association for the Development of the Person Centred Approach, www.adpca.org/articles/ppp.htm

Norcross, J. C. (2002b). *Psychotherapy relationships that work: Therapist contributions and responsiveness to patient need.* New York: Oxford University Press.

Norcross, J. C. & Goldfried, M. R. (1992). *Handbook of psychotherapy integration.* New York: Basic Books.

Orlinsky, D. E., Botermans, J. F. & Rønnestad, M. H. (2001). Towards an empirically grounded model of psychotherapy training: Four thousand therapists rate influences on their development. *Australian Psychologist, 36,* 139–148.

Padesky, C. (1995). *Cognitive therapy of anxiety: Key treatment principles and methods.* Audiotape. Newport Beach, CA: Center for Cognitive Therapy. www.padesky.com

Padesky, C. (2004a). *Socratic questioning in cognitive therapy: Clinical workshop.* Audiotape. Newport Beach, CA: Center for Cognitive Therapy. www.padesky.com

Padesky, C. (2004b). *Guided discovery: Leading and following clinical workshop.* Audiotape. Newport Beach, CA: Center for Cognitive Therapy. www.padesky.com

Padesky, C. (2004c). *Constructing new underlying assumptions and behavioral experiments.* Video. Newport Beach, CA: Center for Cognitive Therapy. www.padesky.com

Padesky, C. (2004d). *Case conceptualisation. An in-session collaboration.* Audiotape. Newport Beach, CA: Center for Cognitive Therapy. www.padesky.com

Padesky, C. & Mooney, K. (1998). *Between two minds: The transformational power of underlying assumptions.* Cork: EABCT Workshop.

Padesky, C. & Mooney, K. (2000). *Applying client creativity to recurrent problems.* Workshop. Newport Beach, CA: Center for Cognitive Therapy. www.padesky.com

Padesky, C. A. (1990). Schema as self-prejudice. *International Cognitive Therapy Newsletter, 6,* 53–54.

Padesky, C. A. (1993). *Socratic questioning: Changing minds or guided discovery?* Congress of the European Association of Behavioural and Cognitive Therapies, London.

Padesky, C. A. (1994). Schema change processes in cognitive therapy. *Clinical Psychology and Psychotherapy, 1,* 267–278.

Padesky, C. A. (1996). Developing cognitive therapist competency: Teaching and supervision models. In P. M. Salkovskis (Ed.), *Frontiers of Cognitive Therapy* (pp. 266–292). New York: Guilford Press.

Padesky, C. A. (1998). Keynote speech, European Association for Behavioural and Cognitive Psychotherapies, Cork, September.

Padesky, C. A. & Greenberger, D. (1995). *Clinician's guide to mind over mood.* New York: Guilford Press.

Padesky, C. A. & Mooney, K. A. (1990). Clinical tip: Presenting the cognitive model to clients. *International Cognitive Therapy Newsletter, 6,* 13–14.

Papageorgiou, C. & Wells, A. (1998). Effects of attention training in hypochondriasis: An experimental case series. *Psychological Medicine, 28,* 193–200.

Papageorgiou, C. & Wells, A. (2000). Treatment of recurrent major depression with attention training. *Cognitive and Behavioral Practice, 7,* 407–413.

Papageorgiou, C. & Wells, A. (2003). *Depressive rumination: Nature, theory, and treatment.* Chichester: Wiley.

Pennebaker, J. W. (2004). *Writing to heal: A guided journal for recovering from trauma and emotional upheaval.* Oakland, CA: New Harbinger Press.

Perry, J. C., Banon, E., & Iannis, F. (1999). Effectiveness of psychotherapy for personality disorders. *American Journal of Psychiatry. 156*(9), 1312–1321.

Persons, J. B. (1989). *Cognitive therapy in practice: A case formulation approach.* New York: W.W. Norton.

Persons, J. B. (1993). Case conceptualisation in cognitive behaviour therapy. In K. T. Kuehlwein & H. Rosen (Eds.), *Cognitive therapy in action: Evolving innovative practice* (pp. 33–53). San Francisco, CA: Jossey-Bass.

Persons, J. B. & Bertagnolli, A. (1999). Inter-rater reliability of cognitive-behavioral case formulation of depression: a replication. *Cognitive Therapy and Research, 23,* 271–284.

Persons, J. B. and Davidson, J. (2002). Cognitive-behavioral case formulation. In K. Dobson (Ed.), *Handbook of cognitive-behavioral therapies* (pp. 86–110). New York: Guilford Press.

Persons, J. B., Mooney, K. & Padesky, C. (1995). Inter-rater reliability of cognitive-behavioral case formulations. *Cognitive Therapy and Research, 19,* 21–34.

Persons, J. B., Gross, J. J., Etkin, M. S. & Madan, S. K. (1996). Psychodynamic therapists' reservations about cognitive-behavioral therapy: Implications for training and practice. *Journal of Psychotherapy Practice & Research, 5,* 202–212.

Persons, J. B. & Tompkins, M. A. (1997). Cognitive behavioural case formulation. In T. D. Eells (Ed.), *Handbook of psychotherapy case formulation* (pp. 314–339). New York: Guilford Press.

Piaget, J. (1952). *The origins of intelligence in children.* New York: International Universities Press.

Powell, P., Bentall, R. P., Nye, F. J. & Edwards, R. H. (2001). Randomised controlled trial of patient education to encourage graded exercise in chronic fatigue syndrome. *British Medical Journal, 322*: 387–390.

Prochaska, J. O. (2000). How do people change, and how can we change to help many more people? In M. A. Hubble, B. L. Duncan & S. D. Miller (Eds.), *The heart and soul of change: What works in therapy* (pp. 227–255). Washington, DC: American Psychological Association.

Purdon, C. & Clark, D. A. (2000). White bears and other elusive intrusions: Assessing the relevance of thought suppression for obsessional phenomena. *Behaviour Modification, 24,* 425–453.

Raimy, V. (1975). *Misconceptions of self.* San Francisco, CA: Jossey-Bass.

Robson, P. (1989). Development of a new self-report questionnaire to measure self esteem. *Psychological Medicine, 19,* 513–518.

Rogers, C. R. (1957). The necessary and sufficient conditions of therapeutic personality change. *Journal of Consulting and Clinical Psychology, 21,* 95–103.

Roth, A. & Fonagy, P. (1996). *What works for whom? A critical review of psychotherapy research.* New York: Guilford Press.

Rouf, K., Fennell, M., Westbrook, D., Cooper, M. & Bennett-Levy, J. (2004). Devising effective behavioural experiments. In J. Bennett-Levy, G. Butler, M. Fennell et al., *The Oxford guide to behavioural experiments in cognitive therapy* (pp. 21–58). Oxford: Oxford University Press.

Rowland, N. & Goss, S. (Eds.). (2000). *Evidence-based counselling and psychological therapies: Research and applications.* London: Routledge.

Rudd, M. D. & Joiner, T. J. (1997). Countertransference and the therapeutic relationship: A cognitive perspective. *Journal of Cognitive Psychotherapy, 12*(1), 39–55.

Ryle, A. & Kerr, I. (2003). *Introducing cognitive analytic therapy.* Chichester: Wiley.

Safran, J. D. (1998). *Widening the scope of cognitive therapy: The therapeutic relationship, emotion and the process of change.* Northvale, NJ: Jason Aronson.

Safran, J. D. & Segal, Z. V. (1990). *Interpersonal processes in cognitive therapy.* New York: Basic Books.

Safran, J. D. & Muran, J. C. (Eds.). (1998). *The therapeutic alliance in brief psychotherapy.* Washington, DC: American Psychological Association.

Safran, J. D. & Muran, J. C. (2001). A relational approach to training and supervision in cognitive therapy. *Journal of Cognitive Psychotherapy, 15,* 3–15.

Safran, J. D. & Muran, J. C. (2003). *Negotiating the therapeutic alliance: A relational treatment guide.* New York: Guilford Press.

Salkovskis, P. M. (2002). Empirically grounded clinical interventions: Cognitive-behavioural therapy progresses through a multi-dimensional approach to clinical science. *Behavioural and Cognitive Psychotherapy, 30,* 3–10.

Salkovskis, P. M. & Bass, C. (1997). Hypochondriasis. In D. M. Clark & C. G. Fairburn (Eds.), *Science and practice of cognitive behaviour therapy* (pp. 313–339). Oxford: Oxford University Press.

Salkovskis, P. M. Clark, D. M. & Gelder, M. G. (1996). Cognitive-behaviour links in the persistence of panic. *Behaviour Research and Therapy, 34,* 453–458.

Salkovskis, P. M. (1991). The importance of behaviour in the maintenance of anxiety and panic: A cognitive account. *Behavioural Psychotherapy, 19,* 6–19.

Salkovskis, P. M. (Ed.) (1996). *Frontiers of cognitive therapy.* New York: Guilford Press.

Salkovskis, P. M., Richards, H. C. & Forrester, E. (1995). The relationship between obsessional problems and intrusive thoughts. *Behavioural and Cognitive Psychotherapy, 23*, 281–299.

Sanders, D. (1996). *Counselling for psychosomatic problems.* London: Sage Publications.

Sanders, D. (2006). Psychosomatic problems. In C. Feltham & I. Horton (Eds.), *Handbook of Counselling and Psychotherapy* (2nd ed.) (pp. 442–449). London: Sage Publications.

Sanders, D. & Wills, F. (1999). The relationship in cognitive therapy. In C. Feltham (Ed.), *Understanding the counselling relationship* (pp. 120–138). London: Sage Publications.

Sanders, D. & Wills, F. (2003). *Counselling for anxiety problems.* London: Sage Publications.

Schon, D. A. (1983). *The reflective practitioner: How professionals think in action.* New York: Basic Books.

Schulte, D. (1997). Behavioural analysis: Does it matter? *Behavioural and Cognitive Psychotherapy, 25*, 231–249.

Schulte, D., Künzel, R., Pepping, G. & Schulte-Bahrenberg, T. (1992). Tailor made versus standardized therapy of phobic patients. *Behaviour Research and Therapy, 14*, 67–92.

Scott, M. J. & Stradling, S. G. (1998). *Brief group psychotherapy. Integrating individual and group cognitive behavioural approaches.* Chichester: Wiley.

Segal, Z. V., Williams, J. M. G. & Teasdale, J. D. (2002). *Mindfulness-based cognitive therapy for depression: A new approach to preventing relapse.* New York: Guilford Press.

Sequeira, H. & Van Scoyoc, S. (2001). Should counselling psychologists oppose the use of DSM-IV and testing? *Counselling Psychology Review, 16*(4), 44–48.

Sheldon, B. (1995). *Cognitive behaviour therapy: Research, practice and philosophy.* London: Routledge.

Short, N., Kitchener, N. & Curran, J. (2004). Unreliable evidence. *Journal of Psychiatric and Mental Health Nursing, 11*(1), 106–111.

Silver, A., Surawy, C. & Sanders, D. (2004). Physical illness and disability. In J. Bennett-Levy, G. Butler, M. Fennell, A. Hackmann, M. Mueller & D. Westbrook, *The Oxford guide to behavioural experiments in cognitive therapy* (pp. 309–330). Oxford: Oxford University Press.

Simos, G. (2002). *Cognitive behaviour therapy: A guide for the practising clinician.* London: Brunner-Routledge.

Smucker, M. & Dancu, C. V. (1999). *Cognitive behavioral treatment for adult survivors of childhood trauma: Imagery rescripting and reprocessing.* Northvale, NJ: Jason Aronson.

Squier, R. W. (1990). A model of empathic understanding and adherence to treatment regimens in practitioner–patient relationships. *Social Science and Medicine, 30*(3), 325–339.

Steketee, G (1999a). *Overcoming obsessive compulsive disorder: Therapist protocol.* Oakland, CA: New Harbinger.

Steketee, G (1999b). *Overcoming obsessive compulsive disorder: Client protocol.* Oakland, CA: New Harbinger.

Strawbridge, S. & James, P. (2001). Issues relating to the use of psychiatric diagnostic categories in counselling psychology, counselling and psychotherapy: What do you think? *Counselling Psychology Review, 16*, 4–6.

Strunk, D. R. & DeRubeis, R. J. (2001). Cognitive therapy for depression: A review of its efficacy. *Journal of Cognitive Psychotherapy, 15*(4), 289–297.

Sullivan, H. S. (1953). *The interpersonal theory of psychiatry*. New York: W.W. Norton.

Surawy, C., Roberts, J. & Silver, A. (2005). The effect of mindfulness training and mood and measures of fatigue, activity and quality of life in patients with chronic fatigue syndrome on a hospital waiting list: A series of exploratory studies. *Behavioural and Cognitive Psychotherapy, 33*(1), 103–110.

Tarrier, N. (in press). *Case formulation in CBT: The treatment of challenging and complex cases*. London: Brunner Routledge.

Tarrier, N. & Calam, R. (2002). New developments in cognitive case formulation. Epidemiological, systemic and social context: An integrative approach. *Behavioural and Cognitive Psychotherapy, 30*(2), 311–328.

Tarrier, N., Wells, A. & Haddock, G. (Eds.). (1998). *Treating complex cases*. Chichester: Wiley.

Teasdale, J. (1996). Clinically relevant theory: Integrating clinical insight with cognitive science. In P. M. Salkovskis (Ed.), *The frontiers of cognitive therapy* (pp. 26–47). New York: Guilford Press.

Teasdale, J. (1999). Emotional processing, three modes of mind and the prevention of relapse in depression. *Behaviour Research and Therapy, 37*, S53–S77.

Teasdale, J. (2004). *Mindfulness and the third wave of cognitive-behavioural therapies*. Keynote address, Congress of the European Association of Behavioural and Cognitive Therapies Conference, Manchester.

Teasdale, J., Segal, Z. V., Williams, J. M. G., Ridgeway, V. A., Soulsby, J. M. & Lau, M. (2000). Prevention of relapse/recurrence in major depression by mindfulness-based cognitive therapy. *Journal of Consulting and Clinical Psychology, 68*, 615–623.

Toner, B., Segal, Z. V., Emmott, S. D. & Myran, D. (2000). *Cognitive-behavioural treatment of irritable bowel syndrome*. New York: Guilford Press.

Townend, M., Iannetta, L. E. & Freeston, M. (2002). Clinical supervision in practice: A Survey of UK cognitive behavioural psychotherapists accredited by the BABCP. *Behavioural and Cognitive Psychotherapy, 30*, 485–500.

Tsao, J. C. I., Mystkowksi, J. L., Zucker, B. G. & Craske, M. G. (2002). Effects of cognitive-behavioural therapy for panic disorder on comorbid conditions: Replication and extension. *Behaviour Therapy, 33*, 493–509.

Van Dusen, W. (1958). Wu-wei, no-mind and the fertile void. *Psychologica, 1*, 253–256.

Waddington, L. (2002). The therapy relationship in cognitive therapy: A review. *Behavioural and Cognitive Psychotherapy, 30*(2), 179–191.

Wampold, B. E. (2001). *The great psychotherapy debate: Models, methods and findings*. Mahwah, NJ: Lawrence Erlbaum.

Watkins, E. (2004). Adaptive and maladaptive ruminative self-focus during emotional processing. *Behaviour Research and Therapy, 42*, 1037–1052.

Weishaar, M. E. (1993). *Aaron T. Beck*. London: Sage Publications.

Weishaar, M. E. & Beck, A. T. (1992). Clinical and cognitive predictors of suicide. In R. W. Maris, A. L. Berman, J. T. Mattsberger & R. I. Yufit (Eds.), *Assessment and prediction of suicide* (pp. 467–483). New York: Guilford Press.

Wells, A. (1990). Panic disorder in association with relaxation induced anxiety: An attention training approach to treatment. *Behaviour Therapy, 21*, 273–280.

Wells, A. (1997). *Cognitive therapy of anxiety disorders*. New York: Wiley.

Wells, A. (2000). *Emotional disorders and metacognition*. Chichester: Wiley.

Wells, A. & Hackmann, A. (1993). Imagery and core beliefs in health anxiety: Content and origins. *Behavioural and Cognitive Psychotherapy, 21*(3), 265–274.

Wells, A. & Matthews, G. (1994). Attention and emotion: A clinical perspective. Hove: Lawrence Erlbaum.

Wells, A. and Butler, G. (1996). Generalised anxiety disorder. In D. M. Clark and C. G. Fairburn (eds), *Science and Practice of Cognitive Behaviour Therapy* (pp. 155–178). Oxford: Oxford University Press.

Wells, A. & Cartwright-Hatton, A. (2004). A short form of the metacognitions questionnaire: Properties of the MCQ-30. *Behaviour Research and Therapy*, 42, 385–396.

Wells, A. & Sembi, S. (2004). Metacognitive therapy for PTSD: A core treatment manual. *Cognitive and Behavioural Practice*, 11, 365–377.

Wenzlaff, R. M. & Wegner, D. M. (2000). Thought supression. *Annual Review of Psychology*, 51, 59–61.

Westmeyer, H. (2003). On the structure of case formulations. *European Journal of Psychological Assessment*, 19(3), 210–216.

White, C. (2000). *Cognitive behavioural therapy for chronic medical conditions.* Wiley: Chichester.

White, J. (1998a). 'Stress control' large group therapy for generalised anxiety disorder: Two year follow up. *Behavioural and Cognitive Psychotherapy*, 26(3), 237–246.

White, J. (1998b). 'Stresspac': Three year follow up of a controlled trial of a self help package for the anxiety disorders. *Behavioural and Cognitive Psychotherapy*, 26(2), 133–141.

White, J. (2000). *Treating anxiety and stress. A group psycho-educational approach using brief CBT.* Chichester: Wiley.

White, J., Keenan, M. & Brooks, N. (1992). 'Stress control': A controlled comparative investigation of large group therapy for generalised anxiety disorder. *Behavioural and Cognitive Psychotherapy*, 20, 97–114.

White, J. R. & Freeman, A. (Eds.). (2000). *Cognitive-behavioral group therapies for specific problems and populations.* Washington, DC: American Psychological Association.

Wilkins, P. (2006). Personal and professional development. In C. Feltham & I. Horton (Eds.), *Handbook of counselling and psychotherapy* (2nd ed.) (pp. 158–165). London: Sage Publications.

Williams, C. & Whitfield, G. (2001). Written and computer-based self-help treatments for depression. *British Medical Bulletin*, 57, 133–144.

Williams, J. M. G. (1992). *The psychological treatment of depression: A guide to the theory and practice of cognitive behaviour therapy* (2nd ed.). London: Routledge.

Wills, F. (2005a). *The influence of trainees' beliefs about therapy on the acquisition of competence in CBT training.* Paper presented at the British Association for Counselling and Psychotherapy Research Conference.

Wills, F. (2005b). *The cognitive behavioural perspective on offending behaviour: A skeptical approach.* Newport: University of Wales Newport, School for Social Studies.

Wills, F. R. (1997). Cognitive counselling: A down to earth and accessible therapy. In C. Sills (Ed.), *Contracts in counselling.* London: Sage Publications.

Wills, F. R. (1998). Amending the cognitive therapy scale for assessing counselling students undertaking training in CBT. Newport: University of Wales Newport, School for Social Studies.

Wilson, G. T. (1997). Treatment manuals in clinical practice. *Behaviour Research and Therapy*, 34, 295–314.

Winterowd, C., Beck, A. T. & Gruener, D. (2004). Cognitive behavioural therapy with chronic pain patients. New York: Springer Publishing Company.

Wright, J. H. & Davis, D. (1994). The therapeutic relationship in cognitive-behavioral therapy: Patient perceptions and therapist responses. *Cognitive and Behavioral Practice, 1*, 25–45.

Yalom, I. D. (1975). *The theory and practice of group psychotherapy* (2nd ed.). New York: Basic Books.

Yalom, I. D. & Leszcz, M. (2005). *Theory and practice of group psychotherapy.* New York: Basic Books.

Young, J. & Beck, A. T. (1980). *The cognitive therapy rating scale manual.* Philadelphia, PA: Center for Cognitive Therapy, University of Pennsylvania.

Young, J. & Klosko, J. (1994). *Reinventing your life.* New York: Plume.

Young, J., Klosko, J. & Weishaar, M. E. (2003). *Schema therapy: A practitioner's guide.* New York: Guilford Press.

Young, J. E. (1994). *Cognitive therapy for personality disorders: A schema-focused approach.* Sarasota, FL: Professional Resource Press.

Index